Integrating 12-STEPS *and* PSYCHOTHERAPY

Dr. Osten's Dedication

This book is dedicated to my husband, Dr. Grady L. Garner Jr.; my parents, Clarence and Nancy Osten; my mother-in-law, Omelia Sheppherd; my brothers, Scott and Jason Osten; and to my two dearest friends, Michael Lango and Dr. Kelly Graham-Hoffmann. My love and gratitude to each of you for all of your support.

Dr. Switzer's Dedication

To my husband Michael. . . . Thanks for riding this current E-ticket ride and looking forward to our next.

Integrating 12-STEPS *and* PSYCHOTHERAPY

Helping Clients Find Sobriety and Recovery

Kevin A. Osten

Adler School of Professional Psychology

Robert Switzer

Chicago School of Professional Psychology

Los Angeles | London | New Delhi
Singapore | Washington DC

Los Angeles | London | New Delhi
Singapore | Washington DC

FOR INFORMATION:

SAGE Publications, Inc.
2455 Teller Road
Thousand Oaks, California 91320
E-mail: order@sagepub.com

SAGE Publications Ltd.
1 Oliver's Yard
55 City Road
London, EC1Y 1SP
United Kingdom

SAGE Publications India Pvt. Ltd.
B 1/I 1 Mohan Cooperative Industrial Area
Mathura Road, New Delhi 110 044
India

SAGE Publications Asia-Pacific Pte. Ltd.
3 Church Street
#10-04 Samsung Hub
Singapore 049483

Acquisitions Editor: Kassie Graves
Editorial Assistant: Elizabeth Luizzi
Production Editor: Stephanie Palermini
Copy Editor: Janet Ford
Typesetter: Hurix Systems Pvt. Ltd.
Indexer: Jean Casalegno
Cover Designer: Anupama Krishnan
Marketing Manager: Shari Countryman
Permissions Editor: Jennifer Barron

Printed in the United States of America

Library of Congress Cataloging-in-Publication Data

Osten, Kevin A.
Integrating 12 steps and psychotherapy : helping clients find sobriety and recovery / Kevin A. Osten, Chicago Lakeshore Hospital, Robert Switzer Chicago School of Professional Psychology.

pages cm

Includes bibliographical references and index.

ISBN 978-1-4129-9898-7 (pbk. : alk. paper)

1. Substance abuse—Treatment. 2. Twelve-step programs. 3. Psychotherapy. 4. Addicts—Rehabilitation. I. Switzer, Robert, Psy.D. II. Title.

RC564.O83 2014

362.29—dc23

2013000549

This book is printed on acid-free paper.

13 14 15 16 17 10 9 8 7 6 5 4 3 2 1

Brief Contents

Detailed Contents

Acknowledgments

We would like to acknowledge our colleagues Lee Faver, Lisa Guralnick, and Molly Herron for the precious time they took from their busy lives to review and edit our chapters and give honest and direct feedback. We are eternally grateful to you.

We wish to thank our husbands for their tireless patience and encouragement in helping to move us forward when we paused too long.

We wish to thank Kassie Graves at Sage Publications for her faith in us, and advocacy to get the book deal signed, sealed, and delivered. Kassie, we cannot thank you enough for all that you have done for us. You truly are a gift, and a pleasure to work with—thank you.

We wish to acknowledge and thank our professors and clinical supervisors for their part in molding us into the clinicians we are today. Thank you for inspiring us to do and be better

. . . and mostly we wish to thank our patients who honor us with their bravery to face difficult change. You have helped to craft us into the clinicians we are today, by providing endless hours of education on the routes of addiction and recovery. May sobriety, serenity, hope, inspiration, and laughter be forever the guiding winds at your backs.

An Integrated View: Comparing 12-Steps and Psychology

A NOTE ON LANGUAGE

As with any field, this area of work has its own specific terminology. For the purpose of this book, the terms *substance dependent*, *chemically dependent*, *alcoholic*, and *addict* will be used interchangeably to describe clients who meet the Diagnostic and Statistical Manual Fourth Edition's (DSM-IV) criteria for someone who is substance dependent. Also, please note that we, the authors, firmly hold onto the belief that a-drug-is-a-drug-is-a-drug. Or, in other words, the *process* of substance dependence is equivalent across individuals regardless of the substance or substances involved. Although there may be some specific differences related to different intoxicants (for example, alcoholics are more likely to have memory loss), in all but a few ways addicts think and behave similarly, whether they are dependent on alcohol, cocaine, methamphetamine, or opiates. Thus, unless otherwise explicitly stated, we are speaking of the substance dependent person in general, not those dependent on a certain substance or class of substances.

A NOTE ON THE PROCESS OF RECOVERY

There are many means and methods that an addicted person can utilize to overcome their addiction. Despite deeply held beliefs by many, there is no "right way" to recover from substance dependence. Although research and clinical experience provide clinicians working with this population some guidance, finding the right combination of recovery techniques, skills, and beliefs sometimes resembles throwing a bunch of spaghetti against the wall and seeing what sticks. Our examination of how therapy can enhance the work of a **12-Step Program** (and vice versa) metaphorically amounts to one option or strand of spaghetti smattered on that proverbial recovery wall.

Even within a specific recovery approach such as a 12-Step Program, there is no set timeline for an individual to work the Steps. The **sponsor** (someone who is sober, involved in 12-Steps, and willing to mentor others) generally sets a suggested time-line for their **sponsee** (the term used to denote the sponsored person) to complete the work for each Step. Depending on the sponsor's style, this can be a very rapid process (all twelve Steps completed in about a month) or a much more relaxed pace (all twelve Steps taking several years to complete). Our experience is that most of our clients have a longer versus shorter timeline of working the Steps; often the first three Steps seem to involve a fair amount of trial and error, requiring a year or so. Also, a **relapse** (a very normal occurrence) almost always brings the sponsee back to Step One—no matter how far along they were in the Step process. A relapse is defined as the act of using an intoxicant after the decision for abstinence has been made and a period of sobriety achieved.

Added to the above, we find that groups of Steps seem to hang together, both conceptually and in practice. For these reasons, and for the sake of simplicity for this text, we adopt the following "timeline" of recovery stages:

1. Pre-Recovery (prior to any sustained effort at abstinence)
   a. No Step work
   b. If client is in therapy, therapists begin introducing 12-Step concepts with-out utilizing traditional 12-Step language
2. Early Recovery: 0 to 12 months of recovery
   a. Steps 1 to 3
3. Middle Recovery: 12 to 24 months of recovery
   a. Steps 4 to 7, when appropriate, combined with ongoing work on Steps 1 to 3
4. Longer-term Recovery: Greater than 24 months of recovery
   a. Steps 8 to 12, when appropriate, combined with ongoing work of any previous Step

This book focuses on the pre-recovery and early recovery stages. Later volumes will explore middle and longer-term recovery stages.

PURPOSE OF THIS BOOK

There has been a long history of disconnection between a 12-Step approach to substance abuse and the psychotherapy approach. For many psychologists, sub-stance abuse and addiction are often mentioned little, if at all, during their training. Frequently, psychologists are told during their early training that substance depen-dent clients may benefit from a referral to a 12-Step meeting. Chemical dependency is often given the attention one would give to an afterthought. As an example, during our training, not one class focused on 12-Step Programs, how they worked, and how psychotherapy could be used to enhance the involvement and benefit of clients in 12-Step Programs and vice versa. Instead, these clients and their substance abuse were often discussed as an artifact of an underlying psychological process. From this viewpoint, their drinking and drugging were the consequence of low self-esteem, self-destructive patterns, or disrupted early relationships. At no point were the authors educated about ideas common to 12-Step Programs: where substance abuse becomes a compulsion, where a person loses control, where a successful treatment must begin with some sobriety, and the reality that for many clients their substance abuse often becomes their focal issue. As a result, there is little reason to question why many of our colleagues feel unprepared to treat most substance dependent clients given this accurate assessment of the clinical training for many psychologists and psychiatrists!

In psychology, counseling, and social work, master's level clinicians often are required to take at least *one* class on addiction. Unfortunately, one course typically cannot address much of the field of addictions, including the pharmacology of the substances of choice, diagnosing substance disorders, behavioral addictions, clinical techniques such as Motivational Interviewing, self-help programs such as 12-Step, and family systems. As one course of study does not prepare clinicians adequately for working with any particular diagnosis, so the same is true when studying addictions.

Thankfully, some schools are offering concentrations in addictions in which both master- and doctoral-level students are able to take a series of courses that explore each of these topics more in depth. However, we have found that 12-Steps continue to be addressed in a peripheral manner; one that considers the work clients are doing in this type of Program to be something that occurs *outside of therapy*. Our position, and the reason and purpose for this text, is to demonstrate and provide instruction on how therapy and 12-Step Programs can work in conjunction with each other.

We see a real danger in clinical practice resulting from the lack of training of clinicians in substance abuse or dependence. For some clinicians, this deficit can have devastating consequences for their clients. Let's look at a case example to illustrate this problem.

John arrived in my office with four months of sobriety from alcohol. He had previously been seen by multiple psychiatrists, including at least one who was very well-known and respected. John had also been treated as an outpatient at several reputable hospitals. At the start of his treatment, John was on four different psychotropic medications, including two mood stabilizers, an antidepressant, and an anxiolytic. John described himself as such "a zombie" from these medications that he could no longer work, yet he was adamant that he had to take the medications because he had a Bipolar I disorder. An initial history revealed a pattern of symptoms consistent with this diagnosis, including hallucinations, as well as episodes of mania and severe depression. However, on closer inspection it appeared that these symptoms were not due to a mood disorder. Instead, they seemed to correlate with a pattern of intoxication and withdrawal symptoms in someone who was dependent on alcohol.

After a referral and several consultations with a psychiatrist, all of John's medications were stopped and he began attending 12-Step meetings. For the next four years, John's treatment included meeting attendance and psychotherapy and not once during this time did he present with an episode of a mood disorder, either depressive or manic. In repeated discussions with John, it seemed likely that none of his prior providers had considered that his alcoholism was mimicking a bipolar disorder, and they apparently had not evaluated him for such a possibility. Lacking this crucial perspective, they medicated him to the point that he had lost his job and was no longer able to function.

The educational deficits of providers may also explain much of the distrust that those involved with 12-Steps have for many mental health providers. Again and again, our clients have told us how others in their 12-Step meetings have expressed concerns and doubts about them seeing a psychotherapist. With further exploration, these fears often boiled down to expectations that clinicians would not support the work of a 12-Step Program or, even worse, would undermine and contradict sponsors and even the Program itself. With many of our clients, we prove that not only are we knowledgeable about a 12-Step approach, but that therapy can serve to enhance the 12-Step work. And make no mistake, this work needs to be done.

Just as in John's case, some clients are misdiagnosed and improperly treated, but the reverse mistake is also made. Clients who have severe emotional problems are not referred to therapy or a psychiatrist by those in 12-Step Programs, even though these individuals desperately need the treatment. Repeatedly, clinicians who specialize in addictions treat psychotic clients who have been told by their mentors in 12-Step meetings that they should stop taking all psychotropic medications, including antipsychotic medications. The consequence of following this advice, even though it is given with the best of intentions, sadly can lead to continued mental health problems for the client, which can also lead the client to relapse in order to self-medicate their psychological symptoms in the only way they know how.

Ultimately, this books aims to assist clinicians in their efforts to assess and treat chemically dependent individuals, and is especially directed toward clinicians who are essentially naive about providing treatment (psychotherapy with 12-Step competency) for these clients. This book recommends a treatment that is consistent with 12-Step meetings and its philosophy, but also with the concepts of psychotherapy. It aims at empowering clients' efforts toward sobriety and recovery, by supporting and reinforcing their efforts in the Program while helping them to fully integrate those changes into their functioning life. At the end of reading this text, students and clinicians alike will understand the core concepts of 12-Step Programs, learn ways of utilizing the language of those core concepts in therapy, and be able to integrate basic psychological assessment and treatment of substance dependent individuals within a 12-Step frame of the first three Steps.

Please understand, this book is only a general introduction to working with addictions. There are many related topics a clinician should master prior to considering themselves adept with this client group. One of these topics is behavioral addictions, also called *process addictions,* such as gambling, sexual, or eating addictions. Although many of the concepts we discuss here are directly applicable to those with behavioral addictions, the treatment of these disorders is not a focus. Also, we are not focusing on specific issues related to multicultural psychology or working with specialized populations. All of these topics may be addressed in future volumes, but for now, the focus is on a more generalized approach to working with the chemically dependent.

Finally, please note that this book is about those who meet the aforementioned criteria for substance dependence. Only a little time will be spent focusing on those who remain at a level of substance abuse. Many of the techniques discussed here can be useful with those who are at a level of abuse, but in many ways this is a related but separate disorder. As such, the treatment of abuse extends beyond the scope of this text. It is recommended that any reader who wishes to work with substance-abusing clients obtain additional training beyond this text.

A BLENDED APPROACH: INTEGRATING 12-STEPS AND THE PSYCHOLOGICAL UNDERSTANDING OF ADDICTION

Context Is Everything: A Primer on the Etiology of and Use of the DSM-IV

The notion and use of assessment in psychotherapy is not without controversy. Some schools of thought, in particular cognitive-behavioral approaches, see assessment as a crucial part of treatment as it informs the clinician what interventions should be provided, as well as giving a benchmark where the effectiveness of treatment can be measured and proven. Philosophically, this approach is very similar to the medical model as described by R.D. Laing in 1971 (Laing, 1971). In the medical model, disease is seen as a result of a disruption of the normal physical functioning of the body, resulting in symptoms. The disease process must be identified or diagnosed through the examination of the person and their history, and it is this diagnosis that guides the treatment. These treatments are then applied in the hope of achieving a cure, thereby signaling the end of the disease process. The DSM-IV operates under this model.

Each edition of the DSM, beginning with the third edition, has taken a syndrome approach to understanding diagnoses. This means that the diagnoses are based on a collection of symptoms that are seen as tending to occur together. Each DSM diagnosis is a grouping of symptoms that are most frequently observed in that particular troubled population; for example, symptoms of depression. The DSM does not generally identify the cause, best treatment, or prognosis for each diagnosis. In fact, the DSM quite explicitly does not attempt to do so. To quote the American Psychiatric Association (APA), document, "A Research Agenda for DSM-V,"

> In the more than 30 years since the introduction of the Feighner criteria by Robins and Guze, which eventually led to DSM-III, the goal of validating these syndromes and discovering common etiologies has remained elusive. Despite many proposed candidates, not one laboratory marker has been found to be specific in identifying any of the DSM defined syndromes. Epidemiologic and clinical studies have shown extremely high rates of comorbidities among the disorders, undermining the hypothesis that the syndromes represent distinct etiologies. Furthermore, epidemiologic studies have shown a high degree of short-term diagnostic instability for many disorders. With regard to treatment, lack of treatment specificity is the rule rather than the exception . . . few question the value of having a well-described, well-operationalized, and universally accepted diagnostic system to facilitate diagnostic comparisons across studies and to improve diagnostic reliability. However, reification of DSM-IV entities, to the point that they are considered to be equivalent to diseases, is more likely to obscure than to elucidate research findings. (2002, pp. xvii-xix; Reprinted with permission from A Research Agenda for DSM-5, (Copyright ©2002). American Psychiatric Association)

Without doubt, this quote nicely details that the DSM-based diagnostic system is highly flawed. So why do most providers rely on it? The reasons for its utilization are as varied as the psychological profession itself. For many providers, usage of the DSM-IV helps provide a standard language for communication across the psychological/counseling/social work fields, helps organize research, insurance companies require a DSM-IV diagnosis for providers to receive payment for services, and/or it is perceived as better than any alternative system.

There are additional reasons to consider using the conceptual framework embedded within the DSM diagnosis. With respect to addiction; a diagnosis of dependence is useful in that it communicates that a person's substance use has shifted to a qualitatively different level in comparison to a nondependent substance use or abuse pattern. This is a helpful differentiation for treatment providers. In particular, it is generally recommended that for most substance dependent individuals the goal of complete sobriety is likely the best, if not the only, treatment goal. For those who have not crossed the line into dependence, other treatments that allow continued substance use, albeit at a reduced level, may be an appropriate goal. However, once a client crosses the line into substance dependence, their treatment often shifts as well.

For this reason, until a superior model is accepted the writers strongly recommend that clinicians assess and rely on the DSM-IV diagnoses for substance related disorders. The DSM-V is slated to rework a good portion of the sections on substance disorders. There are current proposals under consideration for the substitution of the term "addiction" for "dependence," and "use" for "abuse," along with expanded criteria selection and the addition of a severity index. To date, the permanent adoption of these changes is not final; however, the DSM-V is slated for completion and release in May 2013.

The DSM system is expedient, but the authors also wish to impress on the reader that use of the DSM system can in many ways be seductive and encourage laziness. It is easy to forget the variety of limitations of the DSM system (a lack of proven inter-rater reliability comes to mind); instead, we accept its simplicity and clear-cut decisiveness for efficiency. Haven't we all heard, at least once, a fellow clinician pronounce that a client is "substance dependent," as if that somehow clarified the client's clinical picture? In many ways, that diagnosis in and of itself is of only limited value. Although we concur that there is some useful information that is communicated by this *necessary* assessment, it is a vastly incomplete assessment.

For instance, the term "substance dependent" tells us that the client likely requires abstinence, but it does not inform whether the client responds best to inpatient or outpatient treatment. Was the client dependent on multiple drugs or only a particular class and do they require abstinence across all intoxicating substances? This question is important as we have treated clients who were dependent on one group of stimulants such as cocaine or methamphetamine who remained abstinent and *in recovery* for years, yet simultaneously they consumed alcohol in a nonabusing pattern. A simple DSM diagnosis does not indicate if a client is more or less likely to succeed in remaining sober. It does not dictate how intensive the treatment, or the extent of family involvement. Will the client require medications to lower the intensity of their urges? Will they respond best to a confrontational or firm yet supportive approach? A DSM diagnosis can appear to provide the clinician with the illusion of some type of profound and true insight, when truly the devil really is in the details. Thus, we strongly advocate that clinicians take a more complete and nuanced view of diagnoses, remembering the advantages and limitations of the current diagnostic system.

Defining Substance Dependence

Given the above disclaimers, let's examine the DSM-IV-TR's (2000) criteria for Substance Dependence:

A maladaptive pattern of substance use, leading to clinically significant impairment or distress, as manifested by three (or more) of the following, occurring at any time in the same 12-month period:

1. tolerance, as defined by either of the following:
    a. a need for markedly increased amounts of the substance to achieve intoxication or desired effect
    b. markedly diminished effect with continued use of the same amount of the substance
2. withdrawal, as manifested by either of the following:
    a. the characteristic withdrawal syndrome for the substance (refer to Criteria A and B of the criteria sets for Withdrawal from the specific substances)
    b. the same (or a closely related) substance is taken to relieve or avoid withdrawal symptoms
3. the substance is often taken in larger amounts or over a longer period than was intended
4. there is a persistent desire or unsuccessful efforts to cut down or control substance use
5. a great deal of time is spent in activities necessary to obtain the substance (e.g., visiting multiple doctors or driving long distances), use the substance (e.g. chain-smoking), or recover from its effects
6. important social, occupational, or recreational activities are given up or reduced because of substance use
7. the substance use is continued despite knowledge of having a persistent or recurrent physical or psychological problem that is likely to have been caused or exacerbated by the substance (e.g., current cocaine use despite recognition of cocaine-induced depression, or continued drinking despite recognition that an ulcer was made worse by alcohol consumption). (pp.197–198; Reprinted with permission from the Diagnostic and Statistical Manual of Mental Disorders, Fourth Edition, Text Revision, (Copyright ©2000). American Psychiatric Association.)

Note that the diagnosis is simply a listing of symptoms and that a client need only show three of the seven symptoms at any time within a 12-month period to earn the diagnosis. Most often, clients who meet the criteria for substance dependence exhibit far more than the minimum of three symptoms required to make this diagnosis, but not always. This means that two clients can be given this same diagnosis of substance dependence without having *any* symptoms in common! Again, this highlights the danger of reading too much into the diagnosis without understanding the particulars of the individual client. Additionally, please note that the diagnosis speaks of the symptoms as producing a *pattern*. This is a crucial point that cannot be emphasized enough. Therefore, in order for a substance dependence diagnosis to be made, the client's intoxicant use, and the problems it causes in the person's life, must be *repetitive* within a yearlong period of time. A one-time intoxication does not qualify for this diagnosis. Correspondingly, a sporadic pattern, *if not repetitive*, does not qualify for a substance dependence diagnosis.

Fraternal versus identical twins: Why clinicians and 12-Step people often misunderstand each other when they are saying the same thing. A key issue in the diagnosis of dependence revolves around the question of whether the person has a physiological dependence on the intoxicant. In the DSM, there are two ways to determine this: 1) Does the client experience tolerance, most often expressed by the client needing more of the substance to get the same high? 2) Has the client ever experienced a withdrawal syndrome from a substance? Meeting either or both determinations qualifies the person as being physiologically dependent on the chemical.

Tolerance. Tolerance is easy to define. It indicates the point at which a person requires more of a substance to experience the same level of intoxication from the substance. A simple example is the use of caffeine. When starting caffeine use, one regular eight-ounce coffee is enough to keep you running through your day like a cheetah amped up on crystal meth. But, with repeated consumption that one regular eight-ounce coffee doesn't have much effect, and soon you bump it up to two cups. Gradually, you continue increasing your caffeine intake until one morning, as you're ordering a quad shot Americano in the jumbo-size cup, you realize that it *still* won't be enough to get you through the morning. At that point, you might need to think about cutting back a little. Basically, your body and brain have developed a tolerance to the stimulating effect of the caffeine, and you now require more and more caffeine to achieve the same level of energy you got with that first-ever cup.

Withdrawal. Defining the concept of withdrawal is more complicated. Most classes of substances (such as opiates, sedatives, etc.) have their own characteristic physical withdrawal syndrome, including both physical and psychological symptoms. Some of them can be very severe; for example, the withdrawal from opiates or alcohol, which can require medical detoxification protocols to safely manage the withdrawal. For other drugs of choice, the physical withdrawal reactions can be so mild that they're almost impossible to notice. The DSM-IV is quite proficient and thorough with respect to withdrawal symptoms by separately listing withdrawal symptoms and diagnoses for each class of drug (such as Alcohol Withdrawal or Opioid Withdrawal).

There are complicated biological and neuropsychological mechanisms underpinning physiological dependence and its associated symptoms of tolerance and withdrawal. A key concept here is one of active homeostasis: the process by which a system, through its own actions, keeps a variable or set of variables within a certain range.

Consider your home's heating and cooling system as a good example of homeostasis in action. In the interest of being geographically inclusive, during a particularly warm day you decide that fresh air is not your desire and set the thermostat to 70 degrees. This alerts the cooling system to maintain a state of homeostasis where it will keep the temperature in the home at an *average* of 70 degrees. We say average, because the temperature will not always be at 70 degrees. Once the temperature rises above 70 degrees, say 72 degrees, it signals the cooling system to initiate and drop the temperature, thus saving you from having to eat a pint of ice cream in an effort to stay cool. The thermostat allows this cooling to continue until the temperature reaches somewhere slightly below the 70 degree mark, when it signals the system to stop. No longer being cooled, the temperature in the home rises again until the thermostat reads 72 degrees. At this point, your thermostat again signals the cooling system to restart. Using this homeostatic mechanism, the cooling system maintains an average temperature of 70 degrees by allowing the temperature to vary between 68 and 72 degrees.

Our bodies work in a similar manner; blood pressure, heart rate, body temperature, and the level of activity in the brain all attempt to run in a homeostatic fashion. Subjectively, we experience subtle shifts in our mood and sleep, and the brain continues to monitor and regulate our body systems to ensure homeostasis. As the level of brain activity rises, a person goes beyond the normal range of mood and physiological arousal. Consequently, they begin to show signs of overactivity of the brain, including increased heart rate, higher blood pressure, upset stomach, agitation, insomnia, hand shaking, hyperactivity, and a mood that may vary from anxious to manic. As the level of activity increases, eventually it reaches a point where the person begins to have seizures. At yet higher levels of brain activity, death results.

Conversely, as levels of brain activity drop below normal, a person may display a variety of slowing reactions. Their mood may go from sad to depressed, and blood pressure and heart rates drop to lower levels. This can result in the person becoming increasingly inactive, exhibiting increased sleep, and a loss of interest in pleasurable activities. With further losses of brain activity, the person can slip into a coma and, not far behind, perhaps die.

On a cheerier note, it is clearly important for the body to maintain a person's brain activity within a normal range, and thankfully for most, the body is quite adept at doing this. As a hypothetical, John experiences minor fluctuations in his brain's activity. For John, he often experiences the feeling that sometimes he is happy and energetic, while at other times he is a bit down and doesn't have as much get-up-and-go. In this example, John's mood fluctuates but not excessively.

In another hypothetical, Tolbert (aptly named) is developing tolerance for alcohol. Alcohol is a central nervous system (or CNS) depressant. This means that it decreases the level of brain activity, as you no doubt have witnessed if you ever stepped into a bar an hour before last call. As brain activity decreases, Tolbert feels intoxicated, and at this point his brain activity is lower than normal. Once he begins to sober up, the activity of his brain returns to its normal range of functioning.

However, if Tolbert continues to frequently drink alcohol, his body detects that his level of brain activity is generally too low and it begins to compensate by increasing his level of brain activity in an attempt to compensate for the CNS-depressing effects of the alcohol. For Tolbert, this means that if he consumes the same amount of alcohol, it will result in less intoxication. This is what is meant by *tolerance*. If Tolbert does not change the rate or amount of alcohol consumed, then his body continues to attempt to compensate for the too frequent CNS suppression brought about by alcohol consumption. Just as in the description of caffeine use, the same amount of alcohol that got Tolbert very intoxicated early in his drinking career now results in very little intoxication.

Unfortunately, most substance dependent individuals do not follow this pattern. Instead, they respond to the development of tolerance by increasing the amount of intoxicant they consume so that they reach similar levels of intoxication. As a result, the person drinks more and more in order to counteract the body's developing tolerance. Not surprisingly, this cycle does eventually end, as the human body can only compensate so far. After a period of adjustment, a person's body essentially stops developing additional tolerance.

Let's switch to another hypothetical example and discuss Nicole. Nicole is a very seriously alcohol-dependent individual who is chronically intoxicated until the point where she realizes that she has a problem. Nicole begins quitting cold turkey, meaning she suddenly stops consuming alcohol with no biological assistance or medications. It will take time for her body to clear the alcohol out of her system. However, the alcohol and its depressant effects on brain activity will be gone long before her brain realizes that it no longer has to compensate for the alcohol. It will take her body and brain a few days to return to normal functioning. In the meantime, the brain continues to compensate *as if* her brain was still bathed in alcohol. As a result, Nicole's level of brain activity increases beyond normal. This rebounding of activity is especially dangerous when dealing with substances like alcohol. The brain activity can be raised to the point of hallucinations and seizures, either of which can result in death, when alcohol is not suppressing the level of brain activity. Assuming Nicole survives, her brain will realize that it is no longer being artificially depressed, stop compensating for alcohol with high brain activity, and bring her level of brain activity back to normal. This phenomenon, where the rapid withdrawal of a substance results in the brain overcorrecting in the *opposite direction* to the perceived effect of the substance, is called *rebound.*

A similar phenomenon also occurs for stimulant dependence. Our next hypothetical example is a stimulant using individual named Patsy. Stimulant intoxication is accompanied by excessive brain stimulation; with repeated use, Patsy's brain will compensate by lowering levels of stimulation and intoxication, if the dose of stimulant is not increased. If Patsy tries to stop cold turkey, because her body is dependent on the stimulant, she will experience withdrawal marked by a rebound effect.

Although these hypothetical examples are oversimplified, they do help explain many of the key biological features underpinning tolerance and withdrawal, and key symptoms of a physiological dependence. However, these two symptoms of a physiological dependence alone do not meet the criteria for a diagnosis of substance dependence. Remember, there must also be behavioral and psychological changes associated with the intoxicant.

Think about the fact that there are individuals who develop tolerance and/or a withdrawal syndrome on an intoxicant, but never develop the behavioral or psychological changes associated with substance dependence. One of these groups of people are those individuals who use opiates as a treatment for severe pain. If they are on a longer treatment protocol, they may need to have their opiate medication incrementally increased due to the tolerance build up by the brain to the opiate medication. However, once the opiate medication is stopped, as a result of its absence these individuals do not seek the drug out, become obsessed with it, or suffer a decline in their functioning (despite minor withdrawal effects as the medication is tapered down). In effect, these people were physiologically dependent on the drug, but they did not become an addict because they did not develop the psychological and behavioral difficulties characteristic of addiction.

So, what are these behavioral and psychological changes that must occur to qualify for the diagnosis of substance dependence? Generally, many of these symptoms fall under the umbrella of denial: that the use is becoming a problem, that there is a loss of control when using the substance of choice, and that there is a significant rearrangement of priorities to support the ongoing abuse of the drug of choice (despite the clear evidence that the continued abuse is resulting in negative consequences for the person). Taken as a whole, these symptoms are often seen as an expression of craving, preoccupation, compulsive use, and the negative consequences of addiction (such as relational problems with loved ones, work problems, poor health, etc.).

Cravings versus urges. Cravings are a complex phenomenon that can be simply defined as an urge to consume something. Cravings can be triggered or caused and then maintained by internal and/or external factors. In other words, cravings are a complex biological and psychological response that responds to operant conditioning, including discriminative and rewarding stimuli that may exist internally or externally relative to the individual.

We have all experienced some version of cravings. The easiest to understand is hunger, which could be described as a craving for food. And, just like hunger, cravings can be started or triggered by a number of things. A physical need of the body (i.e., cramping after going several hours without eating), a psychological need such as stress eating (think Liz Lemon in the television show *30 Rock*), or simply in response to some external cue or stimuli (I wasn't hungry until I saw that pizza commercial or smelled the fresh-baked cinnamon rolls). Not surprisingly, drug cravings work in a similar fashion.

The word *cravings,* when commonly used by most therapists, has a different meaning than the same word if used by 12-Step participants, which frequently causes miscommunication between the groups. When dealing with someone who is a participant in a 12-Step program, it is an error to term the biological and psychological desire to use as a craving. Myriad terms can be used to describe this biological and psychological desire to use, but we like the term *urge* and from this point forward throughout the book uses this term to describe this phenomenon. Additionally, when a desire is triggered most clients are able to connect to the term urge as it closely reflects their feelings (immediacy, compulsively, determinedly).

12-Step applies a different concept to the word *craving.* According to the 12-Step philosophy, craving begins once someone *has had their first hit or sip of their drug of choice.* At that point, the "phenomenon of craving" takes over and no amount of the substance that is ingested satisfies the addict/alcoholic. In essence, the craving to want more of the drug of choice, or more accurately the high achieved from the drug, never goes away—no matter how much the addict/alcoholic uses to try to satisfy it. In effect, the craving produces a bottomless pit that cannot be filled.

In the beginning phases of addiction, any specific episode of use may end in an unpredictable fashion. Sometimes the addict/alcoholic is able to stop themselves after a time. Other times, the alcohol/addict sets strict limits on how much they will use that night, only to find themselves exceeding that limit by an inch or 92,955,807.3 miles, whatever you prefer. As the using progresses over time, the addict/alcoholic's use continues until such time as some external force stops the using. Examples of some of these forces are: passing out from intoxication, a call from a spouse threatening to leave if the addict/alcoholic doesn't come home, running out of money, running out of the substance, and overdosing.

Keep in mind that the addict/alcoholic does not think, "I had enough. I feel satisfied." Often that insatiable feeling of need, the phenomenon of craving, continues even after the external force has intervened. This is powerlessness: the inability of the addict/alcoholic to predict or stop their using once the phenomenon of craving begins.

Preoccupation/compulsion versus insanity. Another aspect of dependence is preoccupation, a characteristic commonly seen as a person slides into substance dependence. It can be expressed in many areas of a person's functioning. In *preoccupation,* the addicted persons' thoughts, plans, and beliefs may increasingly become centered on the intoxicant. Their thinking may increasingly revolve around the use of a substance, the experience of intoxication, and/or any experiences commonly associated with using the intoxicant, such as sex. Their thinking also begins to revolve about planning for the use itself; where will they go to get it, from whom will they purchase it, how to get money for it, when can they start using it, and so on. As the preoccupation grows, little if any time is spent with other activities or people not associated with using. Their mood may be altered by their use in such a way that the only point of primary pleasure in the person's life is when they are intoxicated.

The preoccupations with the intoxicant and its related experiences can impact a person in multiple ways: 1) this preoccupation often serves to trigger the urge to use. This may set up a feedback loop where the urge to use triggers the preoccupation with details of the use, which then reinforces and strengthens the urge to use. Each feedback loop strengthens the urge to use until the person's self-control is eroded, and the individual seeks out the intoxicant and intoxication. In turn, the use of the intoxicant causes the delay on seeking the intoxicant to erode and shorten the time for each subsequent feedback loop. In essence, the feedback loop becomes over-learned over a very large number of repetitions, ultimately resulting in a repetition of very strong and quick associations of urge, to preoccupation with use, to use. 2) A key aspect of this blueprint is that the person continues with these internal and external patterns, despite any awareness that the use of the intoxicant clearly has a significant negative impact on the person and their functioning. 3) In the end, the addict's preoccupation reorganizes the person's short-term priorities so that the addiction and its related activities become so important that other parts of the person's life are neglected, or simply abandoned altogether.

This concept of preoccupation is addressed in both the texts of *Alcoholics Anonymous* and *Narcotics Anonymous*, but it is done so under the term *insanity*. In the beginning, as the preoccupation (insanity) begins to take root, the addict's perception generally is that their intoxicant-centered thoughts and behaviors are harmless and even make sound sense. *Alcoholics Anonymous (AA)* (2001), or just the "Big Book" as it is known within AA, provides this great example:

> On the way I felt hungry so I stopped at a roadside place where they have a bar. I had no intention of drinking . . . I sat down at a table and ordered a sandwich and a glass of milk . . . *Suddenly the thought crossed my mind that if I were to put an ounce of whiskey in my milk it couldn't hurt me on a full stomach. I ordered a whiskey and poured it into the milk. I vaguely sensed I was not being any too smart, but felt reassured as I was taking the whiskey on a full stomach.* The experiment went so well that I ordered another whiskey and poured it into more milk. That didn't seem to bother me so I tried another. Thus started one more journey to the asylum for Jim . . . *He had much knowledge about himself as an alcoholic. Yet all reasons for not drinking were easily pushed aside in favor of the foolish idea that he could take whiskey if only he mixed it with milk!* (pp. 36–37)

We can question whether or not Jim really had no intention of drinking, after all, why choose a roadside place with a bar? There are, and were (the AA book was first published in 1939), plenty of eateries that do not serve alcohol. Jim's choice of selecting a restaurant with liquor could mean that there was a preoccupation of drinking, even if it was not in his awareness. He may have already been under the compelling influence of his biological urges. This brings us to the example of a phrase used in the text of *Alcoholics Anonymous* (2001) that describes addiction as "cunning, baffling, powerful!" (p. 58). The phrase is loosely used to describe all the ways in which a person can become both preoccupied and compelled to seek the intoxicant, even without being fully aware of any intention to use.

Similarly, the "Basic Text" of Narcotics Anonymous (2008) speaks of preoccupation (insanity) in terms of *obsession:*

> Many of us realize when we get to the Program that we have gone back time and again to using, even though we knew that we were destroying our lives by doing so. Insanity is using day after day knowing that only physical and mental destruction comes when we do. The most obvious insanity of the disease of addiction is the obsession to use drug. . . . Ask yourself this question: Do I believe it would be insane to walk up to someone and say, "May I please have a heart attack or a fatal accident?" (pp. 23–24)

This passage describes how many people in active addiction, caught up in the preoccupied state of mind, create literally insane plans to justify use of the intoxicant and also to somehow prevent the negative consequences that occur from their use. Clients participating in 12-Steps repeat a definition of insanity often heard in the rooms as follows: "Doing the same thing over and over and expecting different results." On a global level, this phrase accurately summarizes the 12-Step perspectives on preoccupation with the intoxicant.

The defined preoccupation that is expressed in the dependent person's behavior is consistent between the 12-Step and the DSM-IV symptoms necessary to diagnose substance dependence. Two DSM-IV symptoms that reflect this consistency are 1) a great deal of time is spent by the substance dependent in activities necessary to obtain the substance, use the substance, or recover from its effects, and 2) important social, occupational, or recreational activities are given up or reduced by the substance dependent because of substance effects. Complicating the assessment, these symptoms are often altered by three variables: 1) the client's prior level of functioning, 2) the client's community, and 3) the specific intoxicant used.

A person's premorbid or predisease functioning may influence their behavior, especially as it relates to their life's circumstances and ultimately their clinical assessment. Let's consider an example. First, sometimes the confluence of mental health issues interferes with the ability to diagnose a substance dependence problem. Consider how it may be difficult to see the negative impact of substance dependence with a chronically depressed and socially withdrawn individual. This person would likely be so isolated in their home that no one would see the amount or length of daily using. Additionally, no one would know that the hangover or crash following intoxication was impeding functioning as those symptoms look very much like the behavior of a chronically depressed person (oversleeping, not eating, low motivation, low energy, sad mood, etc.).

Second, a person's social community may also influence how easily they meet the diagnostic symptoms. For instance, a client may work in a family business that tolerates and supports the person's addiction, as addiction is "normal" within that family. So, although the person may be chronically late, taking cash out of the register, missing shifts, and so on, the family regards this behavior as normal. "Oh that's just George. He's just like his grandfather." Another example is that of a bartender who develops alcoholism. For years and years, the alcoholism is all but invisible in the context of their work environment (a bar or tavern). It would be difficult to note how many shots they are drinking with customers (or alone). Tardiness would be hard to use as an indicator because their shift starts at 7 p.m. (never mind that that they slept until 6 p.m.!). Their mood might be bright and cheery as they start their shift, not because they love their job (as one might assume by watching), but because they know they now get to drink.

Specific community characteristics can also impact diagnosis. For example, some substances, such as alcohol or marijuana, may be quite easily obtained in some communities, significantly decreasing the person's need to devote time and effort to obtaining the substance. Additionally, as we cited in the examples above, different groups of people and places where substance use is normative have the ability to greatly skew awareness of problematic use and/or dependence.

Finally, the specific intoxicant choice can also impact the ease with which a person qualifies for a diagnosis of substance dependence. Dependency on some drugs may have little impact on a person, at least for a time. For instance, when a person first develops a dependency on methamphetamine, there can often be little if any negative impact on the person's functioning, and this impact often continues to remain limited for several years. In fact, a dependency on methamphetamine can have the opposite effect by giving the person more energy and focus, therefore further *hiding* any substance dependence because their performance is *enhanced* not detracted. Other drug use symptoms may progress more quickly. For example, once cocaine use has elevated to smoking the drug, the use may escalate quickly to daily use, frequently severely impairing a person's functioning within 4 to 6 weeks.

In addition to preoccupation, compulsive use is another key component to addiction. As our previous examples of preoccupation highlight, it is common for substance dependent people to lose control of their substance use. For the DSM-IV, compulsive use is captured through two symptoms: 1) the intoxicant is consumed in larger amounts or longer time periods than was intended, and 2) there is a persistent desire or unsuccessful efforts made to reduce or control their substance abuse. Perhaps more than any other symptom of dependence, these two symptoms are most influenced by the client's perspective of their abuse. Both of these symptoms require that the client is cognitively, if not emotionally, aware of some dissonance or difference between what they want (i.e., to drink only two beers tonight when they go out with their friends to the bar) and what they are doing (two beers end up being twelve resulting in a blackout, and therefore not knowing how they ended up in a hotel room with a stranger in the morning). This dissonance is often referred to clinically as the concept of someone being egodystonic versus egosyntonic. *Egodystonic* reflects behaviors, thoughts, and feelings that are at odds with one's self-concept. *Egosyntonic* refers to behaviors, thoughts, and feelings that are consistent with one's self-concept. The text of *Alcoholics Anonymous* (2001) highlights this concept nicely:

> If you ask him why he started on his last bender, the chances are he will offer you any one of a hundred alibis. Sometimes these excuses have a certain plausibility, but none of them really makes sense in the light of the havoc an alcoholic's drinking bout creates. They sound like the philosophy of the man who, having a headache, beats himself on the head with a hammer so that he can't feel the ache . . . Once in a while, he may tell the truth. And the truth, strange to say, is usually that he has no more idea why he took that first drink than you have. Some drinkers have excuses with which they are satisfied part of the time. But, in their hearts they really do not know why they do it. Once this malady [alcoholism] has a real hold, they are a baffled lot. There is the obsession that somehow, someday, they will beat the game. But they often suspect they are down for the count. (p. 23)

Conversely, egosyntonic behaviors are seen as consistent with one's self-concept. For those whose intoxicant use becomes increasingly egosyntonic, the individual is less likely to report either of the two symptoms related to compulsive use. This is often a result of the client's use of defenses, most often denial, preventing the client from having awareness of the true impact of their behavior and insight into it. At perhaps its most blatant level, there are a group of substance dependent individuals who do not exhibit these DSM-IV symptoms, simply because they have no desire to limit or stop their use of the intoxicant. Despite the wreckage that their use is causing, from their perspective they see no reason to even slow down. Since all use is welcome; there is no experience of spending more time or taking more of the intoxicant than intended. For them, all of it is good. The egodystonic people are the ones who can easily meet one or both of the DSM-IV symptoms related to compulsive use; the egosyntonic people will not.

When examining compulsive use, with the exception of some terminology differences the DSM-IV and 12-Steps conceptually mesh very well. However, in both books, there are many stories that highlight the egodystonic symptoms of compulsive use. The text of Narcotics Anonymous (2008) defines compulsiveness in the following fashion.

> At first, we were using in a manner that seemed to be social or at least controllable . . . At some point, our using became uncontrollable and anti-social . . . We may have tried to moderate, substitute or even stop using, but we went from a state of drugged success and well-being to complete spiritual, mental, and emotional bankruptcy. This rate of decline varies from addict to addict. Whether it occurs in years or days, it is all downhill. (p. 7)

The stories in both reference books, and some of the cases we bring forth in this text, help paint a clearer picture of the nature of the addicted mind. In order to more clearly understand the symptoms of compulsion, we encourage everyone to read any or all of the stories in both texts of *Alcoholics Anonymous* (the Big Book), and Narcotics Anonymous (the Basic Text), or any of the other 12-Step Program books and/or pamphlets.

Negative consequence vs. negative consequences! We have a winner! Finally, after examination of characteristics such as cravings, preoccupation, and compulsion, the last concept of *negative consequences* is often a key component of the diagnosis. For the diagnosis, the primary symptom is that the substance use is continued *despite knowledge* of having a persistent or recurrent physical or psychological problem that is likely caused by or exacerbated by the substance. To meet this symptom, the client must have been informed of the negative consequence(s) of their use, or be aware of them. If neither condition is met, the client cannot match this symptom. However, meeting this condition can sometimes be challenging. Take for instance a woman with psychosis who is psychologically dependent on marijuana. She experiences more frequent hallucinations and paranoia almost every time she gets high, and yet she continues to smoke a joint or two every day.

This pattern of use only meets the criteria for this DSM-IV symptom if a) she was informed by someone reliable (such as a family member, her psychiatrist, primary care physician, or case manager) of this negative effect, or b) she is aware, or strongly suspects, that marijuana is exacerbating her hallucinations and paranoia. If neither the *a* condition nor the *b* condition is met, then this symptom's requirements are not fulfilled and it cannot be counted when diagnosing her for substance dependence. Likewise, an IV (intravenous) drug user does not meet this criterion, for example, if they are unaware that they have contracted diseases such as HIV or hepatitis through this use. However, if they experience repeated abscesses (skin infections with ulcers) that they know are caused by their injections, then they do meet the criteria for this symptom.

Here again, there is agreement between the 12-Step Program and the DSM-IV, as one of the main tenets for the Program is belief that rigorous honesty is needed to recover from addiction. The chapter titled "How It Works," in the text of *Alcoholics Anonymous* (2001), states

> Rarely have we seen a person fail who has thoroughly followed our path. Those who do not recover are people who cannot or will not completely give themselves to this simple program, usually men and women who are constitutionally incapable of being honest with themselves. . . . They are naturally incapable of grasping and developing a manner of living which demands rigorous honesty. Their chances are less than average. There are those, too, who suffer from grave emotional and mental disorders, but many of them do recover if they have the capacity to be honest. (p. 58)

This includes ownership of the negative consequences stemming from addictive behavior. Neither the Basic Text nor the Big Book specifies directly that the awareness is to come during or after their using days. However, the stories in both books often speak of that awareness and related honesty as occurring during their using, and being a pivotal reason for attempts to mitigate those consequences.

Modifiers of the substance dependence diagnosis. In addition to making the diagnosis of substance dependence, the clinician must also identify if physiological dependence is present or not, and the course specifier. As far as physiological dependence, if the client is displaying signs of tolerance or a withdrawal from the intoxicant, then "with physiological dependence" is added to the formal diagnosis. However, if the client does not display signs of tolerance or withdrawal, then "without physiological dependence" is tacked onto the diagnosis.

As far as course specifiers, a full and complete diagnosis for someone who has achieved at least some sobriety will end with one of the following six specifiers:

- Early Full Remission
- Early Partial Remission
- Sustained Partial Remission
- Sustained Full Remission
- On Agonist Therapy
- In a Controlled Environment

We will start by exploring the first four specifiers for remission. Note that there are three types of terms used here: "remission," "early versus sustained," and "full versus partial." By "Remission," the DSM-IV means that the person has not displayed the full symptoms of dependence for at least 1 month (specifically, they have not displayed three of the symptoms during that time period). The "early versus full" term indicates how long the person has been sober. So, a person diagnosed as in Early Remission means that they have not displayed symptoms of dependence for at least 1 month, but less than 12 months. A person in Sustained Remission has not displayed symptoms of dependence for 12 or more months.

Both Early and Sustained Remission are also modified by the specifiers "partial versus full." A Full Remission means that for a period of at least one month, the person has not met *any* of the symptoms of Substance Dependence or Abuse. In contrast, Partial Remission simply means the person has not achieved full sobriety. Clients with Partial Remission display one or two of the symptoms of dependence during the remission, but not three or more (i.e., the number needed to qualify for the diagnosis). It is important to note that this *does not mean that they refrain from the use of intoxicants, or even the intoxicant that initially qualified them for the diagnosis of Substance Dependence.* They can display up to two symptoms of Dependence or any of the symptoms of Substance Abuse over the course of at least 1 month.

Taken together, these four specifiers are summarized below:

- Early Full Remission: The person has not displayed any symptoms of Substance Dependence or Abuse for 1 to 12 months
- Early Partial Remission: The person has not met the criteria of Substance Dependence during a period of time lasting 1 to 12 months long. However, they have displayed the symptoms of Substance Abuse and/or only one or two symptoms of Substance Dependence during this period of time.
- Sustained Full Remission: The person has not displayed any symptoms of Substance Dependence or Abuse for at least 12 months.
- Sustained Partial Remission: The person has not met the criteria of Substance Dependence for at least 12 months. However, they have displayed the symptoms of Substance Abuse and/or only one or two symptoms of Substance Dependence during this period of time.

The remaining two specifiers are even simpler. "In a Controlled Environment" means the client has been in remission for at least 1 month, and that they reside in a place where access or the use of intoxicants is restricted. Controlled environment examples are prisons, locked hospitals units, house arrest (ankle bracelet equipped with alcohol sensor), and halfway houses. The other specifier is "On Agonist Therapy." To qualify for this, the client needs to meet the criteria for remission (some sobriety for at least 1 month), and also be treated with an agonist. An *agonist*, in this context, means the person is being treated with an agonist, partial agonist, or agonist/antagonist. An agonist is a substance that acts similarly to the drug or alcohol. For example, the most commonly used agonist is Methadone for opiate addiction. Methadone produces an effect that is similar both to heroin and opiate-based pain medication (such as morphine, codeine, hydrocodone, and oxycodone, to name a few). A partial agonist produces a weaker effect than the intoxicant produces. An *antagonist* partially blocks intoxicants or agonists from affecting the client in most ways by acting on nerve cells, generally blocking receptors on the molecular level. An agonist/antagonist is a substance that, on a molecular level, acts as both an agonist and an antagonist.

Taking the Long View: Applying a Broad Lens to Exploring Treatment Options

For many who treat clients with substance dependence, only one treatment goal is appropriate for these clients. That goal is abstinence. For them, once a client crosses the threshold into substance dependence the client's life has permanently changed. From this point forward, these clients no longer respond to intoxicant use in the same manner as a "normal" non-substance dependent person. Instead, any use of that substance (or any other intoxicant to some) eventually triggers the described feedback loop of urge-compulsion-use—the destructive pattern associated with substance dependence. In effect, the person will always be addicted, and this fact never changes.

The view of abstinence as the only treatment option for substance dependence is highly simplistic. There are many groups of individuals with substance dependence who seem to simply stop using. Some even return to use their intoxicant of choice occasionally, but never slide back into compulsive use. Some individuals seem to simply resolve their addictions without treatment or even external influence. For instance, it is fairly common for IV heroin abusers to lose interest in the drug by the time they reach the end of middle age, and it appears that they simply spontaneously stop using. Similarly, across all substances of choice you can see the gradual decreasing of binge use the further along in life one travels. For example, Figure 1.1 is the diagram illustrating the progression of nonbinging, binging, and heavy (dependent) alcohol use throughout the lifespan. Figure 1.2 is an example of the reported amount of drug use (reflecting all drugs of choice) throughout a person's lifespan.

There are other factors to consider when thinking about a human being's response to their environment and in their choice to use an intoxicant. For instance, some soldiers during the Vietnam War developed a dependence on heroin and/or alcohol

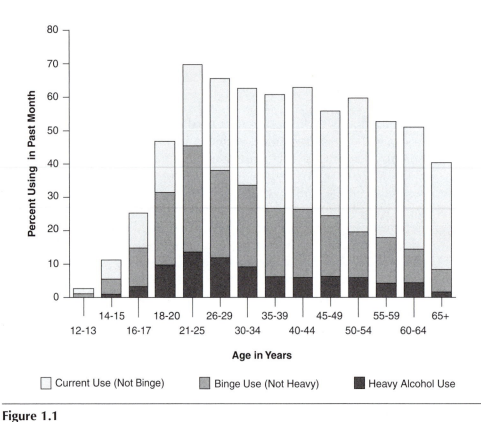

Figure 1.1

Source: Substance Abuse and Mental Health Services Administration. (2011). *National Survey of Drug Use and Health.* Retrieved from http://www.samhsa.gov/data/NSDUH/2011SummNatFindDetTables/Index.aspx.

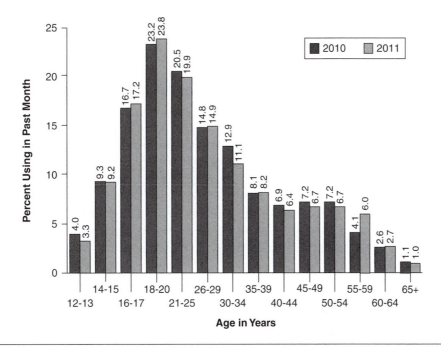

Figure 1.2

Source: Substance Abuse and Mental Health Services Administration. (2011). *National Survey of Drug Use and Health.* Retrieved from http://www.samhsa.gov/data/NSDUH/2k11Results/NSDUHresults2011.htm#Fig2-5

while in Vietnam. However, once they returned to the United States, all interest in those substances disappeared. Many returned to alcohol use once they were home, and this did not escalate into a compulsive use pattern. It is also not uncommon for children and adolescents who develop drug or alcohol dependence in their youth to discover that they are able as an adult to resume use of that same intoxicant without developing a compulsive pattern. The authors have also worked with methamphetamine or cocaine dependent individuals who maintained several years of sobriety, later returning to sporadic use of those substances without the resumption of a compulsive pattern. Clearly, abstinence is not the only goal for every client. More is discussed on this topic in later chapters.

ASAM criteria: Utilizing the most common guideline for treatment planning. Once a treatment goal is set, a treatment plan, ideally in partnership with the client, is then created. One of the most commonly used guides for treatment planning is the ASAM (American Society of Addiction Medicine) criteria. The ASAM criteria relies on a sequence of assessment criteria, or "Dimensions," that are considered when deciding what level of treatment is indicated for a client with substance dependence. Each dimension looks at a specific aspect that is believed to interact with the success of a substance dependent person's treatment.

What follows is a very brief review of some of the main concepts of the Patient Placement Criteria for the Treatment of Substance-Related Disorders, found in the *ASAM PPC-2* (2nd Edition-Revised). For anyone planning on using this approach, it is strongly recommended that they purchase and familiarize themselves with this system (visit www.asam.org). This system is especially useful if you plan on working within a facility or organized treatment program.

The assessed ASAM Dimensions are as follows:

1. Acute Intoxication and/or Withdrawal Potential
   This is primarily a medically based dimension. It involves assessing the level of safety/risk a client experiences given their current level of intoxication, the medical consequences of stopping their use of the intoxicant, the potential for a fatal withdrawal experience (such as with alcohol or benzodiazepines), and the client's ability to monitor a withdrawal, if not life-threatening.

2. Biomedical Conditions and Complications
   Fairly self-explanatory, this dimension identifies any medical issue(s) that might complicate withdrawal or a treatment modality. For instance, a client who has chronic pain from an amputation may have a much more complicated treatment for an addiction to opiates, or pain medication, than a client who does not have a preexisting chronic pain condition. Similarly, a withdrawal syndrome that increases a client's blood pressure may be far more complicated for clients with preexisting problems with their heart or blood pressure.

3. Emotional, Behavioral, or Cognitive Conditions and Complications
   These are also called co-occurring (or the previously used term, dual-diagnosis) disorders. These can include psychiatric or psychological disorders (schizophrenia or severe depression), behavioral conditions (chronic self-defeating behaviors motivated by underlying shame), or cognitive conditions (memory loss due to brain injury).

4. Readiness to Change
   This is taken directly from the writings of Procheska, DeClemente, and Norcross (1992) on their theory of change. This theory and dimension assumes that a person's level of resistance to change, and cooperation with treatment, alters as a person engages in the change process. Thus, the treatment should be amended to respond to the client's stage of change or, as ASAM writes it, the client's readiness to change.

5. Relapse, Continued Use, or Continued Problem Potential
   This dimension is a fairly complex component. It involves a very thorough reviewing of the client's history of relapse, their ability to cope with the stressors involved with abstinence, as well as their awareness and ability to prevent a relapse.

6. Recovery/Living Environment
   This last dimension looks at the systems around the person that may support or hinder their safety, abstinence, and treatment. These factors include family, friends, community, social service agencies, and the justice system. Also incorporated is the presence of those persons in the client's life who pose a relapse risk to the client by virtue of their continued use of intoxicants.

Based on the results of the six dimensions, clinician's determine which level of care is best suited to treat the client's presenting problems. Note that the following explanation of the ASAM level system is a highly consolidated and simplified explanation. Readers are again encouraged to review these dimensions on a more detailed level.

Level 0.5: Early Intervention

Early Intervention is best described as those individuals who would qualify as an *at risk* group. Examples are children or adolescents in homes where one or both parents are struggling with active substance dependence, and live in impoverished areas where drug dealing is a viable means of obtaining income and resources.

Level I: Outpatient Treatment

Outpatient treatment is defined as individual or group therapy sessions that do not exceed a total of 9 hours per week. Support group services such as 12-Step is not considered as outpatient treatment.

Level II: Intensive Outpatient/Partial Hospitalization Treatment

Intensive outpatient treatment (IOP) is a structured program that meets for a total of 9 to 15 hours per week. The days and times of such a program vary greatly. The majority of hospital-based intensive outpatient programs run three to five days per week for three hours per day. The primary mode of therapy is group. Psychiatry services and individual therapy are services that are often, but not always, included. If a psychiatrist is involved with an intensive outpatient program (generally in a hospital-based setting that accepts managed care funding), the psychiatrist is *required* to assess the client's suitability for, and progress in, the IOP on a *weekly* basis.

Partial hospitalization programs (PHP) are programs that run four to six hours per day, for five to seven days a week. These programs are highly structured with a combination of group therapy, life skill development, social work/case management services, and individual therapy. Psychiatrists are *required* to assess the client's suitability for, and progress in, the PHP on a *daily* basis. Due to this expense and other factors, PHP's have steadily declined in popularity.

Level III: Inpatient/Residential Treatment

Inpatient programs are hospital-based and generally (but not always) locked facilities. Anyone admitted to an inpatient program needs a psychiatrist's order to be discharged. Programming varies from facility to facility, but can incorporate individual therapy, family therapy, group therapy, art therapy, psychodrama, psychiatry, social work/case management, comprehensive medical assessment and treatment, activity therapy, and support group meetings. Again, programming varies greatly but can be extremely rigorous where clients are in therapy for 10 to 12 hours per day. Over time, the average length of stay has steadily gone down, resulting in average inpatient stays, if utilizing managed care benefits, of anywhere from 3 to 21 days.

Adult residential treatment facilities for drug addiction are similar to inpatient settings except that the length of stay can range from 30 days to several years, and some of these facilities are not locked. Generally, clients are placed on a "restricted" status on arrival until they earn the trust of the staff by maintaining their sobriety. Once sobriety has been demonstrated, clients are allowed to leave the premises in order to look for work, go to a job or school, attend 12-Step meetings, and so forth. Clients must still attend programming at the facility and adhere to the rules of the treatment program. Most clients access residential treatment facilities after a failed string of inpatient stays where relapse occurs frequently, and sober housing has proven ineffectual in stopping use. Clients often elect, when possible, to go to facilities that are out of town or state to help minimize exposure to triggering people, places, and things. Later in the book, we address these considerations more thoroughly.

Level IV: Medically Managed Inpatient Detoxification

The treatment for clients at this level is primarily medical. Very few clients who are going through an active detoxification that requires medical management are in any fit state to participate in therapy. Due to the high level of medical management, treatment is often confined to physicians and nurses until the acute detoxification process and risk have subsided. The main intoxicants that fit this category are alcohol and benzodiazepines due to their high detoxification lethality. With all the other intoxicants, while withdrawal and detoxification is unpleasant and sometimes nasty, they will not kill you. Therefore, unless you require active medical management, for instance for severe psychosis from acute stimulant intoxication, or have some other medical problem that complicates the withdrawal, you would not meet the criteria for this level of treatment.

Remember that the ASAM method requires clinicians to continually assess clients on the six dimensions at the start and throughout the treatment process. Clients are placed, transferred, or discharged among the levels of treatment based on this assessment. Let's consider these factors as we examine Geri's entry into psychotherapy:

Geri is a 58-year-old single Caucasian man who presented for psychotherapy with severe depression. Geri was referred by a local psychiatrist who had been treating him with medications for six months without success. Geri reported a 10-year history of mounting depression that easily met the DSM criteria for a diagnosis of Major Depression. He also reported a 20-year history of mounting alcohol use. For the past several years, he consumed approximately one fifth of vodka every three to four days. Typically, all of his drinking occurred in the afternoons and early evenings, allowing him to arrive for work sober the next day at a family-owned advertising firm.

Geri had been working for his family for two years. He reported that approximately once or twice a week he either missed work, was late to work, or consumed significant amounts of vodka at work, but "my family never seems to notice." He reported that he had lost several jobs over the past ten years due to the same behavior. During any point in the last five years, he had not abstained from alcohol for more than 48 hours "because the last time I did, I got sicker than a dog, my hands wouldn't stop shaking and my stomach got real upset." He reported spending most of his free time at home alone. Once or twice a week, he visits a neighborhood tavern "where I usually drink alone." Geri was HIV positive and on medications that were very effective at controlling his infection. His health was otherwise good.

Note: Geri easily meets the criteria for Alcohol Dependence, with physiological dependence as he displays withdrawal symptoms, spending a great deal of his time involved in consuming alcohol, and important vocational activities (and likely social and recreational as well) are reduced or given up because of his alcohol misuse. Geri's withdrawal symptoms clearly indicate that he is physiologically dependent on alcohol, and the excessive time and vocational impairment suggest that it has become a key feature of his current life, overshadowing much of his "normal" functioning.

The therapist informed Geri of his diagnosis and explored this with him, including that his depression might very well be closely related to his alcoholism. Geri agreed that he tended to consume too much alcohol, but he denied having a problem with it, stating that he "could control it" and stop on his own. The therapist advised him that suddenly stopping could cause him to experience serious medical problems, and recommended that he be admitted to a hospital for a medically supervised detoxification. Such a program would safely and quickly wean him off alcohol without risking serious medical complications. Geri refused this recommendation and eventually agreed to slowly wean himself off alcohol under the supervision of his psychiatrist.

Note: Alcohol is a dangerous intoxicant for most people to withdraw from, as it has the possibility to cause death due to seizures, aspirating on vomit (or breathing in vomit), or damage due to very elevated blood pressure. A medically supervised detoxification from alcohol is strongly recommended by ASAM. However, Geri refused this plan. A closely medically monitored outpatient weaning was agreed to as a far less desirable alternative, but one that would likely prevent him from endangering his life.

Geri and his psychiatrist created a plan for him to slowly decrease his use while his health was closely monitored. Geri attempted to follow this plan over the course of six weeks, repeatedly starting it, and then failing to reduce his alcohol consumption. During this same time, the therapist identified and explored with Geri how he had previously failed to reduce his alcohol use, how he had lost most of his friends, and how his family indirectly supported or enabled his alcohol use. After six weeks of failed attempts to do it on his own, Geri agreed to an inpatient medically supervised detoxification followed by a course of intensive outpatient psychotherapy.

Defining Substance Abuse

Once a clinician understands the diagnosis of Substance Dependence, the diagnosis of Substance Abuse becomes much simpler. The DSM-IV-TR's (2000) criteria for Substance Abuse is:

A. A maladaptive pattern of substance use leading to clinically significant impairment or distress, as manifested by one (or more) of the following, occurring within a 12-month period:

1. recurrent substance use resulting in a failure to fulfill major role obligations at work, school, or home (e.g., repeated absences or poor work performance related to substance use; substance-related absences, suspensions, or expulsions from school; neglect of children of household)
2. recurrent substance use in situations in which it is physically hazardous (e.g., driving an automobile or operating a machine when impaired by substance use)
3. recurrent substance-related legal problems (e.g., arrests for substance-related disorderly conduct)
4. continued substance use despite having persistent or recurrent social or interpersonal problems caused or exacerbated by the effects of the substance (e.g., arguments with spouse about consequences of intoxication, physical fights)

B. The symptoms have never met the criteria for Substance Dependence for this class of substance (p. 199; Reprinted with permission from the Diagnostic and Statistical Manual of Mental Disorders, Fourth Edition, Text Revision, (Copyright ©2000). American Psychiatric Association.).

Before making this diagnosis, the reader should attend to four unusual features of the criteria outlined below.

First, the diagnosis demands that the intoxicant use represents a pattern that occurs over the course of 12 months. So, a person does *not* qualify for a diagnosis of Substance Abuse if that abuse is both infrequent and unpatterned, even if the individual incidents of abuse were severe. Similar to substance dependence, a one-time intoxication does not qualify for the diagnosis, even if the person engaged in multiple high risk behaviors while intoxicated. Let's look at the behavior of Jacque.

Jacque went out with friends on St. Patrick's Day weekend and got ripping drunk, so much so that he blacked out for the first time. Most of the time, Jacque is able to control his drinking, recognizing when he is approaching intoxication and, on this awareness, slowing down or stopping his use. Six months later, he and his family took a camping trip and one night he once again partied hard and became inebriated, although this time he stopped before he reached a blackout state.

Would Jacque qualify for Substance Abuse? Not according to the criteria. The behavior and its attendant problems must be displayed repeatedly over the course of 12 months to qualify for the diagnosis. Jacque, although there certainly is some concern for his sporadic excessive drinking, does not have a definitive pattern necessary to meet the criteria. Similarly, a person also does not qualify for this diagnosis if once every 2 to 3 years they consume large amounts of drugs and alcohol for one evening with no repeated use within a 12-month long period. 12-Step agrees with this assessment as well. According to both texts, because Jacque is still able to predict (the vast majority of the time) the outcome of his using and limit his intake, he would not be labeled an alcoholic—in spite of realistic concern about the binging incidents.

The second unusual feature of the Substance Abuse diagnosis is that the person must not meet the criteria for Substance Dependence for that specific class of substance. By that reasoning, if a client named Sarah was diagnosed with Alcohol Dependence, then she never qualifies for an Alcohol Abuse diagnosis. Instead, Sarah can only be diagnosed with Alcohol Dependence with perhaps a partial remission; if there was use of alcohol following a period of sobriety. However, if with Alcohol Dependence, she also began snorting cocaine once a month and repeatedly entered into fights with others when intoxicated, at that point Sarah might meet the criteria for Cocaine Abuse. This diagnosis would be added to her original diagnosis of Alcohol Dependence.

Sarah does meet the criteria for Cocaine Abuse as she has a pattern of repeated substance use (cocaine) within a 12-month period that caused recurrent social problems (fighting). Cocaine and Alcohol are different classes of drugs, so they are diagnostically considered separately. The DSM-IV lists the following as classes of drugs: alcohol, amphetamines, caffeine, cannabis, cocaine, hallucinogens, inhalants, nicotine, opioids, phencyclidine (or PCP), along with three groups of drugs combined into one class: sedative, hypnotic, and anxiolytics. For each, a client can qualify for a diagnosis of abuse or dependence.

The third unusual feature to the diagnosis of substance abuse rather than substance dependence is that the client only needs to show one set of symptoms indicating distress or impairment from their intoxicant use. Remember, each of these symptom clusters must be *recurrent* or *persistent*. If these problems were present for the person prior to the substance use, then the symptom must be *more frequent* or *intense* when the person is intoxicated. Using our above example, if Sarah had a history of engaging in fights prior to starting cocaine abuse, then in order to qualify for a diagnosis of Cocaine Abuse, these fights would have to become more frequent or intense while she is abusing the cocaine.

The fourth unusual feature of the diagnosis of substance abuse relates to physiological dependence. Note that the Substance Abuse diagnosis does not even mention physiological dependence. It is based purely on a pattern of maladaptive behavior. It is therefore possible for a person who is physically dependent on a substance to qualify for a diagnosis of Substance Abuse, simply because they do not meet the criteria for Substance Dependence with that physically dependent substance. Also, if a person is physiologically dependent on a substance, but is not experiencing a disruption in their functioning, then that person *does not* qualify for a diagnosis of Substance Abuse or Dependence! An example of a person who does not meet the criteria for Opioid Abuse or Dependence is a hospital patient who was physiologically dependent on morphine for a short time, but never craves or seeks out the drug once released from the hospital, or once the drug is discontinued.

Let's illuminate these points by following a client named Mary:

Mary reports that she has a history of Dysthymic Disorder with a long history of chronic low-level depression that has never advanced in severity. Mary disclosed to her therapist that for the past six months she has grown "fed up" with her feelings of depression, and began "experimenting with cocaine." This involved having episodes of cocaine use two to three times a month. During these times she spent between $50 to $100 dollars on cocaine, using it with friends when she did not have to work the next day. During these episodes, she reported experiencing relief from her chronic depression.

However, while intoxicated on cocaine she also repeatedly engaged in unprotected sex with several men during most of her using episodes. She reported that once she was no longer under the influence of cocaine, she deeply regretted her sexual behavior, not only because of the potential risk of disease transmission, but also because she felt that the behavior deeply violated her internal moral code. She denied experiencing any tolerance or withdrawal symptoms from cocaine. She also denied experiencing any other changes in her behavior or negative consequences resulting from the drug use.

Note: Mary meets the criteria for Cocaine Abuse as she displayed a six-month-long pattern of drug use that she continued despite it causing her recurrent interpersonal problems (the unprotected sexual behavior followed by intense regret). Her use can also be described as egodystonic because her behavior from the drug use "deeply violated her internal moral code." Mary does not qualify for a Substance Dependence diagnosis as she developed no reported tolerance or withdrawal from the cocaine, although one could argue that her Dysthymic Disorder may be interfering with her ability to perceive withdrawal. Some of the withdrawal symptoms from cocaine are similar to the diagnostic criteria for Dysthymic Disorder; namely dysphoric mood, lethargy, and insomnia.

The therapist noted that Mary had previously been reluctant to begin psychotropic medication and a behavioral regimen to improve her symptomology. Mary agreed that she wanted a "quick fix," as the behavioral plan presented by the therapist was "overwhelming" to her. Mary still expressed reluctance to go on psychotropic medications, but agreed to do so after attempting the behavioral plan first. Mary and the therapist reworked the behavioral plan until it felt manageable to Mary. Mary agreed to refrain from cocaine for three months to give the behavioral plan a chance to work without interference.

SUMMARY

While not always in agreement, 12-Step Programs and the mental health/addiction field have a great deal in common conceptually, even if at times the languages are different. Although 12-Step Programs bill themselves as spiritual programs, they utilize a number of cognitive and behavioral techniques that go beyond the spiritual. Conversely, there still is a great deal we do not know about addiction, and therefore we take a "leap of faith" on self-help programs such as 12-Step, even if we do not fully understand why they are effective for some.

Our whole premise for this text is to assist clinicians and clinicians-in-training to bridge the gaps between 12-Step Programs and the field of mental health. In the following chapters, we help you learn how to translate our clinical language and concepts in a way that is synergistic with the 12-Step philosophy, and vice versa. We help you understand each of the first three Steps and the psychological issues underpinning them. We also highlight where science and the 12-Steps diverge and how to navigate this clinically. In the end, we are confident that this book can improve your relationships and clinical work with your clients who are in 12-Step Programs by demonstrating more competent care with this large and active group of people.

QUESTIONS

1. Describe the diagnostic differences between Substance Dependence and Substance Abuse as understood in the DSM-IV-TR.
2. Name three criticisms of diagnostic categories of Substance Dependence and Substance Abuse.
3. What is the difference between the terms "craving" versus "urges," and why is that distinction important for a therapist working with a client in the 12-Step Program?
4. Explain the difference between a preoccupation/compulsion versus the 12-Step term of insanity.
5. What tool is helpful for clinicians working with substance-using clients to determine the appropriate level of care?

Examining the Components of a 12-Step Program: The Benefits and Criticisms

2

The 12-Steps in Context

The 12-Step Program (or, simply, 12-Steps) was created by two alcoholics, Bill W. and Dr. Bob, who were both looking for a means to end their addiction to alcohol. They reached their goal through the use of three tenets that became the core principles of 12-Steps. The first tenant is that if a person hopes to end the cycle of addiction, they must have a desire to stop drinking. The second tenet is that spirituality is a central component to recovery by removing one's will and placing it squarely in the hands of God, as each person understands Him. The final tenet is that there is a healing power that exists in the relationship between two alcoholics when they struggle together to stay sober.

12-Steps was not formed by medical professionals, researchers, or academics. 12-Steps was created, and continues to develop today, through the attempts of those afflicted with addiction and alcoholism in their efforts at sobriety. This is the foundation of all 12-Step Programs.

It is extremely difficult to measure the success of a program like 12-Steps. It is equally difficult to measure success of therapeutic programs that treat addiction. Many programs have initially claimed great success in their "unique" and "revolutionary" treatment for addiction. The Matrix Model and Prometa Protocol are two treatment programs that come to mind. It is easy to jump on the bandwagon of something new. We therapists are not immune to the allure of good marketing. However, we do have a responsibility to thoroughly investigate and assess those marketing claims before implementing the treatment on our patients. These two treatment modes promised high success rates of sobriety and retention in therapy. Sadly, though, after rigorous and scientifically valid studies, those claims were not corroborated by the results. Why is it so difficult to measure success? Well, for one, how do you define *success*? Is it abstinence from all substances for a year? Six months? Until death? Is it abstinence from all substances or just your drug of choice? Or reducing the amount or frequency of drug taking? How are you measuring abstinence? Is it through drug screens, breathalyzer findings, and/or self-reporting?

How often and for how long are you testing those in recovery? Are you observing the drug screens to make sure no one else's urine is substituted? Is the measurement frequent enough to determine use before it becomes undetectable in urine or hair?

As you can see, measurements of success are not easy to capture and document and can be potentially cost prohibitive. Despite these limitations, many treatment programs continue to advertise that if you attend their center, you will attain successful results. Don't believe the hype. Look closely at their definition of what constitutes success and how it is that they are measuring that statistic. Upon close examination, you might find that their claims are not quite the model of success they purport.

It is prudent at this juncture that we expand on what constitutes *success*. Perspectives vary from abstinence-based models requiring no relapses to findings of harm reduction (harm reduction is often a very fuzzy term, but it amounts to determining that someone has the ability to successfully use while minimizing the harm resulting from that use). We encourage you to review different models of substance use/abuse treatment and their perspectives of healing. Given the complexity of the disease, we advocate thinking about substance abuse treatment in a realistic way. Think about considering success in recovery by two measures. First, is the time frame between the client's abusing of substances (or, simply, using) getting longer? Second, are the time and resources that the client spends when using decreasing? Let's take a look at a couple of clinical vignettes to illustrate these measures:

Scenario 1: Successful recovery with complete abstinence.

Jane, a mother of two, started snorting cocaine in her early 20s and progressed to cocaine dependence after two years. After losing several well-paying jobs, she turned to prostitution to support her habit. Although humiliated and profoundly ashamed at the course her life had taken, she felt trapped and without any options. She attempted treatment several times, but relapsed shortly after each endeavor. Finally, in her late 20s, child protective services began investigating her parenting of her children and within a few weeks removed them from her care. Jane worked for the return of her children for nine months, but her addiction prevented her from making consistent efforts.

During a court hearing, the judge told her that either she became sober and a consistent parent, or the parental rights for her children would be terminated. As Jane later explained, "It was either the coke or my kids. I was not going to lose my kids." She began complying with the judge's orders. She entered treatment and completed follow-up services with aftercare, including fully participating in Cocaine Anonymous. For two years, her random monthly drug testing was negative and finally, because of her newfound sobriety, her children were returned to her care.

Scenario 2: Longer periods of sobriety, but not when out using.

Sam had been a heroin addict for ten years when he realized something was wrong. He kept getting ill and was losing weight. He was hospitalized and eventually diagnosed with AIDS. Sam voiced that he wished to stay sober, but it was an ongoing challenge for him to stay consistently abstinent. When he was first discharged from the hospital, he remained sober for 4 weeks before he relapsed. That relapse lasted two weeks before he reentered a detoxification program and was started on methadone. After his discharge, Sam was then able to stay drug free for six weeks before he relapsed, and after two days of using returned for a several-day detox. Since then, Sam has been repeating that cycle with longer periods of sobriety. He was sober for three months then relapsed for two days. His next relapse occurred after three more months, and the next was four months.

Currently, his cycle seems about six months of sobriety followed by a brief relapse. Sam is uncertain why he is unable to remain abstinent. His counselor feels that a relapse is predictable because Sam is simply unprepared to live a sober life, since he needs to make so many fundamental personal changes to himself, his relationships, and his environment. However, his counselor added that with each relapse, Sam seemed to gain more skills and make more changes that propelled a longer time frame for his next sobriety period. The counselor is encouraged that Sam's overall trend seems to be leading toward eventually attaining long-term sobriety.

Scenario 3: Sustained periods of sobriety, but decreasing time periods while out using.

Harry loved alcohol. It was his best and only friend, always available, always ready. He had tried to stop drinking on several occasions, but none had been successful. On his 30th birthday he arrived at work and was surprised to discover that his supervisor had arranged an intervention. His parents, siblings, and coworkers all expressed care and concern for him and his drinking. During the intervention, he agreed that he needed help and his parents immediately transported him to a treatment program where he was first admitted to a detoxification unit and then to an intensive outpatient program.

Harry completed the program but relapsed after three months. He drank for six months before he returned to the program, announcing "You guys spoiled it for me. All the time I was out there I couldn't deny what I was doing. I knew I was killing myself and my life with booze." Harry again completed the program and relapsed after about three months. He continued to drink for about four weeks, but returned to treatment after his employer terminated him for his drinking. After discharge, he again relapsed after about three months, but his relapse lasted for only one week. As Harry explained it, "I'm just thickheaded. I think I have to fall down a bunch of times before I can figure out how to stand."

Note, each vignette represents a clinical success as defined by the clients and the treatment providers. However, the specifics of each "success" are significantly different. Remember this as you read literature and reviews on effectiveness. How did they define success? Was their definition broad enough to capture what is seen clinically?

IS 12-STEPS EFFECTIVE?

In the book of Alcoholics Anonymous, Dr. G. Kirby Collier claims that "any therapeutic or philosophic procedure which can prove a recovery rate of 50% to 60% must merit our consideration" (p. 569). This percentage came from Bill W. himself in a *Saturday Evening Post* article in 1941. This statistic is often repeated by 12-Step members and supporters. Again, beware the hype. Although this may have been true when 12-Step was a small and local group of 20 to 80 people, this is not the reality today. How would that percentage be measured today? How exactly do you measure success with an anonymous population, and furthermore one that is not consistent? People attend different 12-Step meetings all the time, and there is often a wide variance in the tone, content, and even process of specific meetings. This variance is especially strong if you compare meetings that are in vastly different geographical locations. Even within the same meeting, the attendees will change from week to week. How do you isolate one 12-Step meeting group and close off access to that meeting from the membership—especially since that runs directly counter to the 12-Steps mission? There are many problems facing research of the 12-Step Programs.

Although a thorough review is beyond the limits of this text, the published research on the effectiveness of 12-Step Programs is mixed. Some studies show that it is quite effective, some show moderate to weak treatment effects, and some show that it may actually impede progress toward sobriety. However, despite the murkiness of the research, the clinical use of 12-Steps has not diminished. Involvement in 12-Steps is one of the most common treatment recommendations made by those who work in the addictions field.

As treatment providers ourselves, we would love to have a definitive answer to addiction that can provide us with consistent and reliable sobriety statistics enabling us to provide the optimal treatment options for our patients. Alas, to date, there is none. But that is not to say that 12-Steps, the Matrix Model, and other treatment programs and protocols are not effective in treating addiction. Instead, it is up to the clinician and ultimately the client as consumer to determine the most effective treatment for their specific addiction.

Disclaimer: 12-Steps Is an Imperfect Program!

If it is not yet completely clear, just as every other recovery treatment model currently in use, a 12-Step Program is an imperfect program. It does not work for everyone, and some clients have a strong negative reaction to it. A quick and simple search of the Internet or in most libraries reveals a number of works by critics who aim to discredit the Program. Yet, despite its vast criticisms, a 12-Step Program has helped many people remain clean and sober, and live lives more attuned to their personal values—whether honesty, integrity, openness, willingness, and/or humility. It is not for everyone, but it is nonetheless an important part of a clinician's toolkit.

Program of Suggestions

At its foundation, 12-Step is a program of suggestions. It *describes* a method for alcoholics and addicts to stay clean and sober, it does not *prescribe* one. The suggestions are framed from a place of experience, strength, and hope that is intended to help others by listening and learning about how to stay clean and sober. It is absolutely frowned on to tell someone what to do in recovery. An example of this is "You need to just call your sponsor if you feel like you're going to relapse." This sentiment, although that may be the desired message, is framed more like this: "I can really relate to your struggle with relapse. What really worked for my recovery is calling my sponsor on a daily basis. I also called her when I wasn't even sure if I was craving or not." Although the message is the same in blazing letters: "CALL YOUR SPONSOR", the way the message is delivered is very different. The first version can set off people's defenses by telling them what to do. No one likes being told what to do, addicts doubly so. The second version provides a road map for someone to follow, *if they so choose*. It may seem like splitting hairs, but again and again we have witnessed the effectiveness of the latter version. It is one of the cornerstones of Alcoholics Anonymous (AA) to encourage those in a vulnerable position to ask for assistance without the fear of being lectured. It also avoids potential pitfalls of power and authority struggles. To coin a phrase often stated in 12-Step meetings, attendees can take what they need and leave the rest.

Meetings Have the Potential to Be Triggering Events

12-Step meetings aim to provide a message of experience, strength, and hope on how others have combated their addiction and, despite the odds, have remained clean and sober. Meetings, however, do carry an unintentional risk: they can trigger someone to want to use. This is especially true when attendees talk about the joys of using by glorifying the experience of using, or the lifestyle. This is commonly referred to as "telling war stories." It is not that members are forbidden to speak about the alluring aspects of their addiction or addicted lifestyle. Rather, it is hoped that those musings are followed up with stories of the consequences of that behavior or lifestyle and perhaps how the life of recovery has brought about a greater benefit than the drug or lifestyle provided.

Again, it is not always the case, nor is it a requirement that members speak about the positive aspects of being in recovery. Sometimes, the greater message that connects with those in the room are tales of the longing for the addicted lifestyle, except without the consequences, or the struggle that ensues when sober life is difficult and the allure of using to escape is strong. That type of story—that message that recovery is at times hard, ordinary, emotional, or pessimistic—can also provide a sense of kinship within the group.

It may be useful at this point to add a sidebar conversation. Although simplified, one can view the decision tree for staying sober and in recovery as follows:

Table 2.1

	Positive Consequences of Using (reasons to use)	Negative Consequences of Using (reasons not to use)
Positive Consequences of Staying Sober (reasons to stay sober)	Quadrant 1 (ambivalent)	Quadrant 2 (stay sober)
Negative Consequences of Staying Sober (reasons not to stay sober)	Quadrant 3 (use)	Quadrant 4 (ambivalent)

Source: Adapted from Miller & Rollnick. (2013). *Motivational Interview: Helping People Change.* New York: Guilford Press.

If we start at the top of the chart, both columns contain the positive and the negative consequences of that person using. In other words, first the person's reasons to use and then their reasons not to use. In the left hand column are first the positive consequences of staying sober and then listed the negative consequences of staying sober; or, the reasons to stay sober and the reasons not to stay sober. In Quadrant 1 are the reasons to use and the reasons to stay sober. Quadrant 2 lists the reasons not to use and the reasons to stay sober. Quadrant 3 shows the reasons not to stay sober and the reasons to use. Finally, Quadrant 4 lists the reasons not to use and the reasons not to stay sober. Viewed individually, Quadrant 3 strongly suggests the person should use: there are lots of reasons to use and many negative consequences to staying sober. In Quadrant 2, the person should stay sober: there are lots of negative consequences to using and many positive consequences to staying sober. Quadrants 1 and 4 provide ambivalent positions: first, with lots of reasons to simultaneously stay clean and to use (Quadrant 1) and last, with lots of reasons to not use and not stay clean (Quadrant 4).

We hope that a person who is completely mentally "healthy" and perfectly self-aware is aware of all four quadrants at all times. Being fully aware, they then have all the information pertinent to answer the question, "Should I use or should I stay sober?" It is important to note that this is not the case with most substance dependent clients. Their awareness of each quadrant may ebb and flow over time and through the life cycle of addiction. At the height of their addiction, most are very aware of Quadrant 3, dimly aware of Quadrants 1 and 4, and even less aware of Quadrant 2. Early on in recovery, this may switch, and the client becomes very aware of Quadrant 2, less aware of 1 and 4, and only vaguely aware of 3. Later on and with more work, it is hoped that a client's awareness becomes equal across all four quadrants.

Relapse and the time period leading up to relapse typically involve some distortion in an addict's thinking. This commonly occurs through the use of denial and other defenses that alter the person's conscious awareness. As an addict approaches relapse, they may tend to increasingly become more aware of Quadrant 3 and less aware of Quadrant 2. For some, the moment of relapse occurs when they have lost any conscious awareness of Quadrant 2. Their attention becomes focused on how using helps them. This is one of the reasons why telling war stories and glorifying using can be so destructive. It risks activating a distortion where the person focuses on Quadrant 3 and loses contact with Quadrant 1.

Therefore, it is not surprising that a risk for those in early recovery is to be at a 12-Step meeting where they are exposed to material that triggers them into having urges to use. There are additional risk factors that activate triggers, thus making more prevalent the likelihood of someone actually using. They are:

- The time frame within 30 days of last use
- A guarded response in talking about urges to use
- Nearing the relapse point in their cycle
- Any recent emotional upheaval
- Having poor support to talk about urges
- Lack of sponsor and/or good sponsor relationship
- Lack of support for psychotherapy or psychopharmacology

Another hurdle for those persons starting to attend meetings and seeking recovery (also called "newcomers") comes from participants in the meetings who believe that recovery from drugs or alcohol is *dependent on a 12-Step Program only.* They adhere to the original idea of the founders of 12-Step that recovery from the disease of addiction can be overcome only by spiritual means. There is resistance, and sometimes outright hostility, to the use of psychotropic medications and/or therapy as a means of treatment for addiction. This subgroup of people within 12-Step, often referred to as "hardliners," sometimes encourage members to end their use of psychotropic medications and therapeutic treatment.

It should not be assumed that this hardline approach is because of ill-will for the psychological/psychiatric profession. Although that does occur for some hardliners, in our experience most of this group had failed treatment outcomes through traditional psychological/psychiatric practice. One can only guess whether that attitude was generated through poor treatment programs, inexperienced clinicians and psychiatrists, poor compliance or willingness to follow treatment recommendations, readiness to end using, lack of adequate time in treatment, or a myriad of other factors. However, it is vitally important that your client be educated about this subgroup, and that your client is given encouragement to consult you or their psychiatrist prior to abruptly ending any treatments.

Unfortunately, this can become a complicated scenario, especially if the recovering person has chosen a hardliner for a sponsor. It has the potential to pit the therapist against the sponsor and the 12-Step Program. We cover this topic more in Chapter 6 with discussions regarding managing the client-sponsor relationship, and strategies to managing the relationship triad.

A final way in which a 12-Step program can prompt a trigger is by its language and format. One example is the Big Book, which has not undergone any major revisions since it was originally written in the late 1930s. The language is decidedly from that period and is very paternalistic and heterosexist. This terminology has the effect of causing some women and sexual minorities to feel disconnected (and sometimes insulted) by its message. The result is that more than one of our clients has felt alienated and turned off by the Program, thereby increasing their desire to retreat into the safety of using rather than replicating the alienation and rejection they have received in so many other areas of society. It is vitally important that any clients who are not White, heterosexual, male, or Judeo-Christian are aware of the limitations of the 12-Step literature, which is often neither inclusive nor sensitive. When appropriate, more of these limitations are expounded on throughout this chapter. It is important to remember that 12-Steps *does* work for many in diverse populations. But, any success requires openly and frankly discussing the fallacies and benefits of the program.

The Real Threat of Being "13th Stepped"

Meetings can be difficult to negotiate for a newcomer. Many newcomers are often shy in their first couple of meetings as it is a foreign place for them with different social norms than they are used to following from their addicted life. Thus, newcomers are encouraged to look to senior members of 12-Step for guidance as, to how to live a clean and sober life. It is recommended, when looking for a sponsor to find one who is living a life of recovery that they want to emulate. For many newcomers, these suggestions are very useful. However, as described below, it can also come with a risk.

As a result of the lifestyle of addiction, some newcomers enter into recovery without a good sense of themselves or their personal boundaries. As such, newcomers can be vulnerable to being taken advantage of from longer-term sober people in 12-Step, especially sexually but also emotionally and/or financially. This is known as "13th Stepping." It refers to someone with more than a year of sobriety preying on another 12-Step member with less than a year of sobriety for the purposes of having sex with them. There are emotional and financial exploitations that have occurred with clients as well.

For example, someone hoping to 13th-Step a newcomer may follow a pattern of expressing concern about the newcomer's sobriety, then ultimately fostering a codependency, eventually isolating the individual later in order to pressure for sex. Another example is where a shy and introverted newcomer is charmed by an outgoing and flirtatious longer-term sober person, leading to sex. In this instance, the person who has been 13th-Stepped may at best be embarrassed, and at the worst devastated after being duped into sex. However, this is not a given. For those individuals where sex was tied to their using, the sexual flirtation and sex itself can be a comforting (although not necessarily healthy) means to relate to another sober person in a way that enables them to feel confident and skilled.

On the downside, 13th-Stepping over both the short- and long-term can have some fairly damaging consequences for newcomers. It can damage an already fragile trust of a 12-Step Program, create a blanket suspicion concerning all members, trigger someone to initiate using their drug of choice to cope with their feelings, or cause a complete rejection of 12-Step altogether.

The Challenge for Those of Non-Christian Faiths, Agnostics, and Atheists

12-Step is a good match for those individuals identifying as Christian, but it can be a challenge for those of non-Christian faiths, and even a greater challenge for those who identify as agnostic or atheist. For example, the 3rd Step reads, "Made a decision to turn our will and our lives over to the care of God as we understood Him." It does not say Allah instead of God, or use a feminine pronoun to describe God. Throughout the Big Book there are references that ask the reader to come to terms with how they themselves define God, or a "Power greater than themselves." Yet, in the chapter titled, *We Agnostics*, the message can be interpreted to mean that you will eventually not be agnostic, because you will ultimately come to believe in God.

References and applications of spirituality, both in the meetings or when working with a sponsor, can vary greatly. In some 12-Step meetings, the Lord's Prayer, among other prayers, is recited in the opening or closing of the meeting. Some meetings have an even stricter Christian interpretation for God. Still, there are meetings that are conducted through the lens of Buddhism, Judaism, and Islam as well, and even a few that truly take an agnostic or atheistic perspective of a power greater than yourself. How, you say, can a spiritual program be atheistic?

In terms of recovery, that is fairly simple and we talk more extensively about this in the chapter on Step Two. Simply put, 12-Step members are asked to find a power greater than themselves that can restore them to sanity. There does not have to be just one power, nor does it have to be in the guise of a deity. A power greater than themselves can represent a meeting, a sponsor, the Big Book or Basic Text, a friend, a spouse, another inspirational text, or a how-to-guide on sobriety. It is anything that helps the addict/ recovering person acknowledge a power greater than themselves and turn their will over to this power to guide them in sobriety. Of course, the key component is that the power must help restore them to sanity—sadly, a jar of peanut butter would therefore not qualify as a Higher Power.

This also means that the newly recovered person must find a sponsor with either a flexible enough concept of spirituality to allow the newly recovered person to develop their own concept of a Higher Power, or a sponsor who holds a view of a Higher Power that the newly recovered person wishes to adopt. Religion and spirituality can be quite powerfully ingrained and operational in many of us (and yes, that includes the spirituality of an agnostic and atheist). It can be difficult to allow an opposing or even slightly altered belief system to coexist with our own, unless our spirituality is internally secure within us. Sponsors whose belief systems are rigid and/or precipitously attached are in danger of shutting down the conversation and interfering with the newly recovered person's exploration of their understanding and interpretation of their Higher Power. There is further extensive discussion regarding this concept in Chapter 10, and also in the section addressing the navigation of the sponsor-sponsee-therapist relationship in Chapter 6.

Alternative Routes to Sobriety

A 12-Step Program is a multinational phenomenon with a common book and literature and a semiuniform program that binds it together. As such, there is a very high possibility of receiving support from within a meeting, no matter where you are located or attend. That is not to say that 12-Steps is the only recovery program that works. There are other self-help programs that may not boast as many meetings or have a uniform means of overcoming addiction, but their messages and methods also have merit. Some of the most successful men and women in recovery are those who adapt strategies from a multitude of sources and not just one. Some of the recovery programs are SMART (Self-Management and Recovery Training) Recovery, Rational Recovery, and Women for Sobriety.

Not all sobriety happens through therapy, psychopharmacology, or self-help groups. Sobriety can be achieved through spontaneous remission, where the addictive pattern of using phases out through no direct intervention: possibly the result of aging, lifestyle choice change, increased meaningful connection (becoming romantically involved with someone, improved family/friend relationships, a religious experience, etc.), unintentional financial change, and a chronic impairment (brain injury, dementia, etc.), to name a few.

THE 12-STEP MEETING

Why do 12-Step meetings work for so many people trying to recover from drugs and alcohol? Through the years with our clients, we have heard several answers to this question, and there is no doubt that through your years of addiction counseling, you will hear many more and varied responses. As a result, there are several common responses to this question to outline.

The first reason is that the newly recovered person begins to know that they are not alone, that others have experienced what they have and are now living a life of sobriety. The newly recovered person hears stories about the shameful and insane behavior of now-sober people during their addiction. It lets them know that their antisocial behavior is not special; they are not the spawn of the devil or harbingers of evil. Rather, their addiction controlled them (as it has many others) resulting in a state of insanity, and thus insane behavior followed.

Additionally, the newly recovered person has a relatively safe place within an understanding group to share their experiences, both with addiction and recovery. Meetings often operate as a pressure valve to be able to release emotion, and a place to work through complicated feelings about sober life and the temptations to return to using. Moreover, through witnessing and attendance at the meetings, the newly recovered person begins to learn how asking for help lends support and encouragement. Thus, instead of turning to their substance of choice, they begin to turn to their fellow person in recovery.

As well, meetings serve a repository of knowledge on how to stay sober *just for today*. The messages of sobriety are rooted in helping those in the room make it through this one day clean and sober. No need to project to tomorrow about how to keep sober–there's a meeting for that . . . tomorrow. It helps the person in recovery keep the focus on managing their sobriety in small chunks rather than sweeping arcs, thereby guaranteeing an increased chance of staying clean and sober. This is an ingenious function of the meetings. It is easy to get so caught up in the future, that you miss how you can prevent that worried future by acting today. The meetings also have short "bumper sticker" sayings that are repeated often, which help to remind the recovering person what to keep in perspective. Sayings like "Y.A.N.A. = You Are Not Alone," "K.I.S.S. = Keep It Simple Spiritually," or "O.D.A.A.T. = One Day at A Time" are simple instructions and encouragements that do not require a very good functioning memory system or a very stable emotional life to be able to remember.

Finally, meetings serve as an experimental laboratory for learning sober social skills. It is easy to forget that the recovering person comes into sobriety with a whole set of social skills that are geared toward an alcohol or drug culture. That set of social skills necessary for using (i.e., helping the client be accepted, function, and continue their addiction) often does not translate well to the recovery world. Newly recovered people can feel awkward, shy, and out of place in the world, let alone in a meeting where people are behaving in ways that are unfamiliar to them, and they don't know how to respond. All of the insecurities that were neatly covered by the alcohol or drugs are now front and center in the newly recovering person. What a challenge to overcome! Through consistent attendance at meetings and, more important, through fellowship after the meetings, the newly recovered person begins to learn a whole new set of social skills, such as boundary setting, helping others, considering group needs above self needs, and discovering an emotional vocabulary, to name a few.

Does this sound at all familiar? It should. Yalom's principles on why group work is therapeutic are at the heart of 12-Step meetings. 12-Step meetings provide universality (you are not alone in the experience of the insanity of addiction), altruism (maintaining positive feelings about a member even when challenging the behavior of relapse), instillation of hope (interacting with others who have stayed clean and sober through working the Program), imparting of information (ideology of the importance of sharing experience, strength, and hope), development of (sober) socializing techniques, imitative behaviors (of a sober person), cohesiveness (bonding together to help a relapsing member or fellowship), existential factors (owning consequences of addiction), catharsis (telling your worst secrets of your behavior during addiction), and self-understanding (learning about the hidden motivations to relapse). Whatever the flaws of a 12-Step Program, the power of the group process is felt at every meeting.

12-Step Meeting Basics

The only requirement for participation in 12-Step is a desire to stop using alcohol or drugs. Sobriety is NOT a requirement, although that is the main objective of the program. Members can show up to a meeting high or intoxicated to get support to stop. This is contrary to how some meetings encourage (and sometimes require) people to introduce themselves by saying "Hi my name is _____, and I am an alcoholic (addict)." There is no requirement to announce, or even believe, that you are an alcoholic/addict. Again, the only requirement is a desire to stop drinking or using.

There are two different types of meetings: open and closed. Open meetings are available to anyone who wishes to attend—they do not have to desire to stop drinking or have a problem with alcohol or drugs. Open meetings are great for family, friends, or other supports to the recovering person. Open meetings are also useful experiences for those healthcare workers intending to work with the recovery community. Closed meetings are just that; they are closed to those people who do not have a desire to stop drinking or using. No one else is welcome at these meetings.

There are several other different formats for meetings: speaker, discussion, and Step meetings. Speaker meetings are where a person shares her or his personal story of recovery. The speaker is commonly referred to as a "lead," as they are leading the meeting. After the speaker shares, sometimes it is open for personal reflections and other times it is not—it is up to the individual meeting and speaker. Discussion meetings are where members with a desire to speak are encouraged to share anything in the meeting. The shared story may be about recovery, but that is not always the case. Step meetings are where there is reading from 12-Step literature, either focusing on the Steps themselves or another aspect of the Program. The meeting leader chooses a reading that is discussed by the participants.

Most meetings are 60 to 90 minutes in length, although some are two hours. Meetings generally start and end on time. Remember, a meeting consists of two fellow alcoholics/addicts sharing their own personal message of experience, strength, and hope on staying sober/clean. Thus, two people can comprise a meeting, and it does not have to be at a set place and time. A meeting can occur at any given moment, at any given place. That said, most meetings open with a reading of the Preamble of Alcoholics Anonymous, a prayer, or other opening statement by the chair. During the meeting there is a "no crosstalk" rule, meaning that no one is allowed to talk over or on the side with another attendee. The purpose of any feedback is not to tell another person how to stay sober by critiquing their sobriety. Rather, the effort is made to lead by example by sharing your own experience, strength, and hope on how you stay clean or sober.

Meetings may end with everyone joining hands and saying the Lord's Prayer, Serenity Prayer, or another prayer. There is no directive to join the circle in prayer, and members can elect to not join. However, it can be very daunting for a newcomer to refuse to join the prayer, especially if they are seeking connection with the others. Feelings of exclusion can also build for those of non-Christian religions, agnostics, and atheists. They report feeling connected to the meeting and the other people in recovery, and disconnected in those moments of prayer, generating a feeling of difference when they are seeking connection.

Here is a sample of some of the different types of 12-Step Programs currently in existence:

AA = Alcoholics Anonymous (ww.aa.org)

NA = Narcotics Anonymous (www.na.org)

CA = Cocaine Anonymous (www.ca.org)

MA = Marijuana Anonymous (www.marijuana-anonymous.org)

CMA = Crystal Meth Anonymous (www.crystalmeth.org)

OA = Overeaters Anonymous (www.oa.org)

EA = Emotions Anonymous (www.emotionsanonymous.org)

GA = Gamblers Anonymous (www.gamblersanonymous.org)

SCA = Sexual Compulsives Anonymous (www.sca-recovery.org)

SLAA = Sex and Love Addicts Anonymous (www.slaafws.org)

SA = Sexaholics Anonymous (www.sa.org)

CLA = Clutterers Anonymous (www.sites.google.com/site/clutterersanonymous/)

WA = Workaholics Anonymous (www.workaholics-anonymous.org)

DA = Debtors Anonymous (www.debtorsanonymous.org)

For the support system of the recovering person, there are these 12-Step Programs:

Al-Anon = Alcoholics Anonymous Family Group (www.al-anon.alateen.org/home)

Alateen = Alcoholics Anonymous Teenager Group (http://al-anon.alateen.org/home)

Nar-Anon = Narcotics Anonymous Family Group (www.nar-anon.org)

ACOA = Adult Children of Alcoholics (www.adultchildren.org)

CODA = Codependent Anonymous (www.coda.org)

S-Anon = Sexaholics Anonymous Family Group (www.sanon.org)

There are many more 12-Step groups, and more are forming as the need for them grows. Research the types of 12-Step programs in your area so that you can make proper referrals to your clients. It is essential to familiarize yourself with the meetings in your area. Many areas of the country have a hotline established where clients and others can locate a meeting. Sometimes these hotlines even provide telephone encouragement or guidance to someone struggling with substance dependence. On the Internet, www.aa.org and www.na.org can provide a variety of information for you and your clients, including the times and locations of meetings.

We advise that practitioners make a practice to attend some open meetings to get a sense of the style and culture of the meetings. If that is not possible because the meetings are closed, ask your clients to discuss the meetings they are attending.

Specifically, what do they like and dislike about the meeting. By gathering this information from multiple sources, you create a more nuanced and targeted list of meetings that increase your chances to recommend a meeting specifically tailored to a client's requirements. For instance, you may not want to send someone who identifies as having a problem with marijuana to a Narcotics Anonymous meeting if there are Marijuana Anonymous meetings running in the area. Some people do not consider marijuana to be problematic or addictive—even in 12-Step meetings. So, it can backfire to send someone with an addiction to marijuana to a meeting where they may receive a message that their struggle with their drug of choice is not real. Marijuana Anonymous would be a more proper referral. Additionally, while addiction across substances of choice may be similar, there are differences in the lifestyle, culture, and neurological impact of each of the drugs of choice that can create a sense of dissonance for the client in meetings, thereby leaving members feeling more disconnected than connected to the 12-Step Program.

Also, you may find that some specific meetings tend to be more rigid in their application of some aspects of the Program, or emphasize the Step work more than other meetings, or tend to be more emotionally supportive, or have members that have been sober for longer periods of time. In other words, different meetings have different flavors. It is common to build a good knowledge base of the variables in your community by listening to your clients and sharing information with colleagues. Over time, you will find that you can more effectively match the needs of your clients with recommendations for specific meetings in your area.

What occurs after the meeting is over is almost as important as the meeting itself: the activity of fellowship. Fellowship is an activity, usually after a meeting but sometimes before, where members get to know each other, socialize, and practice sober social skills. Fellowship usually means a group of members going for coffee or a bite to eat, or to a movie or other event. The purpose of fellowship is to build sober social skills, accountability, and support. Fellowship allows newly recovering people the opportunity to learn skills important to successful sobriety: listening, being of service, honesty, modeling or witnessing prorecovery decision making, showing up for a commitment, and having fun without the use of drugs or alcohol, to name a few.

Fellowship also develops skills of accountability and responsibility. When a newly recovering person attends the same club or goes to a 12-Step meeting week after week, that person begins to build relationships with other recovering people in that meeting or club. Members begin to notice, and question, when a newly recovering person misses a meeting. Calls are made in an effort to check that the newly recovering member is safe and sober. This helps the newly recovering person acquire a feeling of being cared about and cared for, which in turns spurs on further attendance to that meeting or club. Trust and dependability build as the ongoing relationship develops. Consistent attendance and the formation of meaningful relationships with 12-Step members allow the newly recovering person to begin to experience a decrease in their feelings of loneliness and isolation. It begins to remove the ambivalence of disconnecting from their using lifestyle and friendships as there is now a suitable social replacement.

Another accountability factor naturally arises when the newly recovering person does not feel like attending a meeting. They begin to consider the impact on those relationships that their absence might entail. Not showing up for events and appointments is invariably a part of a life wrought with addiction. Missing a meeting that the newly recovering person had previously committed to attending may feel familiar, like their old using behavior. They may begin to consider the feelings of others; such as if their absence would create worry or concern with the members at the meeting. These sensations can all be powerful motivations for attending a meeting, even if the newly recovering person does not feel compelled to do so for their own recovery.

Finally, it is very common for an addict to arrange their lives so they are not held accountable for their behavior and especially their using. Clients often arrange their meeting schedules so that they are rarely or never going to the same ones. Alternatively, they can attend the same meeting consistently week after week but arrive slightly after the meeting begins and leave right before the meeting ends. It creates the opportunity for them to create a system where they believe no one is really accounting for their presence, making relapse more likely to occur. The accountability of fellowship is one way to break this pattern. If they resume using, others commonly notice, reach out to help, but also simultaneously hold them accountable to take responsibility for the relapse and reengage their sober behavior.

SPONSORSHIP

There is only one official role of a sponsor: to share with the newly recovering person (often referred to as a *sponsee*) how he or she, through the experiences of a 12-Step Program, has stayed clean and sober. Sponsorship can be on a temporary basis as well as permanent. Given that nothing is truly ever permanent, the relationship lasts as long as the sponsor and sponsee agree that the relationship is beneficial.

Temporary sponsorship usually occurs when a recovering person is new to a sponsorship relationship, or had a previous sponsor who did not work out. Think about temporary sponsorship as a test period to find out whether the sponsor is a good fit with you and your program. It sets the expectation that the relationship is a trial and gives both the sponsor and sponsee freedom to end the relationship, if necessary. Recommend that a client find a temporary sponsor within the first few weeks after they decide they wish to be sober and begin attending meetings. Sometimes, clients can identify one or more persons in the meetings who seem to have said things especially useful to them. If that person has long-term sobriety, clients should ask if they would become a temporary sponsor. More commonly, clients are unsure or too anxious to approach an individual. In that case, recommend that the client approach the chair of their preferred meeting to ask them who in the room would be a good option to approach. Most meeting chairs have a list of people who would be willing to temporarily sponsor and are very willing to set up an introduction. Then, once a temporary sponsor has been arranged, the client can either wait until a suitable person is identified to be a more permanent sponsor, or the client can choose to attempt to renegotiate the relationship with their temporary sponsor into a more permanent one.

Using temporary sponsors can reduce some of the tensions around finding a sponsor. Our experience has been that newly recovering people feel tremendous pressure to pick The One: The Sponsor of All Sponsors. There is tremendous anxiety over choosing a sponsor. This is one of those red herrings, as the anxiety is usually not about finding a good fit (although this can be a concern). Most of the anxiety originates in both a resistance to being held accountable (often translated in the addicted mind as rejection, failure, and "Jumping Jehoshaphat! I'm not ready to stop using!"), and a fear of forming and maintaining an intimate and emotional relationship with another human being while stone cold sober. We look at this reaction more closely and discuss interventions to use in Chapter 9.

There are many pamphlets from various 12-Step Programs and non-12-Step programs discussing sponsorship, but as the sponsor-sponsee relationship is an individualized one, there is no ascribed method or "One-Way" to sponsor someone. Sponsors can perform their sponsorship duties through the telling of personal stories of their sobriety (how they worked the Steps or what the Steps mean to them), offering suggestions for change (including how to work the Steps), and modeling sober behavior (including practicing healthy boundaries). It is with hope that the sponsor relationship also provides a safe forum for the practice of rigorous honesty, accountability, and skill building in asking for help prior to picking up a drug or drink.

The sponsor's role initially begins as a much more directive approach to suggesting means and methods of remaining clean and sober. As the sponsee progresses along the program and gains experience in recovery, the sponsor's role changes to more of an advisory role. The sponsor then encourages the sponsee to utilize the program and its principles to make choices that encourage and maintain sobriety. The sponsee's path in the program begins as student, morphs into the role as peer, and finally transforms as teacher (and student at the same time) when taking on the sponsorship role. In this way, the principle of how sobriety is achieved, by giving sobriety back to another alcoholic/addict in need, is perpetually fulfilled.

THE 12-STEPS

These are the 12-Steps of Alcoholics Anonymous:

1. We admitted we were powerless over alcohol—that our lives had become unmanageable.
2. Came to believe that a Power greater than ourselves could restore us to sanity.
3. Made a decision to turn our will and our lives over to the care of God *as we understood Him.*
4. Made a searching and fearless moral inventory of ourselves.
5. Admitted to God, to ourselves, and to another human being the exact nature of our wrongs.
6. Were entirely ready to have God remove all these defects of character.
7. Humbly asked Him to remove our shortcomings.
8. Made a list of all persons we had harmed, and became willing to make amends to them all.
9. Made direct amends to such people wherever possible, except when to do so would injure them or others.
10. Continued to take personal inventory and when we were wrong promptly admitted it.
11. Sought through prayer and meditation to improve our conscious contact with God *as we understood Him,* praying only for knowledge of His will for us and the power to carry that out.
12. Having had a spiritual awakening as the result of these steps, we tried to carry this message to alcoholics, and to practice these principles in all our affairs.

The Steps are an incremental process. Each Step builds on the last. There is no set time limit to work each Step or the Steps themselves in that the program is self-paced. If the sponsee is reluctant to engage with the work of a Step (the most difficult is often Step 4), then the sponsor may make a decision to implement time goals for a Step to be completed. The Steps are built on a base of daily maintenance and the active working of each completed Step. As such, any unresolved work with previous Steps shows up in later Steps, requiring the need to be addressed. The program is not meant to be finite. It is a circular program that requires the participant to work through the Steps on a continual basis.

SUMMARY

The 12-Step Program presented to you here is in a primer format, and it is therefore just a rough sketch of the essence of the program. Part of the difficulty in accurately describing this Program is that its essence lives in the meetings and membership itself, not in the texts and pamphlets of the program. The texts and pamphlets define the work to be done, the method, if you will. The artistry is in the operation of the Steps, and witnessing the power of recovery overcoming the hopelessness of addiction. Nonetheless, it is important to read both the Big Book from Alcoholics Anonymous, in addition to the Basic Text of Narcotics Anonymous. The goal of this book is to breathe life into the Steps and how your role as a therapist can assist in that work. However, the true beauty of the process of recovery as a whole is assuredly in its movement.

QUESTIONS

1. Describe the roles of the following components of 12-Step, and how clinicians can help foster compliance:
   a. Meetings
   b. Sponsorship
   c. Fellowship
   d. Step work
2. Name three criticisms of the 12-Step Program, and techniques for addressing those concerns with clients.
3. Name at least six different 12-Step Programs available today.
4. List four of the twelve Steps in the 12-Step Program.
5. Is sobriety required for attending a meeting? Is labeling yourself as an alcohol/addict required?

A Clinical Perspective on Why a 12-Step Program Is a Useful Tool for Reversing the Damage Wrought by Substance Dependence

3

With all of the imperfections of a 12-Step program, with the ambivalent evidence of its effectiveness, and with the difficulty some clients experience joining the program, why on Earth would any therapist ever recommend that a client participate? The answer is that for all of its imperfections, there is a real clinical case for a client's involvement in 12-Steps. This chapter presents that case.

There are many areas of neurobiological, cognitive, and affective functioning that become altered and/or damaged by substance use. Some of these effects are poor judgment, emotional volatility, impaired impulse control, complications in learning and memory, and the development of antisocial behaviors that become adaptive coping skills during addiction. These five areas are often some of the most central issues to those struggling with addiction. Likewise, each of these areas are addressed within a 12-Step program. As a result, 12-Steps can help in the healing process, or at the very least, function as a de facto brain for these areas that may currently be operating at less than peak efficiency. Our hope is that by the end of this chapter, you understand that given the injury to their brains, the common behaviors of a person in early recovery are perfectly normal, and we hope you understand how a 12-Step program can compensate for the client's deficiencies and assist in the development of prosocial skills.

THE FIRST AREA OF IMPAIRMENT: GENERAL EXECUTIVE FUNCTIONING

The frontal cortex can be fondly thought of as the braking system of the brain, with added abilities to plan, reason, and a whole lot more. Thankfully, one of its many purposes is to make certain a person does not say or act on every thought that comes into their mind. This section of the brain evaluates and filters actions and responses based on several factors such as our learned social norms and skills, risk assessment, and emotional needs, to name a few. It is what prevents us from running into a busy street filled with cars, from speaking while another person is talking, or from hitting someone who is irritating us. Intoxicant abuse and dependency injure this part of our brain. At the time that someone is using substances, these intoxicants are also responsible for impairing functioning of this section of the brain. If you have ever indulged a little too much in your intoxicant of choice, you may note the difference in your words/behavior compared to when you are stone cold sober.

If there is a family history of substance abuse or dependence, genetics may be passed down to the children resulting in vulnerabilities that lead to perpetuating addiction in its various forms. One of these vulnerabilities is likely a weaker braking system compared to people whose family histories are absent substance dependency. This weaker braking system can also be further augmented by poor reasoning ability and emotional volatility, which in turn lends itself to initiating substance use. Chronic substance abuse can compound this harm by further damaging an already underfunctioning frontal lobe.

Substance dependence, or essentially a lifestyle based on immediate gratification, does not do the brain's braking system any favors. By losing the ability to delay gratification through the various weakened executive functions, substance dependence deprives people of the opportunity to experience delayed action in order to obtain greater rewards later on. Over time, delayed gratification is replaced by immediate gratification. Without successful delayed experiences, the framework for achieving sobriety and even success in life is more difficult. Indeed, a newly sober person often has to accomplish a great deal of learning and adapting in order to successfully negotiate a world that demands this ability to delay. Thankfully, the brain operates similarly to a muscle—the more you exercise parts of it, the stronger it becomes. With practice, by controlling their impulses the client can become better at delaying gratification.

The structure of 12-Step meetings provides several protective factors that help control impulses and allows for the building or rebuilding of the impulse control system. One important aid is the rule of "no cross talk" in most 12-Step meetings. As you remember from the previous chapter, no cross talk means that members cannot interrupt someone speaking by responding to what they are saying. Members have to listen fully instead of thinking about what they want to say next. Thus, members have to attend fully to the message of the meeting, and in doing so, build self-restraint. The no-cross-talk rule also forces attendees to learn and employ stress-management techniques.

By virtue of not being able to instantly respond to another person's thoughts or story, attendees learn to tolerate feelings such as irritability, hurt, inadequacy, guilt, and shame. The relationships developed within meetings also support the growth of impulse control. Choosing one meeting to attend consistently, week after week, helps to build accountability and responsibility. In a 12-Step Program, it is known as picking a Home Group. By attending the Home Group week after week, the recovering person becomes a regular face at the meeting, builds relationships with other members who consistently attend, and possibly takes on service work for the meeting. This accountability includes accountability for choices.

Another protective factor of a Home Group is that by sharing and building relationships, other members begin to get to know the recovering person's vulnerabilities and strengths. The group more accurately begins to be able to predict warning signs of relapse thinking and behaviors because they *know* the person well. Members encourage one another to utilize each other in order to manage triggering people or places, which could include helping another to pay off a dealer, cleaning up an apartment after using, disposing of paraphernalia, or making amends, to name a few.

With the building of these relationships within a Home Group, and the process of becoming more accountable, the recovering person builds a link between the risk of loss and relapse. When the recovering person is considering use, they now have to consider the consequences of that choice; namely having to return to their Home Group admitting to a relapse. A relapse can also create feelings of shame/guilt, broken trust, having to start over with clean time, and facing disappointment by members of the Home Group. These outcomes are sometimes enough to prevent the newly recovering person from following through on their impulse to use, and at the same time requires practicing reasoning ability to consider the consequences beyond just the use. Over time, this link between relapse and consequences can become all but irrevocable.

The Steps of the Program also address this issue of impulse control. Step 4 (*Made a searching and fearless moral inventory of ourselves*) and Step 9 (*Made direct amends to such people wherever possible, except when to do so would injure them or others*) are the two most direct Steps that address this problem. Step 4 asks the person to identify their contribution to any struggle or difficulty in their lives. At its core, it asks the person to be accountable. Step 9 involves admitting to past misdeeds and providing justice for them whenever possible. So, for instance, if someone in recovery had stolen $50 from a roommate while they were using, Step 9 asks the recovering person to admit to their misdeed and return the $50.

Steps 4 and 9 help remind the recovering person that they are accountable for their actions. Remember that the Steps are a process and can be worked through multiple times. Some people in recovery like to work Step 4 on a daily basis and Step 9 to decrease the likelihood of an impulsive action by holding accountability front and center in their lives. It is hoped that as they adapt to this method, they become more aware of their reasoning and decision-making processes (thoughts, feelings, and motivations) in order to identify relapse thoughts or behaviors at a very early stage.

Immersing oneself in 12-Step meetings also helps to avoid people, places, and things that can trigger a person to make an impulsive decision to use. Early in the recovery process, this avoidance is a very good thing. The impulses to use can be very frequent and strong for those in early recovery. Given the deficits in the brain function at that point, it is highly likely that if a person is triggered to use, their ability to resist these impulses and stop themselves from returning to use is significantly reduced. For some, their impulse control system has been so injured through using that their impulse control is massively impaired; there just is not enough executive functioning working properly to stop this individual from using, once they are exposed to a trigger and experience an urge to use. Meetings often help such clients avoid their triggers.

12-Step meetings also repeat the message of sobriety. They provide a replacement behavior and thought (sobriety) for any thoughts or feelings of using that may come up during a meeting. From a behavioral perspective, the meetings are attempting to substitute a new competing behavioral and cognitive schema (sobriety) while extinguishing the old behavior and schema (using).

Meetings also model reasoning and planning skills to avoid or cope with a situation that may trigger impulses to use. As mentioned in the last chapter, it is highly probable that at some point a newly recovering person experiences a trigger in a meeting. This can be a positive event as the newly recovering person has the opportunity to respond to the trigger in a prorecovery fashion, such as talking about being triggered in the meeting, attending fellowship afterwards, or focusing on the message of the meeting instead of attending to their triggering thoughts or feelings. In this way, delayed gratification ensures the continuity of sobriety.

THE SECOND AREA OF IMPAIRMENT: JUDGMENT

When working with people in early recovery, it is clear that their executive functioning is often severely compromised. Specifically, this includes their ability to assess their world and their behavior in order to accurately perceive risks, anticipate consequences, and plan accordingly. There are many components that can cause these deficits:

1. As we've discussed above, there is research suggesting that many people who become substance dependent display below-average levels of frontal-lobe functioning prior to initiating their substance use (the frontal lobe is the brain area where most executive functions like planning and anticipating are located). In effect, these individuals may always have exhibited below-average ability to plan and anticipate. For some, their problems with judgment were long standing and were present prior to their addiction.
2. In addition, many substances cause injury to the brain, frequently to the frontal lobes. As a result, the person's ability to plan and monitor their world is further reduced, leading them to make poor choices.
3. Part of this impairment may also be due to habit. Substance dependent people who actively use drugs and alcohol commonly spend a great deal of time and energy living their lives in the immediate present, not anticipating the future or learning from the past. This is their default approach. When placed in a new situation or when under stress, their memory recalls this default perspective, which, to the addict's detriment, is the act of using; thus getting sober and staying sober is certainly a new and stressful situation for most addicts.
4. Finally, substance dependent people have great difficulty conceptualizing, let alone living, a "sober lifestyle." Imagine asking yourself right now to stop your life as a nonaddict, and begin living your life as an addict. Would you know where to go to get illicit drugs and negotiate price, and do so without getting arrested? Would you know how to behave around other addicts? Speak their language? Know how to use the drugs? Bring yourself down

from a high if needed? Anticipate the risks, and construct as clandestine a plan as possible to hide your use? As alien as it would be for you to enter the addict's world and know how to operate, sometimes it is equally strange and unknown for the addict to enter the world of sobriety and function accordingly. The skill sets necessary for leading a sober life are covered in depth in subsequent chapters.

Recovering clients have a difficult time anticipating potential risks of sobriety and relapse, especially if they have never tried to do so before. Learning how to stay clean and sober requires knowledge and practice from an expert source. It is fitting then that the guiding principle in 12-Step programs is for all members, from the newcomer who last abused 24 hours ago to the veteran with 20 years of sobriety, to share their experiences, strengths, and hopes in their journey of recovery. This is the ultimate means of helping everyone stay clean and sober. This sharing begins to counteract the network of poor judgment and reasoning, by taking the individual's mind out of the equation and placing it into a (sober) group consciousness.

The program discusses this issue with its own language. Here, members are cautioned about the dangers of the individual mind, and the "cunning, baffling, and powerful" nature of the addicted mind (*Alcoholics Anonymous*, 2001, pp. 58–59). Most aspects of the phrase "cunning, baffling, and powerful" relate to issues of poor judgment. By "cunning," it is meant that substance dependence cannot truly be cured; that urges to use can reoccur for a person even after years and years in recovery clean from active use. Often, relapses occur simply because of an urge combined with poor judgment.

Phillip was a cocaine addict who had been clean for 1-1/2 years. On the second day at a new job, he joined several coworkers for dinner. They ordered several bottles of wine and he consented to drinking it rather than cope with the embarrassment of refusing. After three glasses of wine, and feeling a bit tipsy, Phillip began having urges to use cocaine. Clouded by the alcohol, he left dinner and purchased and consumed his first bag of coke in 18 months.

The next word in the phrase, "baffling," relates to the addict's ability to use, despite the extreme and negative consequences this use previously had on their life. The full extent of poor judgment is baffling. The last word in the phrase, "powerful," relates to the overall strength of addiction and its related errors in judgment. If allowed, addiction can override or overpower all other elements of a person's life and judgment.

Cunning, baffling, and powerful are the core concepts behind substance dependence and the addicted mind. By sharing their experiences, recently sober and those with more long-term sobriety help each other gain perspective and better judgment. The newcomer with fewer than 24 hours clean can share their experience of the horrors of withdrawal, which in turn reminds the 20-year veteran of the cost of resuming their own abuse. Alternatively, the 20-year veteran is able to share with the newcomer what methods were useful to manage the withdrawal, and can provide hope that the first day of sobriety can lead to day 7,300. For both the newcomer and veteran, good judgment is reinforced by remembering the pains of addiction. Each helps the other, regardless of the individual length of their sobriety.

Additionally, a 12-Step Program can counteract an individual's deficits in judgment by the group operating as a supporting external ego/frontal lobe, or in some cases as a de facto brain. In effect, the recovering person relies on the group consciousness, fellowship, and sponsorship to be the guiding light in considering and making decisions, both in terms of recovery and the challenges of everyday life. Effective 12-Step meetings work by a sharing of the wisdom and judgment of those in attendance. In this way, and because of this, it greatly assists the newly recovering person to consider previously unknown choices that lead to sobriety and a lifestyle that is foreign and at times scary.

One particular judgment error is related to memory. Specifically, the addicted brain gets stuck in a kind of memory loop previously discussed in Chapter 1. The urge-compulsion-using loop often includes preoccupation with memories of seeking the intoxicant, and the great feel of the high, as well as the fun times associated with the high. This loop can play over and over in the mind of an addict, fueling urges and eroding judgment. The rooms of 12-Step meetings respond to this by using the technique of "playing the tape through." This exercise is applied when a person in recovery is having an urge to use. They are encouraged to play the memory through in their minds from the intoxication to the posthigh period. The recovering person is asked to remember how the drug or alcohol crash/withdrawal feels, and list the ways in which fallout from the use occurs for them financially, socially, occupationally, and with their families and support systems (notably anger, disappointment, fear, loss of trust, etc.). In effect, the person is directed to remember all of the reasons, pro and con, to use and to stay sober, anticipating the consequences of each. The memory loop is thus interrupted by the continual reminder to anticipate the consequences.

A 12-Step Program encourages members to put their sobriety before anything or anyone else in their life. In this way, the program is defined as a "selfish program." It is selfish in that the person's priority in their life has to be self-care. Part of this relies on the notion that without sobriety, nothing or no one else matters to the person anyway. This reprioritizing, with sobriety first, often interrupts the errors that put a person at risk for relapsing. Consider the portrayal of the cocaine addict, Phillip. One of Phillip's errors was to consume alcohol rather than face the embarrassment of not drinking. In effect, he placed the avoidance of embarrassment as a higher priority than his sobriety.

Throughout their sobriety, the recovering person is consistently challenged with choosing to make sobriety a priority and making decisions through that sober lens in order to further that goal. So, going to a party where drugs are present, attending a family function where there is drinking, or missing 12-Step meetings are recognized actions that are not furthering sobriety (also known as "working a program"). We highlight many different scenarios of this challenge throughout the rest of the text, and how to process these difficult situations.

The recognition of risks to recovery and relapse are some of the first key steps in the process of making decisions that protect one's sobriety. The tool most often used in 12-Step programs to aid in the recognition of risks is the practice of "rigorous honesty." Rigorous honesty is exactly what it says, to be as completely honest with self and others. This stands in contrast to the typical stance of addicts, which includes secretiveness combined with a strong tendency to fix, manage, or control the people around them. The typical addict has a highly distorted and often simply inaccurate view of themselves and others. Addiction flourishes in a world of half-truths where a person can easily deny the reality of their lives.

For those working the program, rigorous honesty becomes a way to counteract the distortions that support addiction and its associated poor judgment. Additionally, it is a response to the cunning, baffling, and powerful aspects of substance dependence. It assists in helping the recovering person fight self-deception by proverbially spilling the beans any time they can about their thoughts, dreams, impulses, or behavior about using. The hope is that this continual practice of "telling on my addiction" improves the chances of successful recovery. The addicted brain wants to use, and compels the person to seek out the intoxicant and use. Denial and self-deception are two of its most potent weapons. By the act of making their self-deceptive thoughts known, the recovering person begins the process of self-empowerment by making better decisions through the accurate perception of their risks and resilience to better judgment.

Rigorous honesty has some additional benefits. As the person acts in an increasingly honest way, rigorous honesty improves trust with 12-Step members at meetings, improves their support systems, and ultimately improves themselves. One caveat is that this does require that the support system utilizes that knowledge in a way that is helpful to the recovering person and not as a means of initiating shame, blame, or hysteria. It is why addiction requires the holistic effort on the recovering person *and their support system.*

THE THIRD AREA OF IMPAIRMENT: EMOTIONAL REGULATION AND CONTAINMENT

The early stages of sobriety can be an enormously painful and emotional experience for the recovering person. As was mentioned, the emotion-regulation system gets injured by using drugs and alcohol, resulting in the brain's ability to regulate moods often becoming far less proficient. Consequently, people in early recovery tend to feel their emotions stronger, and for longer periods of time than someone with an undamaged emotion-regulation system. Subjectively, the person's feelings may be raw and difficult to tolerate. They may be emotionally labile or unsteady, prone to irritability, and difficult to soothe. Further complicating their emotional fragility, the newly sober person may have greatly reduced neurotransmitter functions and, depending on the neurotransmitters impacted by the using, not be able to feel pleasure, happiness, or even calm. In the end, they feel bad and are highly aware of this condition.

How is that lack of sensations possible? It is explained by how intoxicants work in the brain. We recommend visiting www.learn.genetics.utah.edu/content/addiction/drugs/mouse.html for a wonderfully fun and interactive guide on how drugs and alcohol work in the brain. For the purposes of this book, here is a simplified version of how an intoxicant high is created in the brain.

Each time a person administers their intoxicant, it is not the intoxicant that they feel when they experience a high. It is their own neurotransmitters (dopamine, serotonin, GABA, etc.) flooding the brain that produces the experience of the high. Intoxicants work by signaling the appropriate brain cells to pump out neurotransmitters, and also to block their reuptake. Highs wear off because the brain slowly but surely cleans up and disposes of the flooded neurotransmitters, thereby restoring the brain to a nonhigh state. Administer the intoxicant again, and "Hey Presto!," the intoxicants do their best work as the brain floods itself again and the high returns.

Knowing this, what do you think is responsible for people reporting that after "x" amount of days of using, they stopped getting high *even though they kept on using*? If you surmised that the overwhelming majority of their neurotransmitters have been used up thus leaving little or nothing left to flood the brain, you are correct. Through the process of continuously flooding neurotransmitters over and over again, the brain effectively gets drained of its supply. Simply put, there is nothing left to flood out to produce a high; it is the literal interpretation of brain drain. The brain cannot keep a production pace to match the rate that the neurotransmitters are being used and destroyed; the demand just overwhelms the supply.

The brain does not have an unlimited supply of neurotransmitters, and depending on the type of neurotransmitter, it takes a variable amount of time to produce more. In an effort to protect itself, and as the use of the intoxicant becomes either more sustained or intensified in quantity, the brain attempts different defensive measures to limit the amount of damaged caused by the neurotransmitter flooding. These countermeasures the brain has at its disposal are rather unpleasant. It can destroy parts of the brain that release the neurotransmitters, destroy the parts of the cell that the neurotransmitters connect to, reduce the amount of neurotransmitters it produces, or in the worst case scenario it can kill a cell altogether. These types of defensive measures can be repeated by the brain and occur by varying degrees with every administration that a person takes of their intoxicant. Thus, you have the slow burn method (e.g., alcohol), which takes a longer time for brain damage to show, or the more rapid decline method (e.g., methamphetamine), which has a shorter time for brain damage to show. To what degree the brain suffers damage is determined by the potency of the intoxicant, the impurities and additives in the intoxicant, time and intensity of use, genetic vulnerabilities and resiliency, and good old dumb luck.

It is also important to note a mostly overlooked fact of intoxicant use (with the exception of alcohol). Unless the person is actually growing or producing their own intoxicant, chances are that they are not getting a pure sample. When that idea is uttered, it seems natural that this is the case. Of course, a dealer pads their product with additives; he stretches the supply of the pure intoxicant, thereby increasing profit margins. To give customers a bigger bang for their buck and to get them to keep coming back for more: add some tobacco or other plants to marijuana; add some caffeine, aspirin, or drywall to cocaine, ecstasy, or meth; add some diphenhydramine to ketamine; or add more addictive substances. Drug dealing is a business pure and simple. Clients have disclosed all sorts of techniques on how to extend their supply in order to deal more drugs. What is scary for clinicians is that it is nearly impossible to determine what the short- and long-term neurological and physiological impact of these substances are and will be from all of these unknown additives that clients take in with their substance use.

Human brains do not respond well to the regular addition of intoxicants and sometimes to the other substances that dealers can add to the drug. Brains have a tendency to compensate for this use, which itself can create a host of short-term and/or long-term problems. Some of these problems are: psychosis occurring because the brain's efficiency at clearing out excessive dopamine decreases; depression intensifying because the brain reduces the production of neurotransmitters or the cells have been so damaged that they no longer work efficiently; or memory loss occurring because anandamide has stayed too long in the brain. All of these symptoms arising from substance use are not from the intoxicant *per se*, but rather from the flooding of neurotransmitters that intoxicants trigger and the defensive countermeasures that the brain takes in response.

A 12-Step Program does not directly help the recovering addict's brain heal the emotion-regulation system. Keeping the person clean and sober, the main goal of the program, is often the greatest help to repairing the brain. Additionally, it is incredibly normalizing when people in early recovery hear others in meetings describe events, the emotional rollercoaster they went through, and how their emotions eventually subsided. It helps people in early recovery counter their thinking that there is something wrong with their feelings or their inability to regulate their emotions. Take for example the following experience:

> I received a bad review at work, and at first I was really *angry*. I was *pissed off* that my boss held my addiction against me. Then, after sitting at my desk for an hour, I realized I felt *disappointed* in myself, for having my addiction become a contributing factor to the review. I know I am a hard worker. It just highlighted to me how I failed to live up to my own standards. I feel really *guilty* for using. I know I can't change the past, but I feel *hopeful* that I can improve my performance back to where I want it to be, given time and my sobriety.

In this one sentiment, a whole range of emotions are offered up as an example to the newly recovering person. It assures them that emotions are temporary, they need to be experienced in their context, and that they can be identified, articulated, and processed.

In review, a 12-Step Program offers its members a wide variety of techniques and processes that can aid a member experiencing emotional volatility. 12-Step meetings, fellowship, and sponsorship can function as an emotional container where one can experience their emotions openly, often without judgment, and receive validation of those feelings. Some addicts in early recovery accumulate and store their confusing feelings until meetings, and then use the meetings as a place to process those feelings. In effect, these members are using meetings as a strategy to contain and titrate (continuously measure and adjust the balance) their emotional volatility.

Clients often experience frequent bouts of shame, depression, and discouragement in early recovery stages. These feelings can greatly complicate their attempts to remain sober. Much like the Greek figure Pandora, the meetings and the program also use hope as a way to counteract the potential for members to become lost in these painful experiences. Meetings also include sharing the successes and joys that come from continued sobriety and recovery, furthering this message of hope. As discussed in later chapters, several of the 12-Steps also directly target the goal of finding hope.

Importantly, a wonderful template for teaching anxiety management skills is provided by Step 2, Step 3, and the Serenity Prayer. Recovering people learn to determine what is in their ability to control today ("one day at a time"); what they can turn over and release to their Higher Power, sponsor, or support system for assistance; and what is out of their control and therefore not worth the worry. In effect, the goal is to be aware, observe, and let go.

THE FOURTH AREA OF IMPAIRMENT: MEMORY AND LEARNING

To understand how the memory can work against a client in early recovery, and why addiction is chronic, take the analogy of learning how to ride a bike and then a car. To keep this example fairly short, let's say that a person first learns the basics on a tricycle: balancing, pedaling, braking, and steering. From the first ride forward, the brain begins to build pathways as it learns these skills at their most basic level and up. Next, that same person graduates to a bike with training wheels. They begin to learn how to balance further off the ground with less stabilizing support gear, and continue to perform their other skills at this level (pedaling, braking, and steering), furthering the development of those memory pathways. From this level, they graduate to biking without training wheels, and proceed to learn all sorts of new tricks (that make their parents' hair turn a little grayer each day) like sharp turns, jumping over objects, weaving, and speed racing, and so on. At this juncture of their bike riding career, they are a veteran of several years, if not a decade of experience. As such, the brain has thickened and elongated the pathways of those basic skills through constant repetition of these behaviors. It also continues to form new pathways of recent skills, which in turn create this vast network that comprises all bike-riding skills.

A magic day happens next, a day that is the stuff of nightmares for parents and insurance companies alike; the day that an adolescent finally gets their driver's license. At this point, the teen exclaims "Goodbye BMX and hello BMW!" Maybe BMW is really ambitious, but the poor bike still gets unceremoniously tossed into oblivion in the back of the garage. What do you think happens to that large network of bike-riding pathways that were developed? Does all the knowledge accumulated over all those years of bike riding stay firmly in place? Does it all go away? The answer is both yes and no. The brain does not have an infinite capacity of storage space. If any person were to retain all of the knowledge that they learned, and all memories from life's experiences, their heads would be gargantuan. Instead, the brain has to make efficient use of the space it has allocated for storage.

Let's go back and look at that point when the teenager is about to get their driver's license and their brain is at the peak of bike-riding knowledge and skill. The memory network of brain pathways for those skills was vast. As the years pass and the dust grows on the bike in the back of the garage, the brain begins to weaken and delete some of the memories that are not practiced repeatedly. The first memory pathways to go are the most recently learned skills toward the end of the teen's bike-riding career (the jumping over things, tricks, and speed racing) that did not have the benefit of years of basic skills repetition (pedaling, braking, steering, and balancing). This deleting process continues as long as there is no return to bike riding or to any other tasks using those skills. Subsequently, the next most vulnerable memory pathways are disassembled; the longer time passes without utilizing any of those skills, this memory reduction process continues.

Metabolism begins to slow down somewhere in middle age and conspire against people in an effort to enlarge their waistlines. With a resigned sigh, one might gather what's left of one's dignity and purchase a bike just to show the metabolism who's boss. Amazingly, even though the middle-aged person has not been on a bike, or anything even remotely looking like a bike in a decade or two, they can still ride it—albeit a bit wobbly. Those basic skills that were repeated and forged into memory every time one got onto the bike miraculously still remain. Why? Very simply, we retain what we repeat the most. In the case of this example; a decade of repeating the skills of balancing, pedaling, braking, and steering created the difference. Those memory pathways were very resilient to deactivation because they were continually strengthened with all of the continuous biking. Those pathways were in effect "overlearned," making those skills very enduring. They wait in the background, often without conscious awareness, ready to be refreshed under the proper circumstances.

This is the same for all behavior or knowledge. Memories are retained that are recalled most often, words learned in a foreign language class that were regularly used, and skills such as pedaling or steering that were repeated incessantly. All those memories that are not recalled, all the words learned once or twice but not utilized after that, or those fancy tricks on bikes, all disappear in the brain's effort to use its storage space efficiently.

Understanding this helps to comprehend why it is so difficult to change behaviors or routines, such as eating habits, exercise regimens, or sleep schedules. The longer we have behaved or thought in a certain way, the larger the memory tree that exists, whether it is positive or negative. The memory networks of often-repeated, overlearned behavior patterns are easily activated, difficult to stop, resistant to prevention, and even seem to operate outside of awareness, which is why we can find ourselves thinking and acting in ways that we know are not healthy for us. We may desperately want to eat healthier, lose or gain weight, or start to exercise but we often fall back into our old routines after a few days or weeks.

Let's visualize this in terms of memory structures that are competing to unlearn or retain a behavior such as late night snacking. On the one hand, we have our nightly routine of eating some unhealthy snack. We've been doing this for so long that the routine is an old friend, all but necessary to fall asleep. As the years go by and the waist size of our pants enlarges, we reach an epiphany that our weight has become unbearable. We make a New Year's resolution to stop this, and by golly we are determined to end this bad habit! So, on January 1st with a firm and unshakable resolve, we white-knuckle it through the night and complete our first night without snacking. Congratulations to us, we have formed a new pathway for a new routine and ever so slightly weakened our existing unhealthy pathway. Over time, if our resolve and reinforcement is successful, we might win the battle and the new routine of not eating at night wins out, becoming the dominant memory guiding our behavior. It is rare for old ways of thinking and acting not to resurface as we try to change one of our old behaviors or thought patterns. Instead, what often happens is that we have periods where we lapse into the old behaviors. Try as we might, we have a whole lot of history of repeated behaviors working against us. Therefore, sometimes the old (overlearned) memory network overpowers and prevails over the newer (underlearned) memory network.

Often, a return to old behaviors (e.g., the late night snacking) is done on a whim. An impulsive moment that was not planned or anticipated. For instance, a friend arrives with our favorite nighttime snacks and we indulge without a thought about our commitment. After all, it is not polite to refuse! If not an impulsive moment, sometimes the lapse into old behaviors can be caused by factors such as fatigue, familiar settings, stress, emotional situations, or simply by contact with cohorts who engaged in the same patterns. Our willpower slips, we give up the fight, and indulge. It is possible that we view our relapse of snacking as justified based on what we are currently going through. That next morning, we may brush away the prior night's crumbs and realize that we do not want to stay stuck in our old ways. The desire for our new way of thinking and behaving is strong enough, and so we make the decision to return to our pledge, climb back onto our "no eating at night!" horse, and ride on. Eventually with due diligence, the old unhealthy behaviors begin to feel unfamiliar when reengaged, and our new healthy behaviors feel more comfortable, easier even, than in the beginning. At long last, our new behaviors or thinking possess a larger memory network than our old repeated behaviors or thought network.

This same process is at work when we talk about addictive behavior and thinking, that feedback loop of urge-compulsion-use. Consider all of the thoughts and routines that are a part of that pattern: fantasizing about the intoxicant, where to get it, whom to get it from, how to use it, how it makes me feel; bringing myself down from my high or bringing myself up from my low; managing my crash; lying to hide my use; and justifying my using with excuses, just to name a few. No one is equipped with the foreknowledge of how to perform all of these behaviors; they all have to be learned. The more each of those behaviors or thoughts are repeated, the stronger they become, the easier they are to engage, and the harder it is to change or forget them. Just like riding a bike.

Consider that it is their own memory base and learning that the alcoholic or addict (also the sponsor and therapist!) is up against when they first enter into recovery. Everyone has a large and powerful network of learned and chemically reinforced behaviors. In the case of the alcoholic or addict, it is the antisocial, impulsive, and compulsive thoughts and behavior patterns that drive them to think and behave in a way that is familiar and easier because they have behaved or thought that way for such a long time. Their learning and practice related to the addictive loop does not disappear the day they stop using. Just as in the example of the midnight snacker, it takes time for the brain to deactivate those pathways. In addition, simply stopping using doesn't mean that the addictive pathways go away. All of the addictive thinking, behaviors, and routines remain in place. So, the person can remove the intoxicant, but that does not make this memory network disappear. Once the intoxicant use stops, the obsessive thinking and compulsive behavior initially remain active. This places the newly sober person at risk to relapse or to manifest their addictive thinking and behavior through another method, whether an alternative intoxicant, sex, gambling, exercise or another type of behavior that follows that similar negative feedback loop. As therapists, it is crucial to help recovering women and men develop new routines, thought patterns, and behaviors that are different from their old addictive ones.

To highlight this, take for example the dangers of recovering alcoholics and addicts who continue to smoke cigarettes. Given what you have been reading, take a moment and think of why we recommend that those in early recovery stop smoking. Conventional wisdom used to hold that people in early recovery should not try to stop smoking. After all, they are trying to stop their substance of choice, which can do a lot more damage, so why not let them keep this one vice? Doubly so, it was worried that the stress of quitting smoking would only make it more difficult for them to remain sober from their intoxicant(s). Why risk a relapse in this way? The answer lies in the process of learning and memory, especially when taking into account how that development impacts the absorption of new coping skills.

Let's examine the issue of smoking in more detail. Consider how the habit of smoking continues the same addictive network in the brain that the addict/alcoholic is trying to stop with recovery. Smoking operates on the same obsessive-compulsive-impulsive spectrum as any other substance of choice. For example, smoking can be utilized as a coping skill for emotion regulation. I get angry; I smoke to feel relief. I am nervous about an upcoming exam or meeting; I smoke to feel calmer. Nicotine is not helping the anxiety or anger, quite the opposite in fact. What is producing the calming effect is the deep breathing with each inhalation. Smoking can also be built into a routine, including drug and alcohol use. Complicating matters, it can be built into that routine without the person even being aware of the connection. If I go out to the bar to drink, I smoke as a companion behavior. Furthermore, given that nicotine is an addictive substance, it should come as no surprise that the learning involved for smoking is similar to other intoxicants. It is also then reasonable to understand why continuing smoking after stopping another intoxicant has the potential to hinder recovery efforts, if alternative coping skills are not learned.

When in early recovery from intoxicant use, if the only coping skill I develop for emotions, routines, or behaviors is another obsessive-compulsive-impulsive behavior (e.g., smoking), then those addictive memory networks never get deactivated. This leaves the addict vulnerable to relapse because once a stressor is encountered that smoking is insufficient to relieve, the addict seeks out the next best thing—a more powerful intoxicant. Added to this, if smoking becomes linked to the substance abuse, then actively smoking can directly trigger the memories of using, resulting in biologically mediated urges to use, and in general initiating a real-time ambivalence around staying sober.

Returning to the notion of the substance dependent memory systems, if a client has this large addictive network in their brain that was created and overlearned through the chronic use and dependence on an intoxicant, then that individual needs to learn skills, behaviors, and routines that are *different and new* from the addictive ones. This is where a 12-Step Program can be very helpful. It is the reason that a 12-Step Program has many sayings in a bumper-sticker format that are short, easily recalled, and even some that are acronyms. Additionally, 12-Step meetings tend to repeat similar themes and messages of recovery, thus increasing the likelihood of being learned, especially by those with memory impairments. A 12-Step Program also calls out members for telling "war stories" and in doing so, helps to rewrite the addict's long-term memories from "fun and pleasurable" to the harm that those experiences caused, both to the recovering addict and their loved ones. This, in effect, causes the addict to mentally practice the replacement memory network. The result is that the more often new thoughts and behaviors of sobriety are practiced, the stronger that network becomes. Alternatively, the less the recovering person employs their addictive thoughts and behaviors, the weaker that network becomes. What results is an actual flip in neural networks over time.

Unfortunately, just like riding a bike, twenty years can pass and the recovering person can relapse, and find that their behaviors and use patterns very rapidly resemble the pattern that was occurring prior to their sobriety; or, to use 12-Step lingo, they can pick up the substance (i.e., relapse) and be right back where they were when they left off. This pattern also fits the memory system model previously described. For the addict, even though time and effort deactivate many of those learned thoughts and behaviors, the most repeated (likely the seeking and using of the drug) behaviors and thoughts remain. The urge-compulsion-use loop remains in the background, waiting to be reengaged. It's easy to retrieve that information and just like riding a bike, albeit perhaps a bike from hell, the addict starts anew. The inability of most addicts to completely deactivate and delete that memory system is one of the many reasons why it is said that the person is always in recovery, and not recovered.

THE FIFTH AREA OF IMPAIRMENT: PRO-SOCIAL THINKING AND BEHAVIOR

It is important to remember that because an active or early recovery addict may demonstrate antisocial traits or behaviors, that does not necessarily mean that they have an antisocial personality disorder. As discussed before, antisocial thinking and behavior are necessary components of active addiction. The DSM-IV-TR describes the following as the symptoms of Antisocial Personality Disorder:

- Disregard for right and wrong
- Persistent lying or deceit
- Manipulation of others using charm or wit
- Recurrence of difficulties with the law
- Repeated violation of the rights of others
- Child abuse or neglect
- Intimidation of others
- Aggressive or violent behavior
- Lack of remorse about harming others
- Impulsive behavior
- Agitation
- Poor or abusive relationships
- Irresponsible work behavior

If this symptom list were the only criteria for Antisocial Personality Disorder (APD), almost every alcoholic or addict who walked through a clinician's door would be classified as APD. Fortunately, a majority of the time that is not the case. Over time, it is important to determine whether these symptoms persist independent of active addiction.

Diagnostically, this is a messier problem than it may appear on the surface. For some individuals who met the criteria for APD before they developed an addiction, that personality structure likely continues, hopefully at an increasingly moderated level after they are sober and well into recovery. For many of these people, they continue to meet the criteria until the day they die. For every other substance dependent person who did not meet the criteria for APD prior to addiction, an antisocial adaptation becomes necessary to remain actively abusing intoxicants. Many of these individuals revert to their premorbid non-APD personality structure once they are sober and in recovery for a few weeks or months. However, some do not revert to their premorbid personality style. Instead, they resemble someone with APD well into recovery. For them, it is as if their antisocial adaptation during addiction essentially overwrote their prior personality structure, and now for all intents and purposes they should be considered as having an APD.

Regardless of the status of their antisocial traits, Step work, fellowship, sponsorship, and meeting attendance can assist in molding the fragile identity of the newly recovering individual into one who is prosocial versus antisocial. Specifically, these four components of the 12-Step Program help to build the following prosocial qualities:

- Accountability for current and past behavior
- Unending practice of rigorous honesty
- Creation or rediscovery of spiritual identity
- Ability to redefine personal moral code
- Ability for any member, no matter how early in recovery, to help another recovering addict/alcoholic
- Encouragement of service work/volunteering
- Focus on a message of experience, strength, and hope
- Platform to develop sober social skills and learn healthy conflict resolution

- Experience the ability to trust and be trusted
- Self-esteem developed from vulnerability and humbleness, not false pride or grandiosity

It is hoped that the absence of the intoxicant renders mute the need for antisocial behavior, but just like any other thought or behavior pattern, the pathways of that learning still exist, even with the addiction in remission. It is one of the many reasons that a 12-Step Program strives to help an individual create a completely different life from that of the addiction lifestyle. The values of rigorous honesty, service work, support, and resilience all are opposite to antisocial living.

SUMMARY

There is a clear clinical benefit to a client attending a 12-Step program, regardless of 12-Step's shortcomings. If a therapist is knowledgeable and prepared, the challenges that 12-Step present in terms of its approach or philosophy can be successfully navigated and help to ensure a positive outcome for the client. Although a 12-Step Program does not *per se* heal the brains of people in recovery, its focus on creating a lifestyle that is very different to addiction ensures that progress is made in healing. The mere absence of an intoxicant aids in healing, as will the formation of prorecovery thoughts, skills, and behaviors.

QUESTIONS

1. Name the ways in which substance use impairs general executive functioning, and how 12-Steps helps to undo or compensate for some of that impairment.
2. Name the ways in which substance use impairs judgment, and how 12-Steps helps to undo or compensate for some of that impairment.
3. Name the ways in which substance use impairs emotion regulation and containment, and how 12-Steps helps to undo or compensate for some of that impairment.
4. Name the ways in which substance use impairs memory and learning, and how 12-Steps helps to undo or compensate for some of that impairment.
5. Name the ways in which substance use fosters antisocial thinking and behavior, and how 12-Steps helps to build prosocial thinking and behavior.

A Primer on Therapeutic Practice with Substance Abuse Clients

4

INTRODUCTION

Before proceeding into the clinical work of substance abuse treatment and 12-Steps, let's address the therapeutic setting first. Working with substance abuse is similar in many ways to other clinical work; however, given the nature of the disease there are some notable differences. While everyone approaches office policies in their practice differently, the following outlines clinical procedures specific to our practices, which we hope can serve as examples and a possible framework for your own practice. The chapter concludes by talking about the process of building credibility with your clients.

SUBSTANCE DEPENDENCE AND THE THERAPEUTIC FRAME

The general ground rules for counseling also apply, with only a few caveats, to substance dependent clients.

Fees and Payment Issues

This population frequently has financial difficulties resulting from the consequences of their substance dependence. However, as a supervisor said a long time ago, "If they can manage to scrape together the money to drink and drug, what makes you think they can't do the same to get some treatment?" As heartless as this seems, this is one of the general rules we adopted. We do not reduce our fees simply because the individual has a substance abuse or dependence problem. This approach tends to save therapists a great deal of irritation and doubt that they're enabling the relapsing addict by offering them a reduced fee. Now, we'd be lying through our teeth if we said that we had never offered reduced fees to a financially strapped client. However, it is usually a time-limited reduction that terminates if that client continues to relapse, especially if there's reason to question their motivation to change. In that case, we normally renegotiate the fees to a full fee.

We also recommend collecting fees for services at the time they are provided rather than bill on a monthly basis. Delayed payments can create complications, especially if the client goes on a binge and blows all of their money on the relapse. Collecting fees at the time of service is not a fail-safe alternative, witness trying to collect monies for your time spent waiting during no shows or late cancellations. We recommend that your informed consent document include granting permission to take legal action or to utilize a collection agency for any unpaid debt. Whether this alternative is used or not, it does grant the option to collect what is due, if you choose.

Cancellations and Late Arrivals

As with all clients, consider that the appointment time essentially rents that hour of treatment. That means that the client is charged their fee for that hour, whether they keep the appointment or not, unless they cancel by giving at least a 24 hour notice (or whatever timeframe is specified in the informed consent). If a client is late to an appointment, they are only provided services for the remaining time in their appointment. For example, if a client is 40 minutes late for a 50 minute appointment, then they are provided with 10 minutes of services and billed for the entire therapeutic hour.

Confidentiality and Legal Involvements

In general, this treatment population often requires more outside contacts with authorities, such as work representatives, family members, lawyers, and courts. Expect to frequently be drawn into correlating issues: suitability for organ transplant, potential work termination, coordination with probation/parole officers, divorce court, and court actions related to prior arrests, divorce, and custody battles. It is quite important for you to be knowledgeable about the confidentiality laws in your district and to adequately inform your client regarding these laws. Simultaneously, these outside contacts often raise concerns around potentially enabling the client. Consider the following example:

> Stuart, the client, was referred by a local substance abuse program. He has been dependent on alcohol for decades and now is very ill due to advanced liver disease. He entered treatment only after he was told by his physician that sobriety was a requisite before he could be placed on an organ transplant list, however you were not told this. Instead, the referring treatment program told you that Stuart was referred in order to give him the best chance of continuing his sobriety. Six months into treatment, Stuart requests that you write a letter in support of his efforts to qualify for a liver transplant.

Stuart's case raises many questions: How does writing this letter impact his treatment? By writing this letter, is the clinician enabling him to avoid the consequences of his drinking? Is this a real sobriety or essentially a pause in his alcohol use just to qualify for this procedure? Why didn't Stuart state at the start of treatment that this letter was an objective; he must have known he'd need it? Why didn't the referring agency tell you his whole background? Has Stuart been truly engaging in treatment, or is this just one large manipulation to obtain the letter? Even if it started as a manipulation, does it matter now that he is sober?

Client's Response to Ground Rules

As one might expect, substance abusing or dependent clients often struggle with the ground rules. First, at the start of treatment it is best practices to review the rules while in session and provide all clients with a copy of their informed consent so that they have a reference document for review at any time. Remember that the substance dependence breeds antisocial skills, including rule breaking, manipulation, and lying. Providing clients with hard copies of these documents is a necessary and effective response to both manipulation and any memory problems the client is experiencing.

Also, asking this population to be 100% responsible regarding the rules of therapy is going to be very challenging for them. Likewise, as a clinician, expect that with this population you can be tempted to bend the rules far more than with other groups. Do not give in to this temptation any more than you would for a client from a different mental health population. For this group, bending rules not only demonstrates your lack of adherence to your own required rules, but enables the old behavior patterns that therapy and recovery are trying to change! This is especially true for a client struggling with relapse. Clients engaging in a relapse return to their drug-taking. Many also resume the behavioral disruptions associated with addiction: an active antisocial adaptation, manipulation, and irresponsibility combined with emotional fragility and crisis. Therapists get hit with the splash damage from this just like every other major player in the client's life. This can run the gamut from clients missing scheduled appointments without cancelling, showing up late for sessions but demanding the full session time, dropping out of treatment for periods of time, or trying to convince the therapist to run interference with the client's significant other/spouse. It is not uncommon to feel a strong urge to accommodate the client and bend the accepted rules of treatment. Why not skip charging them for the session they blew off? Or extend the appointment past the end of time? After all, the client is often in great emotional pain already. Holding to your rules only punishes them further. Why not act in a way that relieves some of their pain? However, that's the rub! By relieving their pain, you are often protecting them from the consequences of their actions and supporting their continued drug-taking. By helping, we can end up enabling the problem.

This is not to say that our rules are immutable. We would also be telling tall tales if we didn't say that sometimes a clinician has to bend the cancellation/late arrival rules because of extenuating circumstances. Newly sober people, apart from having impaired executive functioning and impulse control, or because of it, tend to have an extreme level of chaos in their lives. There are often many crises and demands on their time, especially if they are having medical, occupational, or relationship/family problems. Compounding this, many simply lack essential and basic social skills, such as time management and organizational skills (for instance, keeping a calendar). For these individuals, we may loosen the rules sometimes, but again, it is a time-limited proposition. Typically, depending on the speed of improvement and the extent of the problem, we reassert the rules of the informed consent within 3 to 6 months or sooner. Within that timeframe, we address the problems directly in treatment by attempting to remediate any deficits while concurrently slowly increasing the tightness of the rules.

Responding to an Intoxicated Client

As one might expect, it is not atypical for a client to call when they are intoxicated. During this time, remember the age-old wisdom, "Never argue with a drunk." In these cases when appropriate, we advise taking the following actions:

Safety

Intervention is warranted if a client is in medical risk or if they are engaging in behavior that threatens themselves and others. For instance, if a client with a history of heart problems telephones complaining of chest and radiating arm pain after using a stimulant such as cocaine or methamphetamine—have them call an ambulance or offer to call one for them.

If a client calls and says they are being terrorized by auditory hallucinations and the clinician thinks these hallucinations are drug induced, tell them that the hallucinations were likely brought on by their abuse, cite previous examples, and relay that the hallucinations will likely end after they stop using. Other suggestions might be that the client return to a safe environment (home, a trusted friend or family member, a treatment center), call their sponsor, or go to a 12-Step meeting. Ending the conversation shortly thereafter is advised.

In general, avoid long, protracted, repetitive interactions common to conversations with the intoxicated. Again, make brief suggestions and then end the call in order to avoid being pulled into rescuing behavior. Even in the midst of a relapse, if someone acts for them then clients do not learn self-confidence in their own ability to master recovery skills. A 12-Step meeting room is the optimal environment for them as they generally provide abundant resources for resuming sobriety: members willing to "ride out the high" with the client, provide shelter, or escort them to treatment.

Referral to a Higher Level of Care

Escalating the level of service is another option to consider when an intoxicated client calls in a crisis. In the midst of such a crucial time, clients resistant to stopping their drug of choice can be far more willing to consider some form of hospitalization. These crises produce a level of emotional, physical, or financial pain such that they are willing to consider anything that provides them with relief. This is normally the point where the ambivalent client reaches their "bottom." For this reason, it is not uncommon for clients to be admitted to treatment programs when they are very intoxicated and even in a blackout. This scenario is discussed in more detail later on in the text.

Mental Record Keeping

Expect ambivalent clients, and those in early recovery to have more crises than the typical client. The therapist's task is to help provide brief interventions during these times as well as to record the emotional distress of the client. Clients have difficulties recalling and then holding onto memories of the negative experiences associated with their drinking and drugging. As denial or other defenses come to the forefront to minimize the negative effects of the using, a professional can empathically remind and record these damaging experiences in order to help clients maintain a more complete picture of their using experience. The end goal is that by providing this documentation, the client is motivated toward abstinence.

Mitchell was a long-term cocaine dependent client who found it very difficult to remain sober. Typically, he strung together 6 to 9 months of abstinence before he inevitably relapsed. His relapses followed a binge pattern: spending very large amounts of money on the drug, being intoxicated for several days, and getting little or no sleep. During one of these relapses, he contacted his therapist in a crisis. Mitchell was experiencing cocaine-induced paranoia that included auditory hallucinations. He was terrified that every black SUV he saw was filled with "men in black suits" who were going to hurt him. The therapist informed Mitchell that his paranoia seemed due to cocaine and recommended he admit himself to a hospital for medical help. Mitchell refused, but agreed that he would stop abusing cocaine and instead attempt to get some sleep. The therapist ended the call after briefly assessing for other safety concerns.

During their next session, Mitchell discussed his relapse and his phone call. Over the next several months, the therapist brought up the phone call as evidence of the destructiveness of Mitchell's addiction, and his inability to manage his drugging; at the same time, Mitchell was attempting to rationalize and minimize his addiction. Each time this occurred, Mitchell experienced the therapist's comments as an "Aha" moment because in comparison to the therapist, Mitchell's own memories of the event were distant and removed. His memory only generated a certain distant, two-dimensional quality that lacked any emotional significance. The therapist's recollections, and their emotional impact, helped Mitchell to hold onto the severity of his binges.

Involving Family and Significant Others

Addiction is a family disease; the antisocial behavior of substance abuse is deeply embedded and operating within a family system whether the family recognizes this fact or not. If the substance dependent family member is going to change by stopping their use, then the family needs to accommodate this by changing themselves. Surprisingly as it may seem considering the alternative, not all families cope with this prospect gracefully. When a family member is mired in substance abuse or dependence, a number of changes can happen in a family system. There are multiple scenarios: some members gain more power in the family, others can ignore their own problematic or dysfunctional behavior by focusing solely on the problems of the person using, others still may boost their sense of self-worth by becoming the user's rescuer, and so forth. The list could fill an entire text, and indeed there have been many books written about family dynamics and substance dependence. Instead of covering the totality of family dysfunction, a primer is offered here related to the clinician's role in interacting with the family when treating a person with substance abuse or dependence.

It is common for the families of clients in the first stages of the change process (those ambivalent about stopping using) to contact the therapist, especially in response to the client's destructive behaviors. If the client is willing to provide a release of information for you to interact with their family—then by all means welcome these interactions. Families are often unaware that there is a 12-Step Program for them as well, so be certain to educate and encourage their participation in the Al-Anon program. Al-Anon operates in the same way as 12-Step programs by providing a space for families to work through the 12-Steps themselves, in order to learn from each other about best practices while in the support process of their loved one's recovery.

The transition to sobriety seems especially jarring to romantic associations by injecting a great deal of strain and turmoil into the relationship. As the addict becomes sober, both parties experience a dramatic shift in behaviors: from underfunctioning, to a more normal level of functioning, to becoming far more emotionally available and responsible. As expected, these shifts act and react against the emotional, financial, and familial crises that the substance abuse creates, and in turn, the attention it demands. In addition, after spending many lonely days and nights while the newly recovering person was out using, significant others are loathe to now share their loved one with 12-Step and recovery. 12-Step meetings are at a minimum an hour long, not including travel times, and fellowship (a critical component that allows development of a sober support network) may be anywhere to an hour or two in addition to that! The inevitable disappointment felt by the significant other lies in the belief that once clean and sober, the newly recovering person will be more available to them. Discord and resentment often pop up once the significant other realizes the reality of the time requirements of sobriety. Many a relationship has ended over this reality.

Added to the above, many families and romantic partners initially respond with relief, if not direct support, to a loved one seeking substance abuse treatment. However, once the initial crisis passes, it is common for the loved one to increasingly express resentment and anger at the client. This occurs for a couple of reasons. First, because of their substance-abusing loved one, these partners existed in a chronic state of crisis themselves, preoccupied with the chaos brought into their world. As treatment progresses, the level of chaos in the system reduces and individuals realize how resentful they are over the client's chronic inability to meet their obligations. Second, the client may appear to be getting better, so the assumption is that they are then in a better position to receive these angry messages. Within a few short days, family interactions can turn from supportive, to cold, to openly hostile as this dynamic plays itself out.

The client should be notified that their change to sobriety can be associated with higher levels of stress and risk in their relationships and families. In anticipation of this normal course, assist the client with building their communication skills, and coping with the fallout of their actions on the family. As they progress through treatment, check in weekly with clients about the family relationships and monitor how everyone is adjusting to sobriety. If there is too much tension in the system, refer the client to additional treatment for couples or family therapy. This is especially urgent if there are emotional upsets or behaviors aimed by the family at sabotaging the client's sobriety.

The situation can be even more complicated when your client's significant other is revealed to be an active substance abuser themselves, a fairly common occurrence. This then leads many clients and therapists to question: 1) Is their significant other's abuse triggering the client to relapse, and 2) As the client engages more in recovery, are they able to have a rewarding relationship with their abusing partner?

Some partners elect to pursue sobriety along with the client. On the surface, this appears to be an optimal outcome, right? What could be better that the two of them supporting and aiding each other in their efforts at recovery? However, if the couple is unaware of the entanglements this can creates then such an arrangement can often greatly complicate recovery instead of helping it. For instance, has each person developed a sober support network *independent* of the other in order to provide support if the partner relapses? Are they going to separate meetings to openly talk about their triggers or resentments (freeing themselves from worry about the reactions from their significant other)? How are the suggestions from each person's sponsor enhancing or undermining the other? As you can see, there are a great number of boundaries to consider in this dynamic. The key to success appears that the couples must maintain strong boundaries between each other, and not become deeply involved in the other's recovery.

A more toxic relationship occurs when the partner is dependent on the same or similar intoxicant to your client's drug of choice, combined with an unwillingness to enter into recovery. This pattern usually involves the client frequently relapsing or coming close to relapsing, making it clear that the client must choose between sobriety or their relationship, but not both. In general, a relationship where both people are abusing intoxicants is unlikely to survive recovery efforts. Typically, either both parties return to active use or they split up. However, this is not a universal truism. Couples can survive and lead happy, rewarding lives together with one or both remaining sober. For asymmetrical couples, where only one continues to abuse, a reliance on setting strong boundaries is crucial for the couple to effectively function.

The fact of disruptions within relationships can also be used by therapists to achieve positive ends for their clients. Although painful, therapists can guide clients to integrate anger from loved ones into a more complete awareness of the negative consequences of using drugs and alcohol. Relationships that end are a loss, but also an opportunity for clients to form relationships that support their sobriety.

THERAPIST AS A MEMBER OR NON-MEMBER OF THE RECOVERING COMMUNITY

Non-Member of the Recovering Community

We have trained students at sites that work with addictions, and can predict with uncanny accuracy which students will be questioned by the clients as to whether or not they are themselves in recovery. This question is not about whether a student, or clinician for that matter, presents as someone with a substance use disorder. The question signifies a lack of demonstrable knowledge by the clinical team member on recovery concepts, language, terms, and techniques. Clients doubt that you know what you are talking about, which is why they question whether you are also in recovery!

In previous chapters, we made recommendations for clinicians to become involved in 12-Step, and for good reason. By attending open meetings, you pick up on the concepts, lingo, and processes that can provide you with the tools to work with 12-Step clients in therapy. This book (as great and informed as it is) is not a substitute for that practical experience. All clinicians should find the courage to walk through those doors and experience a 12-Step meeting; share the experience of the addict by walking in knowing nothing and no one. You quickly appreciate the client's experience, and the result is that you become a better guide. You also meet other people in recovery who can serve as contacts for newcomers to make a connection. In short, GO! GO! GO! If a client begins to question your credibility treating recovery, you have some work to do, my friend.

Member of the Recovering Community, but Not Participating in 12-Step

We have worked with clinicians who are recovering from addiction themselves but do not elect, for any number of reasons, to participate in 12-Step. For those clinicians (whatever the reasons that 12-Steps did not work), they had to come to a peace with the Program. For the majority in this group whom we met, there was recognition that although it may not have worked for them, it may for their clients. We found them to be an excellent source for recommendations for alternative routes to sobriety, including other self-help recovery programs, spiritual approaches, and sometimes just how to stop cold turkey and not look back.

We have also witnessed clients directly asking these same clinicians why they did not attend 12-Step meetings, and the clinicians were equally as direct and frank about their reasons. Ironically, this approach did not steer clients away from a 12-Step program. Rather, these exchanges often resulted in a client being better prepared for the Program by recognizing its shortcomings. Additionally, in order to work through those difficulties, clients sought out these clinicians to air their disagreements/disillusionments with 12-Step. With this specialized group, as with our approach, the method is to present clients with a selection of routes to sobriety with all of the pros and cons laid bare. Clients who make a more informed decision tend to have greater flexibility in tolerating and working with the imperfections of any program.

Member of the Recovering Community, and Participating in 12-Step

Therapists we know who are involved in 12-Steps themselves have taken several different approaches to being a member and a clinician within this community. Suffice it to say that the dynamics are very similar to being a therapist in a small community. The level of intersection in the therapist's personal and professional identities depends on their ability to manage:

- Determining boundaries in 12-Step with both active and former clients in treatment
- Desired level of separation of recovery program from professional life
- Balancing the 12-Step principles to "pay it forward" with sharing "experience, strength, and hope" and balancing revealing personal information with active clients in treatment
- Determining boundaries of use of information learned through informal channels in 12-Step (meetings, relationship with client's sponsor, etc.) in therapy
- Determining processes for handling of their own relapse with both active and former clients in treatment

Newly Sober Therapists

Some clinicians are drawn to this work because they have unresolved issues in this area. They may be recently sober or exhibit their own pattern of substance abuse. If this is the case, we strongly recommend that you delay working in this area until you are firmly embedded in your own recovery. For most, this will take two to four years of sobriety and recovery work before they are ready to work with clients, usually with four years proving more successful a time frame than two. By jumping the gun and engaging in this work too soon, there is the added risk that the newly sober therapist can become triggered for use, begin working out their own struggles with recovery with the client, or relapsing themselves. Once lost, therapeutic credibility is hard to gain back.

SUMMARY

There are many factors to consider before beginning to practice with people with addictions. Consider the information presented here as a guide to establishing your own policies and protocols for practice. We *highly* recommend that before implementing any procedures, you consult with trustworthy experts on issues related to liability, ethical practice, and state regulations. This information is not meant to discourage anyone from working with this population, but rather it is meant to help add more competency and protection to your practice.

QUESTIONS

1. Name three recommendations for informed consent policies to implement in a practice with substance using clients.
2. What are some options you have as a clinician when responding to an intoxicated client?
3. How might a client's question regarding your recovery indicate a lack of confidence?
4. If you are a therapist in recovery yourself, what are some of the benefits and drawbacks to revealing your recovery to clients?

Assessment Considerations and Techniques

5

ASSESSMENT AS A THERAPEUTIC TECHNIQUE

Assessment is a different process than therapeutic intervention. Typically, a therapist conducting an assessment is far more active and directive than when conducting therapy. The therapist as an assessor also has a clear agenda of what information is required to make a determination about the client and their issues. Therapy, on the other hand, is commonly far less agenda and judgment driven. An experienced clinician can often listen to only a minute or two of a taped session to determine if an interview is a diagnostic or therapeutic interview.

While acknowledging that there is a difference between therapy and assessment, in reality the difference between the two is far fuzzier and less simplistic than presented. A beneficial treatment requires that the actual therapy include an ongoing assessment process. Conversely, it is often not considered that a good assessment also includes elements of good therapy. Think about it. An effective assessment gathers information and essential points from a person's history to gain a holistic picture of the client. In order to selectively explore essential elements of the client's history, the assessor must work around the client's defenses and resistance. These components are then linked together to arrive at an understanding of the client and their operational world. The assessor then builds hypotheses that are further explored in the interview, testing what does and does not hold true. Together with the client, the assessor works to establish trust and provide a foundation of understanding about the client, the client's world, and the parameters of therapy. The work of disclosure, trust, and the construction of a comprehensive and accurate picture of the client is necessarily a fairly fluid process. This is predominantly true for clients who voluntarily refer themselves, but it's also true for most mandated clients as well. Remember, clients present themselves in your office because they are in distress, they want to understand why they are in pain, and they want to obtain relief. These reasons especially hold true for the substance dependent client, thereby allowing the therapist, as an assessor, to begin the important opportunity to lay out and begin assembling the myriad pieces of their addiction puzzle.

Nathaniel, a successful middle-manager, sought treatment complaining that he had lost his "mojo" and his life was without purpose or direction. Nathaniel was uncertain as to the cause or why this malaise had continued for a couple of years. During the first session, the therapist began gathering Nathaniel's history and quickly determined that he was cocaine dependent. As the session proceeded, the therapist worked through much of the client's history; starting with his history of his reported loss of "mojo," and simultaneously tracking the escalation of his cocaine use. Near the end of the session, the therapist announced that there seemed to be a close link between his loss of "mojo" and cocaine use. Nathaniel agreed, saying that no other conclusion seemed possible given his history.

History of Substance Use versus Personal History

As with any behavior, substance use is easily influenced by history and circumstance. For instance, it is not unusual for individuals to engage in frequent binge drinking when attending college, or in some military situations. Often, people also increase their alcohol or tobacco consumption during periods of heightened stress. Some periods of life, adolescence into early adulthood, are known as a time of experimentation with intoxicants. With this in mind, it is beneficial to correlate a person's substance use with their personal history. Simply put, substance use results from the details of a person's life, or the substance is used in an attempt to cope with their current circumstances. However, this relationship often changes in two ways once the person slips into substance dependence. First, it intensifies. It is quite common for a person to increasingly respond to events in their life with intoxication, and in some cases essentially reach the point where intoxication becomes the person's primary coping mechanism. Second, the person's relationship to their intoxicant reverses where the person's life is now responding to their substance abuse. In this tail-wags-the-dog relationship, the newly minted addict now shifts their life to accommodate their substance abuse. Jobs and relationships are altered or lost, information about their substance use is strictly managed, and the person often attempts to control their environment in a way that hopes to minimize the fallout from their continued intoxication. Be alert to the fact that many first-time clients have limited to no conscious awareness of the interconnection between their lives and their substance abuse. Here is a case example highlighting this dilemma:

Amber was referred by a local child protective services after allegations that she provided inadequate supervision for her two children, ages 6 and 8. Amber reported that she began abusing cocaine and alcohol toward the end of high school. As the evaluator (assessor) progressed through her history, many of the losses and failures in her life corresponded with both external events and periods of intensified intoxicant use. For instance, she lost a job at age 22 when she began smoking cocaine, and she was unable to hold consistent fulltime employment ever since. She began drinking alcohol daily at 24, coinciding with a miscarriage and the end of her last long-term romantic relationship. The interviewer continued to track her life and her substance abuse, but at no point did the interviewer suggest a connection between her life's difficulties and her addictions. Toward the end of the interview, the client looked at the interviewer and announced that more than any other topic they discussed, she realized that she had a drug problem, which she acknowledged might be her core problem.

Mono- versus Poly-Substance Dependence versus Cross-Behavioral Addiction

Some clients become dependent on multiple substances. The reader should be vigilant regarding some common patterns or drug-related behaviors that result when chemical dependents abuse multiple substances. Most commonly, multi-intoxicant-dependent clients have one intoxicant they prefer to use above all others (intoxicant of choice or drug of choice). However, having an intoxicant of choice does not mean that the client is devoted only to that substance for the rest of their drug-taking career. Some clients remain faithful to the first intoxicant of choice that they tried and liked, but many others display a shift in preference across their lives. This shift can involve not just the type of intoxicant, but also the method of administration. For instance, a person's drug of choice may be cocaine, where their first use was by snorting. After a few years, once their high began diminishing, they shifted to smoking it. After the high diminished once again, they shifted to injecting it.

Clients may also shift their drug of choice over time. For instance, a client may have started in adolescence with marijuana as their drug of choice. However, after a skiing accident, they were placed on painkillers for an injury. The realized that the painkillers created a more powerful, sustaining, and immensely better high than marijuana. However, after ten years of use, no prescription was strong enough or available enough. At the same time, the online ordering of pills was beginning to draw unwanted attention from family members questioning their actions. In response, after meeting a dealer through online chat rooms and to avoid more complications with family, the individual turned to heroin. For other clients, they may turn to another drug to decrease or prevent withdrawal symptoms from their intoxicant of choice. For example, a client may turn to a benzodiazepine, such as Xanax or Klonopin, when they cannot consume alcohol. Alternately, a heroin-dependent individual may drink alcohol or take another sedative-like substance (such as Ketamine) when they cannot obtain heroin. Over time, these substituted substances can develop into a completely separate dependence. It can be easy to miss these separate or additional dependencies during a clinical interview. The client often negates concern about the use, casting it as "not a problem" and justifying its use in very logical ways. This can become quite problematic if this client completes treatment with their efforts only focused on their reported primary drug of choice. After leaving treatment, the untreated secondary substance dependence often blindsides the client as it begins to take over their life (even without the primary drug of choice present), often resulting in the need for additional treatment.

In addition, behavioral disruptions can occur with substance dependence to the point that the two dependencies can become inexorably entwined, assuring that it is a folly to treat one without treating the other. As an example, methamphetamine use can become so integrated with a person's sexual behavior that both become compulsive—one triggers the other. A case example best illustrates this:

Dimitri was an attractive gay man in his mid-30s when he initially presented for treatment. He had been smoking methamphetamine for the past seven years. At the start, he smoked it once every month or two. For the last two years, he developed a new cycle. His binges lasted two to four days, followed by two days without use, with the resumption afterwards of another binge.

Typically, he displayed very high levels of sexual activity during his drug-taking binges by masturbating throughout most of the binge, having multiple sexual partners, or seeking out additional partners at online sex sites. He estimated that he had engaged in sex with approximately a dozen men over the prior week and declared that this was typical. Dimitri stated, "as soon as I get high I think about sex, and as soon as I think about sex I think about getting high. And sex is everywhere for me. I can't even stand in line at Starbucks without finding a guy in the store and imagining him skull-fucking me."

Dimitri's therapist (a male) after the interview examined his counter-transference reactions to the client. He noted feeling that Dimitri was seductive to the point that he "oozed sexuality."

The key with Dimitri is that both his drug taking and his sexuality are compulsive, meaning that they are mutually triggering, thus the term *cross addicted*. If the client went to treatment and the program or therapist only focused on skill building for the methamphetamine dependence, then you can immediately see how the deck is stacked against him as soon as he is discharged and has a sexual thought or urge.

Through proper assessment generated by rich inquiries and information, therapists, in their capacity as clinical interviewers, can and should find a wealth of material around the interplay between substances and behavioral compulsions. In the case example above, when and how did sexual behavior and methamphetamine become so conjoined for Dimitri? What function does the sexual preoccupation serve for him? How did each of the sexual and drug compulsions develop for him? How did they interact prior to becoming so entwined? Are there ways in which his current behavior reflects or expresses these patterns he described in therapy?

In the last chapter, it was discussed that, when a client ends their primary drug of choice, the compulsive thinking and behavior of substance dependence can be transferred to another intoxicant or behavior. This is another reason why the clinician's task of developing an alternative sober brain network, one that is different from the dependent brain network, is so vitally crucial.

Assessment of Co-Occurring Disorders

Rarely does a client present solely with a substance abuse or dependence disorder. More commonly, it is accompanied by problems with impulse control, emotional regulation, mood, judgment, and/or reality testing. Disorders such as psychosis, depression, mania, anxiety, Post-Traumatic Stress Disorder (PTSD), and personality disorders commonly present simultaneously with substance use disorders. These additional issues are called co-occurring disorders (COD), and they can complicate the assessment process because of necessary questions such as:

- Were the CODs present prior to the development of dependence and, thus, are they expected to continue once sobriety is achieved?
- Are these CODs simply an artifact of intoxication? Will they disappear once the person is sober for a while?
- Are they a result of dependence that will disappear once the person has gained a period of recovery?
- Are these CODs an artifact of early, middle, or late recovery that will resolve on its own?

- Is the COD a result of a social, emotional, characterological, or interpersonal adaptation to substance abuse? Is this adaptation temporary (meaning that it will fade once the person stops abusing intoxicants), or is it now permanent (meaning that some or all of the changes will continue for the remainder of the person's life, regardless of their substance use)?
- Is a COD an actual, independent disorder that was caused by the substance use damaging part(s) of the person's brain?
- Are CODs a necessary part of the process of attaining sobriety that should not be treated? Or, in other words, since one of the reasons people stay sober is that withdrawal and initial sobriety are very painful, by removing this pain do clinicians make it easier for the person to consider returning to substance abuse?
- How necessary is it to treat a COD?

There are many factors that influence CODs. The interplay between preexisting psychiatric disorders and substance use is not clearly defined. In some instances, substance use creates the COD, and in others it is the reverse. In addition, here are other issues to consider while assessing CODs.

Mental Status Changes with Intoxication and Withdrawal

Substance intoxication can mimic almost any other mental disorder. Individuals high on stimulants, phencyclidine (PCP), or *Lysergic acid diethylamide* (LSD) can easily appear hyperactive and/or psychotic. Those intoxicated on sedatives can appear depressed or possessing a cognitive disorder. If you look at the DSM closely, you recognize that almost every class of psychological disorders also has a related diagnosis for those symptoms being caused by substance intoxication. Simply put, the effects of intoxication often mirror severe psychiatric symptoms.

It should then come as no surprise that substance withdrawal can also mimic many, if not all, of the mental disorders. A person withdrawing from alcohol can appear psychotic, a person in stimulant withdrawal can appear severely depressed, or a person in sedative withdrawal can appear highly anxious. At this point, the reader should recall the prior discussion of homeostasis. In particular, as the client's brain functioning changes with dependence and its attendant withdrawal, and as the brain attempts to reregulate itself, this physiological process frequently mimics other mental disorders.

The picture is further clouded when individuals are substance dependent and prone to binges of use that may or may not be punctuated by intervening episodes of sobriety and withdrawal. For these individuals, the interviewer may notice a pattern of problems that appears to fade in and out or be cyclical. Assessors are strongly recommended to be *very conservative* when diagnosing a client who is currently actively abusing intoxicants, given that intoxication and withdrawal mimic the symptoms of other psychiatric diagnoses. It is also strongly recommended that clients be reassessed often to determine what psychiatric symptoms remain or worsen throughout their first year of sobriety. Also, if a client is being seen in an urgent care, residential, or hospital-based program, it highly recommended to conduct drug testing on all clients during their initial presentation and sporadically thereafter to confirm treatment compliance. It is especially warranted if a complete history isn't available, you question the reliability of the client's story, or they present out-of-character psychiatric symptoms. The option of drug testing in an outpatient once-a-week therapy practice is solely at the discretion of the private practitioner.

A caution here: regardless of their cause, we are not suggesting that you ignore and not treat any symptoms of a CODs. We encourage clinicians to *actively treat all psychiatric symptoms and COD*. However, you should be aware that the addition of substance abuse greatly complicates the assessment and subsequent treatment of a client's symptom picture. For instance, episodic depression that predated substance dependence should be treated in a different way than depression resulting from substance intoxication, or depression resulting from substance withdrawal, or depression that developed after sobriety that seems to be triggered by situational stressors. Each of these cases may present with very similar symptom pictures, but each should be treated differently. Remain alert to the multiple sources of symptomology before you pursue treatment. Forewarned is forearmed.

Post-Acute Withdrawal Syndrome (P.A.W.S. or PAWS)

Classically, the treatment of substance dependence occurs in two stages. The first stage is detoxification, where the person completes an acute withdrawal phase. The second stage is all of the rest of treatment and recovery. That first stage has been seen as an acute phase that occurs over the course of one to two weeks maximum. Many consider that a third stage should be inserted right after the acute withdrawal stage. This stage is called post-acute withdrawal syndrome or, more commonly, PAWS.

PAWS is thought to begin during the very early phases of sobriety and to continue for three to six months. Some argue that it may continue for as much as two years after the person stops using. The typical symptoms of PAWS include:

- Urge to use substance of choice or alternative/secondary intoxicants.
- Sleep disturbance. Includes any form of sleep dysregulation (hypersomnia, insomnia, and intense or disturbing dreams, including dreams about using drugs/alcohol).
- Emotional dysregulation (ED). Includes problems regulating mood (ranging from emotionally overreacting to underreacting, including emotional numbness). Often paired with problems with impulse control or judgment, in addition to anxiety, depression, obsessive thinking, guilt, and sensitivity to stress.
- Behavior disruptions. Includes interpersonal skills and compulsive behavior.
- Cognitive problems. Includes difficulty with concentration, problem solving, a sense of not being able to think clearly, confusion, and memory problems (often involving learning new information or accessing previously learned information).
- Physiological problems. Includes altered or intensified experiences of pain, reductions in coordination (including eye-to hand coordination), and physiological damage done from intoxicant of choice (dental problems, STD/HIV, cardiovascular, respiratory, endocrine, etc.).

These symptoms are intermittent and largely determined by the intoxicant(s) of choice (whether stimulants, depressants, etc.). However, they may also be triggered by environmental or social events that can create a considerable level of distress, thereby placing the client at significantly greater risk for relapse. PAWS may also be a product of the distinct physiological phenomena caused by changes in the brain over a longer-term course of use. This explanation is especially strong with regard to drugs such as stimulants, alcohol, and benzodiazepines.

Irrespective of the etiology, when treating clients in active recovery, PAWS must be considered in both the diagnosis and treatment. In terms of assessment, the importance of these symptoms is directly related to: 1) the degree to which they provoke or cause relapses in a client, and, 2) the degree to which they interfere with the person's pursuit of a satisfying life.

Preexisting Conditions or Disorders

Classically, a co-occurring disorder (COD) precedes substance dependence and typically fuels the development of the disorder. In this scenario, a client turns to an intoxicant in an attempt to treat the underlying disorder themselves, commonly referred to as self-medicating. *Self-medicating* becomes especially problematic when the substance use fails to successfully treat the psychological symptoms or distress. The substance use then compounds the person's distress by both augmenting the psychiatric symptoms through intoxication and/or withdrawal and the development of dependence (physical and/or psychological). Let's highlight this in a case example.

Rolando was raised in a home with little supervision. He thought that he had always been a dissatisfied and moody person, even into his early childhood. By his late 20s, he was dependent on alcohol. At the age of 32, he was mandated into treatment by his employer. At the time, he was consuming a fifth of vodka every other day and presented as a "typical" alcoholic to the treatment staff. Although desiring sobriety, Rolando was unable to remain sober from alcohol and required three more admissions over the next few years until a clinician, who had witnessed each treatment, noted some patterns in his mood.

Armed with a suspicion, the clinician conducted a very detailed history that revealed that Rolando experienced his first depressive episode around the age of eight. His first hypomanic episode occurred during his early 20s when he began cycling between hypomania and depression. He enjoyed the highs but dreaded the lows in his moods. He turned to alcohol as a way to numb out some of the depression and to add further enjoyment to his hypomania. Rolando thought that he was more moody than others, but had no awareness of the severity of his mental problem. He thought that his depressions were just another manifestation of his alcoholism.

In reality, it was the shifts in his mood that ultimately were interfering with his sobriety. The immobilization of depression would socially isolate him, making it easier for him to relapse, and his hypomania would diminish his ability to resist his urges to resume drinking. Once identified, Rolando was prescribed a mood stabilizer, and weekly counseling was added to his treatment. These new additions seemed to work and he has been sober now for four years.

Rolando exhibits many of characteristics commonly seen in a preexisting condition. For instance, clients may or may not be aware of the existence or name of a psychiatric condition, although possibly experiencing it for a lifetime. A thorough history, sometimes with a reliable historian, can provide the clues that reveal the condition. However, clients may not be the best source to obtain that history, especially if they have had a long-term substance dependence or if the dependence started early in their lives. With your client's consent, gain additional historical information from multiple sources, for example a primary care physician, family members, partner/spouse, or an employer or employee assistance program representative (if work referred). Substance abuse can also be started and maintained for multiple reasons, including self-medication, and it's possible that the client is not even aware of their motivation. If the preexisting condition is left untreated, it invariably interferes with the person's sobriety. Repeated relapses by a client are a clue that the clinician should consider that something else (possibly a previously unidentified mental condition) may be interfering with the client's progress.

Assessment Problems Associated with CODs

Substance dependence itself can cause multiple problems for the individual. The first involves coping skills, or rather the lack thereof. For the typical dependent individual, their intoxicant(s) becomes their best friend and at the same time their worst enemy. When they feel sad, they get high. Happy? Of course they get high. Angry? You guessed it; they get high. Conflict with partner or spouse? Right again; they get high. Over time, a person's coping skills (apart from getting high) simply fade away from disuse, and the intoxicant becomes their primary (and possibly only) coping mechanism. Sadly, this leaves them with very few ways to regulate themselves and as a result they are vulnerable to stress, prone to distraction, and interpersonally limited.

Correspondingly, substance dependence produces an unprecedented level of wreckage on the lives of those people surrounding the dependent person. Wreckage in the form of failed relationships, family rejection, broken friendships, isolation, financial problems, legal issues, job loss, diseases, brain damage, physical illness, and profound traumatization, not to mention a host of past misdeeds that fuel desperation, guilt, and profound shame. Given that substance dependence shrivels the normal coping skills used for combating problems, imagine how a sober person confronted with their list of misdeeds might immediately want to relapse! Additionally, the client's triggers commonly involve the people, places, and things they previously associated with using. For your newly recovering client, basically this means feeling alone and unsupported in the midst of the largest crisis of their lives. This may cause or simply intensify many of the symptoms associated with PAWS, and the resulting likelihood that the client retreats from sobriety back into their known and familiar world.

In addition to coping deficits and losses, substance dependence is often associated with changes to the person's character functioning. For the typical individual, addiction requires that they begin altering many areas of functioning, including perception, emotion, social, and interpersonal. Increasingly, the person's focus is on maintaining the addiction, and this effort can involve a host of dynamics commonly labeled as antisocial (emotional withdrawal/blackmail, lying, manipulating, cheating, stealing, physically harming others while in an intoxicated state, etc.). *A friendly reminder that this antisocial adaptation is a common response to the demands of substance dependence; it does not necessarily mean that the client has Antisocial Personality Disorder.* Upon sustained sobriety, the therapist can assess whether those antisocial character traits that are necessary for substance dependence remain or begin to fade away. Similar with other CODs, if a client had some beginnings of Antisocial Personality Disorder prior to the substance dependence, the substance dependence only exacerbates those traits. For some unfortunate people, the antisocial adaptation that was necessary for substance dependence can overwrite the person's native personality structure. For these individuals, their character style likely remains antisocial whether they are abusing intoxicants or are in sustained full remission. This topic is expounded on below.

Substance dependence can also be associated with the emergence of a new mental disorder that was not previously exhibited by the person. For instance, the use of some substances is correlated with the development of later mental difficulties, such as Korsakoff's Syndrome (a neurological disorder caused by a lack of thiamine [vitamin B_1] in the brain), depression, and even psychosis. For some individuals, these new disorders can occur during the active phase of the illness, and then continue even after the person has been abstinent for long periods of time. Thus, it is possible for a COD to be solely present through the substance use itself, without preexisting prior to the onset of substance dependence, and not as an artifact of PAWS, coping skills deficits, or losses due to addiction.

Synopsis of COD Assessment

When considering diagnosing a substance dependent client with a COD, consider the following:

1. Mental status changes associated with intoxication and the withdrawal of all intoxicants used (whether dependent on these or not)
2. PAWS and its associated symptomology
3. Preexisting disorders
4. The biopsychosocial (BPS) problems associated with dependence (biopsychosocial is an approach that posits that biological, psychological, and social factors all play a significant role in human functioning in the context of disease or illness)

The question of CODs and the theoretical arguments of their causations (are they a separate mental disorder, an expression of the psycho-social-emotional consequences of addiction, or something else) goes well beyond the focus of this book and, in fact, beyond the interest of most clinicians. Instead, the authors recommend you use a "clinical Occam's razor" (a principle of economy, or succinctness, which states that among competing hypotheses, the one that makes the fewest assumptions should be selected).

Do the symptoms significantly interfere with the client's quality of life and/or increase the likelihood of relapse? For the first year of recovery, focus on whether the symptom's end results increase or decrease the likelihood of sobriety.

Assessment of the Response to Antisocial Adaptation

In several ways, the treatment of substance dependence mirrors the treatment of the antisocial personality disorder. One key prognostic sign for a client is the degree to which that antisocial adaptation is egosyntonic (to what degree does the client believe their adaption is acceptable to themselves and their self-image). Consider these two cases:

Loretta is a married female in her mid-50s. She was married to a "loving husband," had a successful career as a nurse, and was engaged in a satisfying social life for much of her life. However, much of this changed in her early 40s when she was in a car accident that injured her neck resulting in chronic pain. Over the next ten years she had multiple surgeries and treatments, yet none seemed to provide her with much relief from the pain. However, opiates seemed to help.

By her late 40s she was getting prescriptions for pain killers from several of her physician colleagues. However, as the months passed these physicians became increasingly reluctant to provide her with medications. With few remaining options, she began stealing medications from the hospital where she worked, covering it up through a variety of phony documents and lies. Finally, because her husband was threatening to leave her, Loretta sought treatment. During the first interview with Loretta and her husband, Loretta was quite focused on her pain, the injustice it brought to her life, and her sense of herself as a victim. However, as her husband outlined her lies and the consequences of her addiction, Loretta shifted position from one of defensiveness to guilt and shame.

Ed is a single man in his mid-40s. He was diagnosed with ADHD in middle school when he began displaying behavior problems both at home and at school. These problems escalated as he aged, resulting in two psychiatric hospitalizations during his adolescence for belligerence, fighting at school, and multiple runaways from his home. Ed graduated high school and was accepted to college, but dropped out before the end of his first year for unknown reasons. Ed mostly works as a salesperson in a variety of positions. He described himself as a gifted at selling because he can "read people." Ed frequently changed employers and rarely held a job more than a couple years, initially blaming this on employers lacking ethics. However, he later admitted that he had lost many jobs due to problem behaviors directly linked to his alcohol use (such as drinking on the job, showing up late, missing work, or being intoxicated at work).

Ed sought out treatment after being arrested and convicted of a DWI (Driving While Intoxicated). This was his third arrest for this offense. Also, he was arrested a few times as an adult for disorderly conduct. Ed began drinking alcohol in high school, which likely shifted to alcohol abuse by the age of 18. He clearly met the criteria for alcohol dependence by the age of 25. Currently, he consumes about twelve beers and a "few shots" a day. He experiences shaking hands and anxiety in the morning, which abates if he "takes a shot of medicine" (drinks alcohol) in the morning. Ed describes his life as a "success."

Most failures, including his DWI arrest, he perceives as evidence of unfair treatment or being picked on. Ed did express guilt over the DWI arrest. However, as this topic was explored it became apparent that Ed did not feel guilt for his behavior; rather, he felt anger with himself for being caught. The interviewer saw Ed as likeable but untrustworthy. He relied on a high level of denial and minimization, making him very "slippery to interview." He continues to deny, and not own up to his drinking problem and the consequences it has on his life—even when the facts are laid out for him.

Notice how both Loretta and Ed adopted an antisocial position. They exhibit a behavior pattern that is highly self-centered, ignoring and also denying the impact of their behavior on others, and lying on multiple occasions. Neither expresses guilt or remorse about their behavior. Both display a pattern of risk and hurt to themselves and those around them, while denying this pattern. The key difference between the two is *their response to this antisocial adaptation.*

For Loretta, the adaptation seems a recent occurrence. Although it is possible, if not likely, that she had antisocial elements to her character structure prior to the substance use, this all changed once she became dependent on pain killers and her character shifted to a more substantial antisocial position. However, given her response at the end of the vignette, she has not yet fully accepted responsibility for her actions or their impact on others. Some additional therapeutic work is mandated, but it appears she can access parts of herself that are (or can become) appalled and remorseful over the evolution of her behavior in response to her substance dependence. The same cannot be said for Ed. His antisocial adaptation seems chronic, early, and well embedded in his persona. It is comfortable for him; as far as can be determined, it is who he is. Remember that his response to his third DWI was not that he was putting other peoples' lives at risk by driving; it was that someone caught him. It is likely that he does not feel that his drunk driving is harmful to anyone, least of all himself.

In assessing antisocial adaption, ask the following key questions:

1. How chronic is the antisocial adaption?
   The more chronic the adaption, the less treatable the person.
2. How egosyntonic is the antisocial adaption?
   The more the person experiences the adaption as egodystonic, generally the more amenable the person is to learn more prosocial skills.
3. To what degree can the person access emotions related to the egodystonic position?
   In effect, is there a willingness to own the consequences (including their emotions) and behaviors that substance dependence has on them and on others? If so, this attitude can provide a motivation to change.
4. As the recovery phrase goes, how "sick and tired of being sick and tired" are they with their dependence on substances or at least the consequences experienced from them?
   This is relevant only to assess the severity of the antisocial traits. A client with more ingrained antisocial traits wants the behavior (disruptive, rebellious, unfriendly, disagreeable, and so forth) without the consequences of the selfish behavior. Ed's response to his DWI is a prime example.

Given the above, a complete assessment of a substance dependent individual also includes an assessment of the often interdependent systems around them, including family, friends, significant others, and employers. Each category is usually impacted by the addict, and each system can play a part in maintaining the addiction and/or the person's efforts to abstain. It also provides opportunities to assess the strength and perseverance of antisocial behavior in the client's psyche and life.

Assessment Techniques

Evaluating a client who is substance dependent is very similar to interviewing any other client. However, to prepare for work with substance dependent clients, it is important to become familiar with the clinical descriptions and criteria of substance abuse and dependence for all classes of intoxicants. Also become knowledgeable about the pharmacology of intoxicants, especially the physical and mental manifestations of intoxication and withdrawal. Also, review the ASAM (American Society of Addiction Medicine) criteria to determine appropriate levels of treatment based on symptomology. Finally, build recovery resources (lists of treatment centers, 12-Step meetings for clients and their families, other substance self-help groups, etc.) and referrals. On an individual client level, background materials, previously completed interviews, and other treatment records may be of great assistance, especially if the client's treatment is mandated or the client is resistant.

When looking at taking a drug history, there are also certain specifics that help understand the etiology of both the pattern of substances and the intoxicants the clients choose to use. There are several substance-abuse-assessment tools available on the Internet or in other substance abuse books, but we recommend that they contain these crucial questions:

1. What is the client's history of substance use?
   a. When did the person first become intoxicated and on what substance?
   b. What intoxicants have they tried, even if just once?
      i. Did they continue to use that intoxicant and if not, why not?
2. At what point did their use become routine, even if the use was sporadic, such as once a month?
3. Did their use change over time? If so, when and how?
4. Did they continue to consume their substance of choice in the same way? Or did they change to another method (drink, snort, smoke, etc.)?
5. Did they begin to show symptoms of dependence? What symptoms and when?
6. Have they used other substances to lessen withdrawal symptoms or enhance their primary intoxicant's high?
7. Have they used other substances to lessen side effects of being intoxicated (i.e., to come down), or to help with any immediate and intense rebound from the drug episode (i.e., to avoid a crash)?
8. Did the intoxicant negatively impact their lives? When and how?
9. Have they attempted to control or lessen their level of use?
   a. If so, what have been their successes and failures?
10. When was their last use?
11. In general, what do they currently think and feel about their use?

Responding to Denial: Watch for Signs and Symptoms and Seek Out Details

The use of denial by many clients is not a deliberate or conscious act. Its function is to allow the continuation of the use in spite of the consequences that continue to accumulate. Admitting to a behavior's negative consequences generally causes a person to reconsider the benefits of that behavior. "I had no traction walking on ice in my flats, which caused me to slip and break my ankle. I think I should wear boots next time." Sounds perfectly logical right? Wearing flats + ice = bad decision. One would think that the same formula would hold true for substance use. "I just got fired for coming into work drunk. I think that I should not stay out until 4 a.m. drinking on a work night." Again, it would appear a given that: "Drinking until 4 a.m. + going into work at 9 a.m. = bad decision." Instead, a substance dependent person has a different formula running in their head: "I just got fired because my boss has been on my case for weeks! I don't know what she is talking about; I'm not still intoxicated. I stopped way before 4 a.m." Therefore, late-night drinking + fired = victim (bad decision by someone else)! This example highlights how denial makes it very difficult to discern the objective truth of a situation. However, the job of the adept interviewer is to clarify the reality of the person's functioning, despite the haze of their denial, while maintaining a positive collaborative relationship with the client.

One of the clearest examples of denial is when the client engages in vagueness and slippery language when asked a question. Classic examples of this are:

- Question: "How much are you drinking?" Answer: "I drink from time to time."
- Question: "Have you ever abused drugs?" Answer: "I smoked a little weed when I was a kid."
- Question: "What problems are you having with drugs or alcohol?" Answer: "I've never had a problem with drugs or alcohol."
- Question: "Tell me specifically about your pattern of drinking." Answer: "I drink a couple of times a week, weekends mostly."
- Question: "Your work associates say you smelled of alcohol after you came back from lunch the other day; does this happen often?" Answer: "I had a drink or two at lunch."

Notice how each of these statements lacks specificity and uses language that avoids giving a complete answer. For each of these answers, gently attempt to have the client move from generalities to specifics by asking for specifics. Look at how each of the above answers actually clouds the reality of the client's poor level of functioning.

"I drink from time to time."

The question here is what does "time to time" mean? It is used to avoid detailing the extent of the actual use. With one client in particular who was asked multiple questions to define what "time to time" meant, the client finally disclosed that use was at least one to two pints of fortified wine five to six days a week. The client rarely went 36 hours without consuming alcohol, and when they abstained they showed signs of alcohol withdrawal.

"I smoked a little weed when I was a kid."

So why is this answer problematic? The client is admitting to smoking marijuana in adolescence, right? Wrong. The answer completely evades addressing two things. The first evasion is the answer to the question of past substance abuse; the client only admits to smoking "a little." Smoking a little doesn't constitute abuse, so why even bring it up? Perhaps it may be that the client truly abused marijuana and does not know how to talk about it? Maybe the client doesn't have any other substance history to report but this? Perhaps the client read on the Internet that marijuana is impossible to abuse, so how could he have abused it? The answers to this point are varied and great, and they require further exploration. The second possible evasion is addressing any current substance abuse. When clients who are referred for substance abuse begin with a seemingly innocuous answer to this question, it often either marks a discomfort to discuss substance use or a denial about current levels of use.

"I've never had a problem with drugs or alcohol."

This is perhaps the quintessential expression of denial. Rarely is a denial of substance use an unconscious act. However, note that it is not uncommon for a person to consciously deny their use—a more common term for this is lying. The defense of denial is more often applied to the person's understanding of their substance use, not the actual specifics of the abuse. Thus, a person with a chronic self-destructive addiction might deny having a problem with drugs and alcohol but will be able to recalls the specifics of their substance use. When a therapist in their role as an assessor utilizes methodical questioning, clients are able to articulate a fairly detailed history consistent with that addiction. They know many of the details of their problem; they simply fail and/or resist putting them into perspective to see the problem.

"I drink a couple of times a week, weekends mostly."

The key issue here is defining quantities or the client's minimization perspective. How much does the client drink each night? What type of drinks and quantity? What size are the servings? What constitutes "a couple of times"? What is the client's definition of "weekend"? For some, the weekend begins on Thursday and ends on Tuesday. For others, to use on "weekends mostly," means that they drink large amounts of alcohol in a binge pattern.

"I had a drink or two at lunch."

Again, the issue here may be minimization. What does "a drink or two" mean? Consider the difference between these two drinks: a 12-ounce bottle of Miller Light, and a 6 ounce dry gin martini. The beer contains approximately ½ ounce of alcohol while the martini may contain as much as 2–3/4 ounces of alcohol. Both are counted equally as "one drink." More than one client has reported consuming "only a couple of drinks every day or so," but when the alcohol content of these drinks is calculated it adds up to consuming a fifth of liquor every 2 to 3 days!

That is not to say that every episode of vagueness illustrated in the examples above is due to denial or minimization. Many severely dependent individuals have impaired memory from substance use. The impaired memory can be from the long-term damage of the substance use itself or the impairing of the memory system during intoxication (think blackout). This can be very worrisome for some alcoholics because the reality is that they may be missing years from their memory due to intoxication for most of that time period. Individuals' memories for the times they were using may also be impacted by many other factors, including poor self-care while using (e.g., inadequate nutrition, hydration, sleep, etc.), emotional trauma, and physical abuse, to name a few.

CONTEXT IS EVERYTHING: THE IMPORTANCE OF LISTENING TO SPECIFIC WORDS AND HOW THEY ARE SAID

With any good assessment interview, it is very important for the interviewer to pay particular attention to what the client says (content), and how they say it (nonverbals, such as body language and tone of voice). With some clients, what they don't say can be even more important; this seems especially likely if they use avoidance or vague language. Some other clients are adept at using words and phrases in an answer that are heavy with meaning or affect, and embed them in such a way that they do not stand out. Filtering the client's material for these nuggets of meaning and further exploring them is a technique, if not a central technique, of experienced interviewers.

Linking Social History to Substance Use History

Substance dependent people often have a limited self-awareness and are typically very limited in insight, or their ability to understand what motivates their behavior based on their needs, fears, and history. This is not to say that there is necessarily a structural or character defect that prevents this awareness (although sometimes there is), but merely that this is a function of the dependence itself. In its most blatant form, a client may fail to understand how the development of their substance dependence was triggered by events in their life, and also how the dependence now impacts their life today. The following case highlights this concept:

Tina is a 32-year-old single female who is dependent on alcohol. Upon admission, she reported that she had started drinking alcohol around the age of 12 and developed dependence by the age of 18. She stated that during her mid-20s, alcohol became a problem for her following two DUI arrests and the loss of a relationship where her significant other repeatedly told her he could no longer tolerate her alcohol abuse.

Tina denied that alcohol ever interfered in her life. However, a close inspection of her history revealed that after parental conflict in the home she experienced a significant drop in school performance around 8th or 9th grade, and she did not complete high school. Tina began drinking alcohol at school around 10th grade. As high school continued, she increasingly missed school due to intoxication or hangovers. She eventually dropped out of school "just before they kicked me out."

Clearly, Tina's alcohol abuse significantly impaired her school performance. However, her inability to see the connection between these was clear evidence of her denial and lack of insight.

Reviewing Medical and Medication History

It is crucially important to review a client's medical and medication history. There are several reasons for this:

1. Chronic intoxicant use often impacts the client's medical status by damaging the body through the substance itself or opportunistic infections that are common with substance use (STDs, injection site infections, MRSA [**Methicillin-resistant Staphylococcus aureus**], transference of contagious diseases such as TB or the flu, etc.).
2. Physicians are not always well versed in addictions and may fail to consider their impact on other medical conditions. For instance, a client may be diagnosed with

Irritable Bowel Syndrome (IBS) when, in fact, their history of IBS is primarily due to irritation caused by the intoxicant abuse.

3. Physicians, especially general practitioners, may attempt to treat what appears to be an emotional problem with medications failing to detect that the emotional problem is a result of substance dependence. It is not uncommon for an alcoholic to complain of anxiety or depression to a physician and receive psychoactive medications as treatment. These medications fail to treat the substance dependence and therefore the emotional symptoms. At their worst, the prescribing of medications may advance the substance dependence by lessening the effects of withdrawal through the use of sedatives, anxiolytics, antipsychotics, and other mood stabilizers.

4. Some substance dependent people "doctor shop" (see a variety of physicians at the same time) in order to obtain their prescribed intoxicants or to obtain a variety of medications. By going to different physicians for different prescriptions, the substance dependent person fails to raise any red flags with any individual physician. However, if one physician could see all of the prescriptions that a substance dependent person has prescribed to them, the physician would probably have a coronary!

5. Some medical problems and medications are highly sensitive to substance use and therefore alter the criteria for diagnosing a substance abuse problem. For instance, consuming two 12-ounce beers a day is generally accepted as a non-problematic level of alcohol use for most adults. However, that may not be the case if the client is a poorly controlled diabetic who cannot consume such a large amount of sugar (alcohol is a sugar) and remain healthy. Likewise, this level of alcohol use may be inappropriate for a client on opiates for pain medications (in this case, alcohol and opiates would have a synergistic intoxifying effect).

6. Medical problems, especially chronic pain, can be an important factor in the development, maintenance, and cessation of addiction.

The authors are *not* suggesting that you begin practicing medicine without a medical license. In lieu of that scenario, it is recommended that a primary care physician who is practiced in providing care to substance abuse or dependent patients be added to the treatment team. Also, be alert to the fact that not all psychiatrists are proficient or even competent to work with substance abusing or dependent clients. Careful screening of expertise is warranted for all referrals. If one is available to you, an addictionologist (a medical doctor who is board certified by the American Society of Addiction Medicine and who specializes in diagnosing and managing patients with addiction disorders), or a psychiatrist board certified in the treatment of addictions, can be an invaluable aid to treatment, especially when the client struggles with concurrent pain or CODs that require psychoactive medications.

Assessment Interventions for Resistance and Negativism

There are several key assessment tools for further exploring a client's history; notably clarification, restatement, reflection, and finally confrontation. The first three are all basic counseling skills you received early in your education. The last skill, confrontation, is a wonderful technique if exercised properly along with the other three, but it also has the potential to be devastating, if used directly and out of hand. As each technique is employed, separately or in combination, utilize it with the attitude of an explorer who simply wants to further understand the client and their life's events. The use of these techniques typically occurs when an assessor comes up against one of the client's defenses. When this defense is coupled with a substance dependent person's antisocial skills, many interviewers perceive this interaction as a situation where the client is attempting to deceive or con them. It is very easy for the interaction to develop into an adversarial exchange, essentially rupturing the rapport with the client. If the rapport is broken, "good luck," as it is almost impossible to continue conducting an effective and reliable evaluation.

Typically, it is not useful or wise for an evaluator to take a directly confrontational approach with a client. This is especially true with a client who does not have a prior relationship with the evaluator. Instead, the evaluator should use clarification, restatement, or reflection as the means of confrontation. By asking "I don't understand what you mean," "Help me understand this," or "I'm having troubles fitting what you just said into what you said earlier," adversarial interactions can be avoided while still seeking more information. This is especially true if the evaluator directs the queries in combination with an effect of mild confusion or curiosity. Again, your goal should be to understand the client by obtaining and assembling their correct life story as free from distortion as possible. The most effective skill to dispel any distortions is to utilize the client's own words as precisely as possible. Paraphrasing only allows the client to weave around what you missed. It is hard to hold onto statements that contradict each other when they are reflected back to you in your own words.

A final thought is that there are times when a client *does* attempt to trick or con an evaluator. Many times a clinician's perception that the client is providing misinformation or deceptive techniques is correct (and this alone is a useful thing for the evaluator to include in their assessment) and is recognizable by the client's reluctance to admit to their deceits, even in the face of their own words! However, directly confronting this duplicity in an interview is typically not productive. At this juncture, note the discrepancy, listen for evidence that continues to support or refute it, and file it away for another day.

Determining the Usefulness of Collateral Information and Contacts

Most substance dependent individuals work hard to obfuscate information (by hiding intended meaning in communication and making communication confusing, wilfully ambiguous, and harder to interpret) among the people in their world in order to attempt to minimize the negative consequences of their addiction. To this end, they may expend herculean efforts to fix, manage, and control others around them. As an assessor, your job is to pierce this secrecy in order to get a clearer picture of the client's actual functioning. This is especially central to the task facing those who are performing legally related or mandated evaluations.

Collateral information and contacts can greatly assist in understanding the client and seeing past their denial. Prior to seeking out collateral sources, clinicians are advised to evaluate the needs for these and the likelihood that the client will consent for you to make contact. How important is the information you are seeking? Is it possible to obtain this directly and reliably through the client? If necessary (as in the case of an intervention), will a particular collateral contact allow or aid in enlisting other sources to support the client's treatment? Does the collateral contact support or oppose the client? Are there ramifications for the client if you contacted the collateral contact?

Systems-based approach

Substance dependence has been described as a disease of the family. We would expand that to say that substance dependence is a disease of systems. Thus, no assessment of a substance-dependent person is complete without evaluation of the systems in their lives and their impact on the client and vice versa. These systems directly contribute to a client's recovery, either supporting it or sabotaging it. When considering assessing a client's support system, consider the following:

Family and romantic/partner/spousal relationship systems. To what degree has the family compensated for and accommodated the client's addiction? Typically, substance-dependent people cannot fully meet their obligations and responsibilities to their family or significant other. As such, these designated systems may respond to the dependent's under-functioning by picking up the slack or over-functioning. Dad loses his job so mom picks up a second one. Does the significant other call work, providing all manner of excuses for their hung-over or currently high partner's absence? Children may step up and fulfill major parental duties if one or both parents are substance dependent. Over time, these roles may become concretized to the point that the family resists changing them (i.e., sabotage the recovering person's sobriety).

Related to the above, a family's communication patterns may mimic the defenses of an addict. To what extent does the family system have rules about denial, secrets, and not sharing information outside of the family? Is the family able to recognize the substance dependence problem, and are they dissatisfied with it? In addition, how much anger is there at the addict for their behavior, and how is the anger manifested? Last of all, how motivated is the family to change in order to support a new, sober outcome?

There are multiple ways to evaluate family and relationships systems. A suggestion is to compile both family and couple interviews in addition to individual interviews. This allows the clinician to get the story through individual interviews, and then to observe the dynamics between people in a group/family/couple interview. The key question here often becomes one of time and the available resources of the client, family, and clinician.

Occupational systems. It is hard to imagine an occupation that would not be impacted by the behavior of a substance dependence employee. In fact, you might not think some employment types are impacted by substance dependence, but there are many. For instance, bartenders cannot count money, remember orders, or protect patrons if they are intoxicated beyond the ability of fulfilling their duties. Self-employed people may be able to manage for a while, but eventually their declining performance loses customers or clients. Evaluations of job functioning, especially attendance and performance records, usually provide a wonderful timeline to document the severity of substance use. Work contacts are often accessed through an employer's human resources department, or the company's employee assistance program.

Several areas need to be assessed in evaluating the occupational system. Is the client's employer aware of the problem? Have they enabled the problem, and if so how? Do they support the person's recovery, and if so how? How motivated is the employer to change in order to support a new, sober outcome (this may include allowing time off for treatment, as well as setting limits or consequences for future impairments in work functioning)?

Drug and Alcohol Testing as a Means of Assessment

Ask any former cigarette smoker, and almost everyone responds that quitting is very difficult, if not the hardest thing they ever did, and that it took many tries to finally quit for good. Why is it then so hard for people (including clinicians!) to believe that this is also true of the vast majority of substance-dependent individuals? Addiction is a disease of relapse. This phenomenon of relapse is also coupled with the tendency to consciously and unconsciously deny the use as well as to try to fix, manage, and control information related to the use. Again and again, clients deny their intoxication with a straight face, despite the blaringly obvious symptoms of alcohol on the breath, extremely dilated or constricted pupils, or any other clear evidence to the contrary.

For a person attempting to remain sober, admitting to a relapse can be a daunting task. The admission is often perceived as an acknowledgement of failure, the person is riddled with shame and disappointment, and potentially the relapse opens doors to many negative consequences. There is little wonder that clients are reluctant, if not blatantly resistant, to such admissions. However, from a clinical perspective such admissions are central to recovery, as clinicians often change their treatment recommendations based on a relapse. The stakes may be even higher for a therapeutic community. For example, in a recovery home, a client who has relapsed or who is in the midst of a relapse may be viewed as a risk who jeopardizes the safety of the other members of the community who are attempting to remain sober. For these communities, relapse and especially multiple relapses often result in a referral out of the program for protection of the other members.

Drug and alcohol testing can be a very useful tool. However, it is important that it be is done correctly. Most drug testing is urine-based testing. A minority use hair-based testing, which is more accurate. In healthy people, urine-based testing detects most drugs that have been consumed in the prior 48 to 72 hours. The exceptions are PCP and cannabinoids. PCP can be detected up to 7 days after a single use, and in heavy users up to 30 days. For cannabinoids, they can be detected from 2 to 7 days after light use, and 30 days or more in heavy users. Also, alcohol is most commonly tested by breathalyzer, which detects it from 6 to 24 hours after use.

The time windows of detection are very important when attempting to detect relapse or use. Since most drugs are cleared from the urine within 72 hours, it is very important that clients are given no warning of a test being administered and little time to complete a test once they have been informed. For this reason, the actual dates of testing are best determined randomly. The easiest way to do this can be by using dice. Also, it is best to have a client provide a sample within 6 to 12 hours of being told of the test. However, even following these rules, it may be difficult to detect use. For instance, let's say Sam is dependent on cocaine. Typically, he uses it every two weeks, smoking large amounts of it over a 48-hour time period. During any binge, he will test positive for cocaine on the two days that he is using and for three days afterwards. He has two binges a month, so he would test positive for cocaine during ten days of a typical month. Thus, if you test him once a month, your chance of detecting abuse is 1 in 3. Not great odds. It would not be unusual for Sam's abuse to remain undetected for multiple months using this method. If Sam can predict when a test occurs (assume not on weekends or not the week after he has completed a test), then he might be able to go many months undetected.

SUMMARY

Clinicians have various assessment tools available to them in evaluating substance use, abuse, and dependence. Apart from the practical and traditional assessment methods, therapists are encouraged to consider contextual factors with the data collected from clients. Careful listening skills, ability to detect nuanced inconsistencies, and recognizing defensive structures are essential for proper evaluations. Whenever possible, it is recommended that clinicians involve a multidisciplinary approach to assessment with substance use clients given the aforementioned propensity for denial as well as the wide-reaching biopsychosocial impacts on functioning.

QUESTIONS

1. What is a co-occurring disorder? What are some complicating assessment questions that need to be considered when evaluating for co-occurring disorders?
2. What does PAWS stand for? What are some of the traits of PAWS?
3. Name three factors that help to determine whether antisocial behavior and thinking is a part of substance use or a more formal diagnosable condition.
4. Name four questions that help understand a client's context of current and past substance use.
5. How does denial show in diagnostic assessments? What are clinical techniques to use to assess beyond the client's denial?
6. Name three compounding problems that medical and medication history can have on substance use.
7. Name a therapeutic technique to utilize for dealing with a client's resistance and negativism in a clinical interview.

Therapy Considerations and Techniques

6

THERAPEUTIC FRAMEWORK CONSIDERATIONS FOR SUBSTANCE ABUSE/DEPENDENCE WORK

Similar to assessment, therapeutic work with substance-dependent people greatly benefits from skill sets that may or may not have been emphasized in a clinician's training. However, even clinicians who have received no explicit training in this area will find that they already have many of the tools in these skill sets that they need. This chapter not only covers therapeutic technique, but also discusses the role of the therapist with the client and the systems involved in recovery.

Motivational Interviewing as the Foundation for Subsequent Treatment

Substance-dependent clients can be a difficult group. They bring to most treatments a challenging mix of ambivalence, manipulation, and a tendency to become resistant or oppositional. These traits can be magnified as the client moves closer to ending their use. In some of the most difficult dependency cases, negativistic clients refuse to recognize a problem that is blatantly obvious to everyone else, becoming outright defiant if you press them toward recognition. Complicating matters, their underlying interpersonal dynamics around issues of receiving care and owning responsibility seem to directly interact with a clinician's efforts in counter therapeutic ways. It is little wonder that some professionals feel unprepared to work with this population.

Typical psychotherapeutic treatment approaches often have poor results when they are directly applied to people with addictions. As touched on in the assessment section, the client's antisocial adaptation and their defenses often sabotage prescriptive approaches. Other, more empathic-centered approaches, if not prescriptive enough, can lead the therapist to a position of emotionally caretaking and ultimately enabling a client who is acting in a self-destructive manner. Interpretive approaches to substance dependence may intensify the problems by clearing away the client's defenses, raising their anxiety, and ultimately triggering more substance abuse. To be clear, some substance-dependent clients respond to some or all of these approaches and improve. However, for *most* substance-dependent clients, approaches that are solely prescriptive, empathy-focused, or interpretive do not result in long-term sobriety. Instead, it is recommended that clinicians adapt a more integrative approach for therapy, relying on an approach known as *motivational interviewing* as the core of their treatment, especially for clients in the early phases of recovery.

Motivational interviewing is a set of techniques that seeks to remove the clinician from the power struggles and resistances that this population is prone to engage in with clinicians. In many ways it borrows from a client-centered, Rogerian technique. Its aim is to help the client articulate their values, goals, and behavior, then check each statement for consistency. In this approach, one of the key points here is that the therapist's job isn't to make an assessment or to decide what to do about these voiced values and behaviors. Instead, the therapist's job is to empower and assist the client so that they can, to the best of their ability, fully articulate and assess their own components to complete the bulk of the work necessary to recover. Most importantly, it is the client's role to identify areas where they are dissatisfied and where they desire change. For a further description of this technique, we suggest *Motivational Interviewing* by Miller and Rollnick (2013), as well as attending some continuing education workshops.

Motivational interviewing greatly minimizes the problems that beset other treatment approaches by putting responsibility for change clearly where it belongs, with the client. It also allows a therapist the space to form a treatment contract and alliance with a client who previously was highly resistant to even considering that they had a problem. Once that contract is formed, the therapist may find that they can begin shifting to other approaches for the remainder of treatment. However, this shift is more of an evolution than a dramatic change and is determined by conditions in the therapeutic relationship and process of recovery. If a client regresses or the treatment alliance is threatened, a clinician's return to motivational interviewing is often appropriate. The following case demonstrates the usefulness of motivational interviewing:

Jefferson is a 42-year-old man who was mandated into treatment by his employer after missing too many days of work. After several sessions of motivational interviewing, Jefferson identified that he had a significant problem with crystal meth and that his drug use was interfering with his work, friendships, and family relationships. After identifying the problem, the therapist asked Jefferson if he knew what and how he needed to change to be more satisfied with his life. Jefferson considered stopping all meth use, but he discarded that idea in favor of reducing his meth use. The therapist responded that "some people can control their drug use and some people can't. It sounds like your plan is to control your level of drug use and reduce it. How can you tell if your control is working?"

Eventually, Jefferson defined his controlled use as using meth no more than two days a month, and not 24 hours prior to work or a significant social obligation. For three months, Jefferson and the therapist monitored this effort, and Jefferson's repeated failures at self-control, before Jefferson labeled the effort a failure. Jefferson voiced that his only option seemed to be total abstinence, to which the therapist replied "there are multiple ways to attain that goal and multiple things that can help you: inpatient treatment programs, outpatient treatment, 12-Step groups, some other group approaches, church-based approaches, and some people just stop using on their own." Jefferson asked what the therapist recommended, and the therapist suggested an intensive outpatient program and 12-Step groups, but emphasized that "there's no guarantees. It's more about your decision, how motivated you are, and what you want. The change has to be yours for it to work."

As treatment progressed and Jefferson increased his involvement in treatment and invested in the goal of abstinence, the therapist became more active and prescriptive around issues such as the client tracking his urges, attending meetings, and attending to self-care routines. This process was working well until about three months into sobriety, when Jefferson abused meth over a weekend. At that point, the therapist moved back to a motivational interviewing approach, helping the client to articulate the events of the weekend and the consequences of it, and arrived at a spontaneous reiteration of the treatment goal of sobriety.

There are several aspects of this interaction to note: 1) the therapist assessed Jefferson as substance dependent during the first interview, and expected that he would very likely not be able to control his use. However, ultimately the decision was Jefferson's as to whether he could or could not control his use. In this example, the role of the therapist was to help Jefferson clearly articulate this issue and to act as a recorder by remembering the issue and tracking it across sessions (thereby making it difficult for Jefferson to forget or become defensive). 2) The therapist continually reinforced Jefferson's ability or agency to decide and then held him accountable to those choices. This is evident when reviewing Jefferson's decision whether to stop or reduce his use, and when the clinician asked him to define exactly what it meant to meet his goal. The client was the sole decider on the motivation for change and its expression. In the language of motivational interviewing, "change talk" needs to be voiced by the client before most change occurs. 3) The therapist began injecting concepts and phrases from 12-Steps, in effect priming the pump for later treatment (we'll talk more about that in subsequent chapters). 4) Note how the therapist shifted back to a motivational interviewing approach following the client's relapse. If the client, at this point, decided to resume some level of substance abuse, then the therapist would resume a full motivational interviewing approach, essentially equivalent to the approach taken at the start of the treatment.

Recovery Must Always be at the Forefront

Although similar in many ways, treating substance dependence has unique factors that are unlike treatment of any mental disorder. Perhaps the biggest difference is that for most substance-dependent individuals, treatment will fail unless sobriety is the *primary* treatment goal. It is very difficult, if not impossible, for these clients to make progress on any issue without addressing their substance dependence. It makes a lot of sense when you think about it; how can you fix any problem if you continuously create more problems each time you use?

For example, take a client who experienced severe childhood abuse resulting in a Post-Traumatic Stress Disorder (PTSD). As the client grew up, they were unable to cope with the anxiety and pain of intrusive recollections and re-experiences caused by the abuse. Unable to soothe their feelings through cognitive, relational, emotional, or other natural means, the client turned to alcohol. Over time, this developed from alcohol use, to abuse, and finally into alcohol dependence. Once the use developed into dependence, even if the PTSD could somehow be therapeutically cured, this dependence would continue. We say "somehow" because it would be highly improbable (if not impossible) to treat the PTSD without addressing the addiction. If a clinician attempts to treat the PTSD while allowing the alcohol dependence to continue, the client is unable to fully experience their feelings and think clearly because of intoxication, active withdrawal, or simply being hung over. These conditions usually produce impaired memory, emotional volatility, diminished judgment, and poor insight, which are many of the same conditions as a person suffering from trauma or PTSD! This is not a good indicator for successful clinical work.

With some exceptions, sobriety is the primary treatment goal for most substance dependent persons. One such exception is if the client is experiencing a mental disorder that is preventing them from attaining sobriety. Some examples of this might include the presence of an active and florid psychosis, debilitating depression or mania, PTSD with high levels of anxiety, and extreme emotional lability as seen in severe Borderline Personality Disorder. The underlying issue here is the emotional, neurological, interpersonal, social, vocational, and spiritual disruptions associated with active substance dependence that typically sabotage treatment progress. Another example is a client who is not yet ready to recognize and address their substance dependence. Alternate approaches can be attempted, including motivational interviewing or harm reduction. However, the goal of these approaches is often to maintain a therapeutic relationship while the client works through their resistance to accepting their lack of power over controlling their using.

Some clients also respond to an approach that is directly contradictory to the one espoused here. There are clients who reduce, and sometimes stop, their substance use simply by linking the development and maintenance of their substance dependence (e.g., substance dependence as an expression of long-term struggles with shame and self-defeating behaviors), and addressing those factors in treatment. Although this form of treatment can be successful, it is rare, and often the opposite reaction occurs. Noticeably, as the therapist begins to explore and work to resolve the underlying issues related to the substance dependence, the client's use increases—sometimes dramatically. For this reason, avoid this type of upside-down treatment (insight before sobriety) and favor the reverse approach (sobriety before insight). Although there are exceptions, for most clients the only workable approach is to make sobriety the primary goal of treatment. Yet, this recommendation is based on consideration of a client's goals, the therapeutic relationship, and the client's current willingness to recognize and address the substance use problem. There is no one right approach. Instead, we recommend being flexible and monitoring which approach is more effective for individual clients.

Understanding the Role of Defensive Styles and Therapeutic Responses

It doesn't take too long in working with substance abusers to note a classic defensive style: the attempt to fix, manage, and control their worlds. This is often used in seamless conjunction with the previously mentioned styles of denial, minimization, and rationalization. It is truly amazing to realize the number of plates that substance-dependent people keep spinning in order to keep their use going. These "plates" include events, people, and places in the world rotating around the person, including the therapist. Indeed, you can feel like a spinning plate yourself after some sessions with clients in active substance dependence! For instance, the client may strategically cancel or postpone appointments (to later in the week) to avoid a session that immediately followed a relapse. The client may tend to become oppositional or argumentative, especially as the therapist begins treading on sensitive areas that call attention to the substance dependence, such as rate of use, behaviors the client may engage in that support continued drinking or drugging, and so forth.

There are several ways to understand these defensive stances:

1. The defenses are of interest because they continue to support the client's ability to use their intoxicant of choice. Additionally, they protect the substance abuser from the negative consequences of their use by not only blocking their own awareness of these consequences, but also the recognition of others to the extent of their substance use, up to and including blocking the very existence of the substance use itself! Then, with the negative consequences managed, the individual is free to enjoy the positive effects of their substance of choice.

2. The underlying or unconscious experience of a substance-dependent client is often quite painful. Substance abuse and dependence tend to ravage a person's life, forcing them to experience repeated losses and failures. These often evoke strong and profound feelings of shame, guilt, humiliation, rage, aloneness and/or isolation, depression, worthlessness, hopelessness, and helplessness. These feelings are often difficult for even a sober person to resolve. Consider the difficulty coping with such experiences with underdeveloped coping and impaired neurological functioning. In many ways, the client resorts to these defenses because they must—the emotional consequences of acknowledging the reality of their situation is overwhelming and unbearable when sober. They are doing the best they can with what they have.

3. It is difficult for those caught in the grip of substance dependence to see the benefit of sobriety. Consider that when a person abstains from substances, their subjective experience of effect is often overly sensitized. As the person becomes more aware (i.e., clear-headed when sober), they are faced with the losses and conflicts occurring within their lives, thus further compounding their emotional oversensitivity. To make matters even more overwhelming, the person is not used to, or sufficiently skilled at, the demands of a sober life (i.e., structuring their daily lives, self-care behaviors, money management, and solving problems, especially complex and multistep problems, etc.). Nor are they especially skilled at communicating their needs and engaging in behaviors that create close interpersonal relationships. It is little wonder that many recovering addicts experience the initial phases of sobriety as noxious or essentially punishing.

4. Substance abuse temporarily and sometimes permanently alters the way the brain functions. In particular, this added barrier makes it difficult for the person to see consequences of their actions and make complex, long-term plans. In some ways, the client's defensive strategy can be seen as an extension of the organization of their brain and its impaired biological functioning.

5. Clients in the early phases of recovery have a tendency to be very ambivalent about treatment. Most have arrived in a therapist's office because some aspect of their lives is not working, not necessarily because they want to stop using. To a greater or lesser degree they want to change, and simultaneously

parts of them do not. Change is often resisted by this population, and their awareness of the relationship between their life dissatisfaction and substance use is sketchy at the best of times. The antisocial adaptation often functions to prevent the addict (and those involved in their life) from understanding the reality of their use and thereby the need to end the pleasure of intoxication and avoid the difficulty and pain of abstinence.

Much of the work a clinician and client address during the first year of recovery focuses on the client's defensive style coupled with building sobriety skills. It is critical that the practitioner understand that by addressing defenses, the client is being stripped of their emotional armor that exposes them to painful elements that their using covered up. Simultaneously, addicted clients have very poor internal and external resources to cope with this pain. You can see why clients would resist these efforts. The artistry of the clinical work is in balancing the process of tearing down a client's defenses while simultaneously building up their coping skills. It is this therapeutic dance that assists the client in learning to tolerate emotions, adopt a new sober identity separate from the antisocial behaviors committed during their using days, choose sobriety when relapsing provides more immediate relief, and develop sober social skills through maintaining the therapeutic relationship. The artistry is also in the timing: push too hard and too early in the treatment without properly resourcing the client, and you'll rupture the therapeutic relationship. Push too little, and progress will stagnate.

12-Steps and other support groups can greatly assist the therapeutic efforts with these defensive behaviors. It is often easier to hear feedback from others who have experienced and suffered from substance dependence than from a therapist. The artistry of 12-Steps, in particular, is that members speak from their own experience to bring about awareness in another. An example of a type of 12-Step intervention that confronts defense mechanisms goes something like this: "I hear what you are saying about your boss having it out for you. I know that when I was using heavily, I was missing work and everyone else had to pick up the slack because I was doing such a poor job because I couldn't function most of the time. So, yeah, my boss had it out for me too. I know he had good reason, though, and I deserved to be fired. It was a gift because it made me realize how bad my addiction had gotten." This type of intervention often fails to trigger the client's oppositional and blatant resistance because the client witnesses others taking responsibility for their same behavior.

The sponsor-client relationship is another method and means of addressing defenses. It is different from the meetings, as the sponsor may be more directly confrontational with the client. However, factors in this relationship make it easier for the client to incorporate this feedback, even if confrontational. First, 12-Step members are encouraged to find someone whose sobriety they wish to emulate, and pick them for a sponsor. In effect, they reap what they sow! Second, the client can fire the sponsor at any point they desire. No one is keeping them in that specific relationship but themselves. Third, the sponsor has the experience of active substance dependence, just like the client, and has already experienced many of the challenges the client faces. Thus, the sponsor can easily be more empathic to the client's suffering while still having the advantage of their intuitive ability to detect deception. As it is so eloquently said in a 12-Step community, "It's hard to bullshit a bullshitter." Fourth, the sponsor is doing this as part of their own work toward achieving recovery. A sponsor is not paid and has no real investment in the client showing up apart from wanting someone to be sober. Whereas a clinician can be more easily discounted because they're being paid for the work, this line of defensive thinking does not work with a sponsor.

It is highly recommended to incorporate the client's outside 12-Step work to enhance overall treatment outcomes. In later chapters, we discuss how to accomplish this incorporating the actual Steps of a 12-Step program. For now, we continue on with utilizing the other tools of 12-Step, namely the meetings, readings, and interpersonal relationships, including sponsorship.

The Fine Balance of Addressing Sobriety and Social Skill Development in Early Recovery

Interpersonal relationships are a key component to the success of recovery and a 12-Step program. They assist first and foremost by beginning to teach sober social skills through modeling in 12-Step activities such as meetings, sponsorship, and fellowship. Predominantly, the sober social skills most often learned in a 12-Step environment are setting boundaries, taking responsibility, developing language for emotions, expressing these emotions, managing expectations, factoring in your impact on others, and assertiveness. Additionally, 12-Step programming provides a social environment that more often than not has a reduced level of intoxicant use cues. Remember from Chapter 1 that the social life tradition in 12-Step is called fellowship, and the other important interpersonal relationship in 12-Step is that of the sponsor.

As can be expected with any person with social skill challenges, newly recovering substance-dependent clients may have difficulties with the social world of 12-Step—a world with few secrets and accountability structures that may feel simply too uncomfortable for those in early recovery. This is especially true for those who are ambivalent about remaining sober. Even for those more committed to sobriety, negative feelings and beliefs about themselves can make it very difficult to engage with others. Feelings of shame and defectiveness are often the culprits here. Compounding these difficult feelings, there may be a whole host of psychological issues that interfere with allowing oneself to be socially vulnerable and connected, including issues around trust, abandonment, power, and self-sabotage.

To elaborate on the concepts presented above, often these clients feel overwhelmed by their past behaviors and experiences while using. In effect, they are trapped in beliefs along the lines of "I have seen horrible things and I have done horrible things while I was using, so I am a horrible person." They also often internalize the experiences of degradation, helplessness, and hopelessness of their addiction, surrendering any prosaically sense of self-efficacy. Without being aware of these internalizations, these clients find friendship and even sobriety too uncomfortable. They sabotage it. For some, this is an expression of self-punishment; for others a feeling that they do not deserve it; and for others a sense that they are doomed to fail, so why try?

For most therapists, these issues are a beacon that draws the therapist to explore them, often with the eventual agenda of tracking them to their roots in early experience. The risk here is that these psychological issues are seductive and lure the focus of therapy away from sobriety and onto a more comfortable playing field where the therapist feels more skilled and competent. In effect, the treatment shifts toward resolving the emotional components to dependency. Ultimately, this can easily end in the treatment stalling as the focus shifts away from the development of sobriety skills and relapse prevention efforts. Taking the proverbial therapeutic eye off the sobriety prize usually results in the client returning to abusing intoxicants. Knowing this, therapists should focus on a dualistic-approach with a primary focus of the maintenance of sobriety, and a distant secondary focus on supporting the building of sober social skills as learned in 12-Step rooms.

Address the psychological issues related to sober socialization and the underling emotional struggles *only to the extent that they interfere with the client's ability to learn and implement new sober social skills*. Otherwise, the focus should be on the maintenance of sobriety. Once the person has gained some stability and sobriety, typically after their one-year anniversary of sobriety, then most clients can increasingly tolerate the anxiety and discomfort brought on by addressing their internal issues. However, with recovering clients, sobriety needs to be closely assessed during high emotional times regardless of the length of sobriety they have achieved. In effect, sobriety remains the primary goal of treatment, irrespective of how long the client has abstained.

Navigating the Complicated Terrain of the Sponsor-Sponsee-Therapy Relationship

The sponsor relationship is often the most challenging relationship in the treatment of a person in early recovery. In addition to challenging a client's ability to maintain a relationship with poor sober social skills, clients may view the therapist and sponsor as in the same role, that of guide or helper. This can create a psychological environment where the client may readily engage in triangulating strategies.

Sponsors can feed into this dynamic due to a general distrust of therapists. This is not unjustified given the wide range of quality and/or even incompetent care that substance dependent people receive from both the mental health and medical field. Sponsors may challenge the advice of therapists on many fronts: the need for psychotropic medication, the need for return to work timelines, risk assessments, need for abstinence from all intoxicants or just select intoxicants, need for a higher level of care, or a number of other treatment recommendations. The best response to this issue is to provide competent treatment. In addition, thoroughly explaining to the client your rationale for recommendations and how to convey these back to the sponsor builds trust. It can sometimes take many months, but the vast majority of resistant sponsors come around and eventually begin to support the client's treatment.

On the other hand, sometimes the client is not always accurate about relaying what the sponsor says and vice versa. If there is sufficient doubt that a client is communicating either honestly or accurately the sponsor impressions or recommendations, recommend that your client sign a limited release of information that is specific to recovery tasks, treatment recommendations, or whatever seems to be in dispute. *However, all matters of decision making regarding 12-Step involvement (meeting attendance, Step work, fellowship requirements, sponsor assignments, etc.) are to remain the sole purview of the sponsor.* Never countermand a sponsor's direction unless the sponsor's instruction places your client at imminent risk for relapse or harm. Disagreeing with a sponsor's approach to 12-Step recovery is not enough reason to interject yourself into their direction on 12-Step work.

In later chapters, we discuss where you as a therapist can be helpful in *furthering* the work in each Step. However if the client is having difficulty with the sponsor's direction, social-skill training with the client to more clearly articulate his or her concerns and needs may be highly effective. Such a discussion frequently allows the sponsor to bring their wisdom and experience to bear on the client's needs, providing a reality check and sometimes reframing the issue simply as a function of recent sobriety. Here is an example of this technique in action:

> Aaron, an alcoholic with less than a month's sober time, sought out treatment, stating that he could not cope with his anxiety. He also explained that he had been attending AA for six months and had a sponsor who was quite opposed to him starting psychotherapy. Aaron was asked to tell his sponsor that the therapist had a notion of what caused those fears, that some therapists were not helpful with alcoholism, and to give the treatment a chance to work. Over the next several months, the therapist focused on Aaron's sobriety and his anxiety, including referring Aaron to a new psychiatrist who slowly weaned him off of the antianxiety medications he had previously been prescribed. Part of this treatment also included working with Aaron's defenses, helping him resolve some of his ambivalence over remaining sober and how, ultimately, this allowed Aaron to keep a distance from his sponsor. Six months later and still sober, Aaron related a discussion with his sponsor wherein his sponsor voiced pleasure that he had sought counseling.

Despite best efforts, clinicians sometimes find themselves in a highly triangulated position with a client and their sponsor. This triangulation can continue in the face of best efforts to disengage, and concern arises that it may be interfering with the client's ability to remain sober. This is a good time to conduct a single, multiple, or periodic family session(s) with the client and their sponsor. Clients and sponsors who have participated in these sessions have reported that they have been useful and conducive to enhancing their working relationship. The family session should focus solely on helping the communication between sponsor and sponsee, clarifying any confusion, and should not be about taking sides on an approach to 12-Step or recovery. Remember that sponsors are not therapists themselves (most often) and are vulnerable to their own agendas and poor communication skills. Family sessions are a useful tool if conducted with the therapist imposing strict boundaries.

Some clients also struggle with their sponsors around the definition of the role of a sponsor and the expectations on the sponsor's level of involvement. Some expect too little and view their sobriety as a self-driven process seeking little guidance or support from their sponsor. Still others expect too much by feeling entitled to a sponsor's availability at all hours, expecting unfailing empathy, and all but positioning the sponsor as responsible for their sobriety. For many, simply discussing their expectations can clear up these errors. This requires an understanding of what is reasonable to expect from a sponsor. Although there is wide variation, typically someone in early recovery can anticipate that a sponsor has some form of contact *initiated by the sponsee* (to demonstrate motivation for recovery), several times a week, if not daily (including email, text, and phone messages). It is best when a sponsor and sponsee have at least one face-to-face meeting a week; this often involves attending a 12-Step meeting together. Additionally, a sponsor provides some mentoring, including helping the client understand meetings and the Steps by imparting the gained wisdom of their journey in recovery.

Beyond these basic tenets, sponsors vary a great deal. Some are very active, meeting with a client repeatedly every day. Some are very directive, to the degree that they all but issue marching instructions. Others still are much more hands-off and instead give advice through suggestions and recommendations. Some have a large fairly tight knit "family" of recovering people that includes grandsponsors and other individuals being sponsored within the group. To be sponsored by someone in this group can mean essentially being adopted by this family. In addition to the wide variation among sponsors, similarly there seems to be as wide a variation in what a sponsee finds useful in this relationship. Ultimately, the effectiveness of a sponsor/sponsee relationship comes down to the compatibility of fit between the two.

For many clients, multiple emotional dynamics are triggered during early recovery. This includes issues with dependency within relationships, power struggles, trust, and self-defeating patterns. These issues present big challenges for untrained sponsors as they can be represented by one or more of the following dynamics: 1) a continued expression of what initially fueled their descent into addiction, 2) a result (or regression) in the face of the emotional stresses and anxiety common to early recovery, 3) a response to additional losses and stresses occurring after the client's recent sobriety (e.g., now that they're sober, the family feels comfortable expressing rage at the client for past misdeeds), 4) a full-fledged emotional disorder (such as a depressive episode), 5) excessive unstructured time, and 6) an expression of ambivalence over the desire to remain abstinent. Let's review a case example that highlights this challenge:

> Penelope had been sober for three months when she announced during her session that recently she was experiencing more urges to relapse. Penelope and her therapist reviewed new events in her life and identified that a high level of emotional reactivity was one the causes of these urges. Further exploration revealed that Penelope was disappointed with her sponsor whom she felt was not sufficiently available or supportive. Penelope and the therapist explored and articulated these feelings and made an action plan for Penelope to inform her sponsor of her urges as well as to discuss her needs and feelings about their relationship.

> The next week Penelope reported surprise at the willingness of her sponsor to discuss her concerns and that they resolved to have somewhat more frequent contact. In addition, her sponsor also discussed that emotional reactivity was a common occurrence in early sobriety. Together, they identified ways that she could cope with the issue, adding a meeting and reducing her unstructured time.

Unfortunately, this type of interaction does not always resolve itself so smoothly. Some sponsors lack the ability to resolve such conflicts, leading to a seemingly endless cycle of frustration for the client and sponsor. Sponsors also lead lives of their own, sometimes preventing them from meeting what may be very high levels of need from a sponsee. Still other sponsors are just a poor match for the client. Clients should attempt to resolve sponsor conflicts directly and assertively after working on developing the social skills necessary for this with the therapist. Failing this, a client should consider changing sponsors. If this is done, it should be done in as healthy, open, and direct a manner as possible. This means that the client cannot just drop the sponsor without telling them and then avoid anything to do with that sponsor in the future (meetings, fellow 12-Step members, fellowship, etc.). This handling of the problem happens more frequently than not, creating awkward dynamics that could have been avoided.

Consequently, clients are encouraged to tell the soon-to-be former sponsor of their decision, thus allowing the relationship to close on positive terms (most often).

The best rate of success occurs when the client is able to articulate a way that the former sponsor can still play a role in their life, such as being another recovery support (even if an infrequent or distant one). This result is also important, if for no other reason than that the client is likely to encounter their former sponsor given that the 12-Step community is a small one. Most sponsors handle this discussion well, and these discussions go best when clients are open and honest. This is also due to a general understanding within meetings that sponsor-sponsee relationships are only effective if both parties realize a positive return.

If a client is considering leaving a sponsor without first attempting to resolve conflicts or frustrations with that sponsor, it may not be appropriate except in some conditions. However, there are a few exceptions. Exploitation of any kind (economic, housing, occupational, etc.) by the sponsor is an automatic dissolution. Significant verbal or emotional abuse in their relationship might be an exception, only if the client wishes to address the behavior, confronts the sponsor, and then the behavior still continues. Essentially, physical abuse (a certainty) and sexual exploitation (13th Stepping) make the immediate termination of the relationship a necessity. At this early stage of recovery, if a sponsor suffers a relapse then a client should transition to another sponsor as soon as possible.

"Intervention" as a Therapeutic Technique in the Prerecovery Phase

Working with prerecovery clients can be very challenging. Certainly an approach built around motivational interviewing has been shown to be very effective. However, one of the treatment areas that is most often neglected for these clients is systems-based interventions, or interventions aimed at the level of the family or the workplace. For many clients, this is one area of intervention that should be considered as the using behavior is tolerated, maintained, and sometimes inadvertently supported by others around them. It has been pointed out how denial by the client works wonders in active substance dependence to minimize awareness of the negative consequences on themselves and their support systems. In part, this occurs because their family and/or work allow it. Significant others usually don't set limits, and may not even be aware of their hurt and angry feelings about the addict's behavior. Employers fail to suspend, demote, or fire the addict, either entirely ignoring the underfunctioning or fearing that enforcing consequences further harms the addict.

Working with a systems-approach with these families or employers offers the therapist many options. Typically, these emphases include the following:

1. Clarifying the distorted boundaries that often occur as a result of the underfunctioning and over-functioning dynamic
2. Identifying and realigning the amount of enabling and rescuing occurring within the system
3. Diminishing the level of secrets and denial within the system
4. Processing feelings of vulnerability, hurt, and/or anger that often arise as denial about the loved one's addiction recedes
5. Helping members to establish a more honest intimacy

Some systems realize that the situation in untenable without significant activity from a therapist. At times, this awareness occurs in the midst of a person's treatment for some other presenting problems. Other times, a client may contact a therapist asking how they can best intervene with a substance abuser.

One alternative to consider at this point is called *an intervention*. Interventions are organized attempts by members of a system to call attention to how the substance dependent person's using is affecting them, and often offering an option for treatment or other help in ending the using. The hope is that the end result is the addict sees more clearly their problems and the destructive results on everyone. Interventions can be organized by any system where the individual is a member. Typically, these are done within families, though they can also be done at work or among a group of friends. Although each intervention is unique, here is a recommended list of factors to consider and include if considering an intervention:

Participants

It is often best to have individuals involved who are valued to the struggling individual rather than a larger number of people with cursory involvement. Interventions are much more effective with key people physically in attendance. Thus, Aunt Gertrude may be more effective if she traveled from halfway across the country. The mere fact that she traveled to be there has a demonstrative impact. It is emotionally powerful to see people you care about taking time from their lives to gather in one room for you, to reveal their concern.

Concur on Message

Typically, interventions work best if everyone agrees to a "main message" when the substance dependent person is present. If everyone is telling them a similar message it is more effective. This type of message sounds something like this: "Jacqueline, I love you so much and it just pains me to see you come home looking thinner and thinner from all of the cocaine you are doing. It is ripping out my heart seeing you waste away." During this process, if there is one dissenting voice among the many, the effect can be to further the denial of the addicted person, causing an ineffective and unsuccessful intervention.

Be Specific

When the beloved support system members speak, it is often best if they are as specific as possible. Give as many concrete and descriptive examples as possible. It is important to dispel the denial that they're using, and it helps them to see that the consequences from this use are not hidden, contrary to the distorted belief of the user.

Take a Stand Against Enabling and Rescuing

Interventions are more effective when the support system announces how they are going to stop or reduce their enabling or rescuing behaviors with the addicted person. Again, the more specific they can be in outlining how they were previously enabling, the less likely the addict to live in the fantasy that no one knows their secret addiction. One caution: clearly this approach requires the support-system members to be prepared to change their behaviors. This can be very challenging for everyone and often requires a great deal of support, treatment, and/or personal work prior to the intervention in order to effectively make this change.

Express Concern and/or Love

Interventions commonly work best when they include expressions and experiences of love and concern. Hammering away about the destructiveness of their using, or talking about participants' disappointments is of little value. After a time, the addicted person returns to what they know and are good at—tuning this message out.

Timing

This is often the most idiosyncratic or peculiar of all the factors discussed here. Generally, interventions are very ineffective if they are done while the addicted person is intoxicated. The adage, "Don't get into an argument with someone who's drunk," are wise words indeed. However, sometimes incidences occur where the support system is able to convince a highly intoxicated person to sign themselves into treatment. In most of these cases, the addict agreed because they were in a black out, and therefore so trashed that they had little power to resist. This approach is not recommended—given how much can go wrong in that scenario, intervention success seems about as likely as betting against the house in Las Vegas. For the vast majority, interventions are done when the addict is sober or only minimally intoxicated. For best results, interventions should be performed when the addicted person is in great psychological or physical suffering from the using (hung over, guilt-ridden, or in active withdrawal).

Listen

It is important to allow room for the addicted person to speak, and to really listen and hear what they say. In particular, others should be listening for any sign or hint that the person is accepting any of the information that is related.

Be Ready to Act

Those organizing the intervention should be prepared to respond immediately if the addicted person acknowledges the problem. It may be useful to have a therapist appointment scheduled that day, an appointment with a family physician who has been informed about the intervention, or a local treatment center ready to admit the individual on arrival. If the addicted person says they are willing to accept help, then the support system should immediately act to convey the person to some form of treatment as soon as possible.

Never a Slam Dunk

The interveners should be prepared for a non-successful outcome—the addicted person does not agree to enter treatment. In these instances, hopefully the intervention is the beginning of the conversation, and the support system starts acting differently toward the addict, regardless of the intervention's outcome. This change is demonstrated by holding to the limits that were conveyed during the intervention. In effect, the intervention becomes the start of a conversation within the system that may eventually result in the addicted person ending their use.

Resources

There are multiple support groups for friends, family members, and children of alcoholics and addicts in a 12-Step arena. Refer friends and family members to these groups. They can be a great source of support to these individuals. Like those newly sober who walk into any other 12-Step program meeting, the support members realize that they are not alone, nor is their "family secret" uncommon. Attending a 12-Step program and listening to other members in the meeting share similar stories quickly reveals to the support system members how they indirectly contribute to the addict's behavior. It is an especially great tool for those who wish to remain in close relationships with the addicted person, but wish to limit or avoid being drawn into the chaos and negative consequences of the addict's using. This type of relationship typically requires a fair amount of effort from the family or support system member, frequently involving significant boundary setting and higher levels of self-reliance than are seen in most other types of relationships.

Employers

Employers also can contribute to an addict's use and/or recovery. There are multiple laws that impact an employer's response toward an addict. On a federal level, these laws include the Americans with Disabilities Act (ADA), the Family Medical Leave Act (FMLA), and the Rehabilitation Act of 1973. There may be additional state statutes that guide the behavior of an employer that should be learned. Despite these laws, employers are not required to allow an addicted individual to have chronic impaired work functioning. Commonly, employers may mandate a client to be triaged or referred to treatment by an employee assistance program (EAP) or a human resources professional. Assuming the client gives consent to share their privileged information, it can be very useful for treating professionals to have some communication with a client's place of employment. Consider the following vignette:

Natalie worked as a programming specialist at a fairly large company. She was referred to the treatment center by the EAP associated with her employer. Natalie explained that her employer had mandated her into the center as she had been drinking at work "a few times." Her employer also authorized the treatment program to speak with the EAP as a precondition to her continued employment, and Natalie agreed to this communication.

During communication with the EAP, the program was told that Natalie was a valued employee and that her employer wished to do anything possible to support her treatment. Natalie was admitted for a detoxification program and then completed an eight-week-long outpatient treatment program. Over the course of the next two years, Natalie relapsed five times. Each relapse was responded to with support from her employer and Natalie's involvement in treatment.

After the fifth treatment, her outpatient therapist voiced concerns that Natalie's motivation to change seemed very low, and the therapist felt that Natalie was "playing the system, but had no intention of stopping drinking." The therapist discussed this with Natalie, but felt that these discussions were ineffective. The outpatient treatment team for her last two treatments echoed the same sentiments. Armed with this perspective, the EAP was consulted and the employer presented Natalie with some limits. She was told that her relapses would no longer be responded to without consequence, that the next time her drinking interfered with her work performance she would be formally written up and suspended for one week. If there was another infraction, her employment would be terminated. Within two months, Natalie was terminated. Her termination precipitated a crisis and a four-month-long relapse. She appears to have stayed sober since that time.

THERAPEUTIC INTERVENTIONS IN SUBSTANCE ABUSE/DEPENDENCE WORK

The Therapist as a Method Actor

Those afflicted with substance abuse and dependence are not like most clients. They exist in an ocean of ambivalence, intermittently able to acknowledge and own (to some degree) their intoxicant use, its consequences, their desire to change, and hope for change. To complicate things, this intermittent awareness is often coupled with a tendency by the client to lapse into power struggles, to conflict with authority, and to attract imbalanced relationships that enable the use. For therapists, this combination of dynamics makes it very difficult to form a therapeutic relationship, therapeutic contract, and ultimately a working alliance.

Trevor arrived for treatment at the insistence of his live-in girlfriend. Two days prior, he had spent the night drinking alcohol and snorting cocaine, arriving home late the following morning, sleep deprived and possessing a much depleted bank account. Trevor arrived for treatment acknowledging his guilt, reporting that he was making a disaster of his life with his drug and alcohol abuse and that it had to stop.

An assessment revealed that he was experiencing alcohol abuse, cocaine dependence, and a chronic mild depression that might be attributed directly to his substance abuse. Trevor was presented with treatment options, and he chose complete abstinence from all intoxicants, frequent attendance at 12-Step meetings, and twice weekly psychotherapy for the next four weeks. Three days later, Trevor arrived for his appointment and immediately announced that he kept the appointment, reluctantly.

As the therapist inquired about this, Trevor announced that he did not see the need for all this treatment. He felt that he had simply overreacted during the prior session, and he doubted that his problem was even vaguely related to his substance use. The therapist observed that Trevor's pronouncements were made with a resentful, challenging tone, and was fairly certain that challenging his statements would easily escalate into an angry conflict. The therapist instead reverted back to motivational interviewing to determine what it was that the client was seeking.

Wide variations in awareness are not uncommon when working with substance abusing or dependent clients, especially those in the first two stages of change. These shifts can occur at any point and without warning. For the therapist, these vacillations can be confusing, unpredictable, and seemingly cripple progress. The client shifts are thankfully fairly predictable in their context if not their timing. A client usually begins denying the reality of their dependent need on intoxicants and the impact of their using, reassured that it is of little consequence, or that their intoxicant use causes none of the few problems they are experiencing. Without a doubt, these clients stir strong reactions in therapists, ranging from an enmeshed caretaking mode to a controlling stance where a demand is made to acknowledge the reality of the wreckage around them.

Needless to say, neither of those extreme responses and their variations is particularly helpful when a client is wrestling with their ambivalence. Remember, change is the client's choice, not the therapist's. The client selects the goals of treatment and the therapist has the choice to accept them for treatment or ask for an agreement of a modified version of the initial client goal. When the client engages in one of these radical shifts in their commitment to their recovery, the therapist's role must also shift if the relationship with the client is to be maintained. Here are the roles you can adopt that are most helpful during these early ambivalent times which may extend far into sobriety:

The Cheerleader

For most of these clients, it is easy to lose a sense of hope, especially hope that they are capable of change. It is hard for them to balance their desire for recovery with their experiences of relapse. The slow and inconsistent pace of change challenges their natural need for instant gratification and becomes more frustrating with each relapse, which spurs high levels of emotional pain, which leads to a desire to use, thus reinforcing the cycle of relapse. In your role as cheerleader, identify the client's resiliency and strength, and assist them in utilizing those positive qualities toward their recovery efforts.

Take nothing for granted, and particularly look within the antisocial behaviors to search for skills that can be utilized for recovery. For instance, manipulation involves positive skills such as sensitivity to detecting people's needs, persuasiveness, determination to reach a goal, and anticipating consequences. Every one of these skills can be redirected from an exploitive use to an empathic route to obtaining and maintaining recovery.

Reinforce your faith in their ability to create a sober life that is fulfilling and gratifying. There remains a great deal of stigma and unrealistic expectations about substance dependence and recovery in the support systems of the client. If an addict's substance use isn't being enabled, they are then generally yelled at, demeaned, punished, and demoralized with each relapse by some or all of their support system. Unless someone in the support system is actively involved in a recovery program, and usually this is, at best, a peripheral involvement, the therapist's office will be one of the few places where the client receives positive support for their continued efforts in sobriety, even after relapses. It is therefore crucial that hope is kept alive until the client can generate that hope on their own.

The Expert Advisor

In this role, the therapist acts as a mental health/recovery expert, simply passing on their clinical knowledge and expertise to the client or support system. This can be a very effective tactic to avoid stirring a client's combativeness by remaining neutral, and yet challenging the client's ambivalent thinking and behavior through the relaying of information. For example, a client during an initial consult was told, "You meet the criteria for alcohol dependence and it appears that your body will become ill if you suddenly stop drinking. However, the only person who can determine if you're an alcoholic is you, and you're the only one who can determine if it's a problem you want to change." At a later point in treatment, this same client questioned if they must stop all consumption of alcohol. The therapist, in the role of the expert advisor, stated the following: "For most clients with your issues, trying to limit the amount of alcohol they consume is a losing proposition. Their two long-term choices seem to be either no alcohol or out of control drinking. However, this isn't true for everyone. You're the only one who knows what's best for you."

The Recorder of Events

One of the symptoms of denial is memory problems or a type of out-of-sight, out-of-mind mentality. A client can forget painful or shameful aspects of events (i.e., their part in it, the emotional intensity of it, the significance of the event, etc.) or the entire event itself if it allows them to continue using. For most clients, these events are not actually forgotten as implied; rather they choose not to access those particular details or whole events and often even actively resist efforts to recall them. The therapist's memory serves as a fact checker and data recorder, providing clients with a more accurate picture of events when the client is unable to hear and accept them. Consider the following:

> Juanita spent several months struggling with the concept that she had lost the ability to control her drinking. After repeated failed attempts at control, she reluctantly agreed with the notion that sobriety and 12-Steps offered her the best route forward. She remained sober for five months until a work Christmas dinner that included very fine wine and single malt scotches. Juanita decided to drink alcohol at the dinner, and was successful in consuming only one glass of wine and a glass of scotch.
>
> During her next session, Juanita questioned if she now could return to some form of controlled drinking. Her therapist replied, "To stop drinking is to give up something that you enjoy. Nobody wants to do that. The problem for you hasn't been drinking; it's that in the past you haven't been able to *stop* drinking. If you remember when we started, you tried several ways to limit your drinking and each time you lost control. I'm game to try that again, but might I ask if anything has changed since the last time you tried to control it?"

Juanita and the therapist continued to discuss it, and eventually she decided to try to return to drinking with a new plan to control it.

Juanita returned one week later stating that the experiment had been a disaster. She lost control after 3 days, drinking all night long and missing the next day's work. The therapist replied "Total sobriety is a hard pill for many to swallow. It's the last option. You've tried several ways now to control your drinking, but you haven't found a way to do it. Only you know for sure, but it looks like your choices are out-of-control drinking and all of its consequences, or total sobriety and all of its consequences."

The Devil's Advocate

If a client is unable to sustain moderated use, and dependency is developing, there are invariably a great deal of losses and suffering experienced by the client as their use spirals upward in intensity. To counter the client's ability to use denial and justification to enable further use, your role as Devil's advocate is essential. At this stage, the client's support systems are either enthralled in enabling patterns or have given up completely due to the failure of the client to control their use. Your key role as Devil's advocate is to keep an ongoing assessment of the risk and consequences of the using, knowing that the client will either ignore or acknowledge this assessment, but not want to confront it while using.

Two major defensive structures are at work at this point: justification and denial. Justification is used to displace responsibility for using onto other people, events, or things. Some examples include:

- "My boss made me so mad, that I had to drink when I got home to calm down."
- "You know I was doing well, not using at all, but then I got a call from a friend inviting me to this great party. I'm not going to live as a hermit for the rest of my life."
- "I wasn't looking to use, just to have sex. But then he pulled out some meth. What could I do?"

Denial is a different animal than justification. Denial often shows itself in the relentless avoidance in linking consequences of the using to the use itself, or recognizing that the use and amount of the use are becoming more frequent. Some examples include:

- "I didn't get fired for my drinking; I got fired because I was late to work." (Late to work because of being too hung over to make it to work on time)
- "Yes I am using on both Friday and Saturday, but it won't go beyond that." (This, after initially claiming that the use would not extend beyond Friday night)
- "I don't use on purpose. I just use when I get upset." (Client choosing people and scenarios that spur him to become upset, such as inserting himself into family drama where he has no place being involved)

The approaches to working through the client's denials or justifications for their using differ depending on the client's defensive structure, intensity of dependency, and severity of enabling in their support system. The main goal is to assess and then reveal the connections between the client's behavior and thinking and reformulate these problem areas when possible. The role is especially relevant in terms of cutting through some of the denial about the impact their intoxicant use is having on their personalities, their lives, and the lives of others. We must confess that during the prerecovery phase, we clandestinely begin introducing 12-Step concepts and language to the client in subtle ways. It is a method of priming the client for recovery. An exchange might go something like this:

Client: I don't know what happened. Last week I was able to go out and have three drinks and then stop myself. I mean no problem, game over, I was done. I went home and everything. But this past Sunday, I told myself I was going to follow the same plan, three drinks. Before I knew it, I woke up the next morning after blacking out. I don't know what happened; I was out of control and again unable to stop my drinking.

Therapist: Sounds pretty frightening, especially blacking out again. You know that is the sixth episode where your attempt at planning and setting limits failed (Devil's advocate). *Your using continues to be pretty unpredictable. It seems that you are unable (powerless) to determine when you are able to hold to three drinks and when you are going to go on another binge and black out (introduction of 12-Step concepts).*

Client: No. I think I can still control this. I just have to figure out why sometimes I can limit to three and why I drink to excess other times. I think it has to do with my job stress. You see, every time I am stressed about my job, I go off on a bad run.

Notice that the client does not have to agree with your assessment. Often in the prerecovery phase, they will not. They are continuing to struggle to find that magic combination that lets them control their using. What is important is to break their denial or justification and introduce 12-Step concepts along the way without using 12-Step language that might set off the client's defenses. It is precisely why the word "unable" is better than "powerless" at this juncture in the therapy. It introduces the client to the concept of powerlessness but utilizes the client's own language.

The Predictor of Risks/External Frontal Lobe

As is discussed in preceding chapters, substance-dependent clients typically have impaired or below-average functioning in their frontal lobes. This means, in part, that the client finds it difficult to predict the consequences of their actions. There are times that the therapist can assist the client in this function either by supplying the potential consequence, or by helping the client to explore their plans in order to predict the consequences. Consider that your client, George, had been in treatment for five months and sober from cocaine for the past three, when he mentioned that over an upcoming weekend some longtime friends were having a July 4th party and he was considering attending. Think about the therapist's role in this scenario:

Therapist: Have they had other parties like this?

George: Oh yeah, I've been to many of them!

Therapist: What were those like?

George: I had a lot of fun. It's great to see those guys.

Therapist: So you've had a lot of fun there; did that include using cocaine?

George: Yeah it did, especially the last couple of years. I'd get pretty strung out there.

Therapist: So let's play that out, what do you think it'll be like if you go there?

Helping clients predict consequences not only may save them from relapse, but also begins to familiarize the client with a technique referenced often in 12-Step meetings. This type of systematic evaluation of consequences of choices is called "playing the tape through," and it is highlighted later in the book.

The Hardcore 12-Stepper

This role is often useful for those who are already attending 12-Step meetings. It involves the therapist speaking as a neutral expert giving voice to the sobriety approach of a hardcore 12-Step member, and framed as only one of many different approaches to achieve sobriety. Let's revisit George to see how this role is applied:

After exploring the consequences of the 4th of July party, George comes to realize that spending time at a party where people use drugs might trigger a relapse. At the same time, not going means distancing himself from the fun tradition of partying with his friends.

George begins by questioning this summary, wondering if he could attend the party and remain sober. The therapist responds with, "It would suck to have to miss what you enjoy about that party. At the same time, there's no way to predict if you will be able to stay sober. If I put on the hat of a hardcore 12-Stepper, I'd say it's a bad idea. There are too many temptations at that party. It's essentially a Barber Shop for you, and if you hang out at a Barber Shop, it's only a matter of time until you get a haircut. It also sounds like you are questioning your powerlessness when it comes to cocaine. I wonder if there is more work to be done with Step One with your sponsor. Now if I take that hat off, I guess I'd wonder if that applies to you. What do you think?"

The All-Knowing and Impossible-To-Deceive Parent

As noted in the previous chapter, most substance-dependent individuals in their using days rely on antisocial skills in order to survive. Likewise, people in the lives of an addict tend to take on roles of caretaker or enabler, and are generally over-functioning while the addict is irresponsible, needing care, and generally under-functioning. Not surprisingly, these support members often expect the therapist to function similarly. Remember, holding boundaries and limits, such as charging for a missed session because of the client's hung over condition, or ending the session on time despite their late arrival, are effective strategies to hold the client responsible for their actions and raise awareness of your expectations. It is recommended that the therapist reconfirm these boundaries when a client has relapsed by probing them on these unacceptable behaviors and holding them accountable.

The Non-Directive and Neutral Ally

Out of all the shifting roles in therapy, this has to be the bottom line in your work with clients. At the crux of it all, the client is the consumer. Only they decide which goals to choose and implement as they ultimately carry the responsibility for their choice. That is not to say that you cannot add input into the creation or modification of those goals. Once a treatment contract for sobriety is established, and given the inexperience of clients to living a sober life, be more directive earlier in treatment, and then decrease this approach throughout the course of treatment as the client gains the necessary insight and skills for recovery. However, when a working alliance has not grown and especially when the client is in the first two phases of change, then it becomes increasingly important that the therapist be nondirective, or, in the words of motivational interviewing, "change talk must be made by the client."

Making General Therapeutic Techniques Work in Substance Abuse Treatment

In the previous chapter, the basic skills of clarification, reflection, and restatement were demonstrated as extremely helpful in assessment. Similarly, these techniques are effective as therapeutic interventions if they are applied properly in the context of substance abuse and dependence. For instance, restructure the client's content in relation to 12-Step concepts and language. To demonstrate

Client: So it's been another week. I ended up drinking a couple of days, and one of those turned into a bender. I drank more than I wanted to, but it wasn't as bad as the other time. Now, my girlfriend's all up in my face saying I'd promised her I'd get a handle on this. I don't know. I don't think I'm ready to say I'm an alcoholic. We've got to find a way to stop me from going on those really bad benders.

Therapist: So I hear that you want to try to find a way to bring your drinking under control, so you can drink without making such a mess for you that it feels unmanageable?

In this example, the therapist is summarizing what the client is saying, but also restating it in a way that is consistent with 12-Step language. It mentions the word "unmanageable" and draws from the concepts of Step One. Use of 12-Step language makes it easier for clients to hear that you understand their struggles; all the while you are simultaneously priming them for involvement in 12-Step meetings.

Although a full discussion is beyond the scope of this text, it is relevant to note that the use of interpretations in the early phase of recovery is associated with some controversy. For many psychotherapists, especially those who use insight approaches such as psychodynamic or existential, addiction is seen as an expression of underlying pathology. From this viewpoint, addiction is treated by resolving the underlying issues motivating an individual to abuse substances. This process often involves bringing hidden motivations into the client's awareness. These clinicians consider the high frequency of relapse and failed treatment as due, in part, to these underlying dynamics not being addressed rather than because there is a skill deficit around sober behavior.

Positioned on the other side of this issue are therapists who are more in line with traditional substance abuse counseling. These clinicians suggest refraining from interpreting to clients, especially clients who are in the early stages of recovery. Interpretations, if made at all, should be limited to interpreting denial and other defenses that cloud the person's ability to assess their substance abuse and the parts of their life that support this abuse. The theory here is that early on in recovery, clients have very poor stress tolerance and coping skills. Interpretation, especially of defenses, initially can increase a client's tension and anxiety. Lacking other ways to respond to this tension and lacking the sober skills to cope can trigger increased urges to use, and ultimately relapses. Which side of the controversy is correct? Alas, we cannot say.

Utilizing interpretations can be effective with those people who abuse substances but are not yet dependent. Carefully evaluate if these clients have sufficient self-soothing skills to cope with the emotional material from the interpretations, in addition to the self-reflection and help-seeking skills necessary in posttherapy. It can be a useful technique with those who have some solid time in recovery, typically six to twelve months for most clients. However, even with these two groups of clients, closely monitor how the clinical work is impacting their sobriety, titrating as necessary so as not to trigger a relapse.

There are certain cases in early recovery when some limited interpretation is useful. For example:

1. Co-occurring disorder clients who are unable to remain sober, despite first attempting treatment focusing only on their substance abuse or a noninsight based approach (such as medications and cognitive-behavioral therapy). For these clients, insight is suggested because other approaches have repeatedly failed.

2. Ambivalent clients who demand such an approach. This includes clients who are attempting to control their substance dependence through interpretation rather than abstinence. For each of these clients, inform them of the potential risks, especially that the treatment may trigger urges and that often interpretation may be ineffective at treating dependence. Agree to this, but also include a time limit to the treatment of typically three to six months. Also monitor the client's substance use and urges during the time period. At the end of the time period, the treatment is reevaluated. If the client's status is stable or improved, continue the approach for an agreed time period; if not, return to questioning this approach. This approach may be mandated with a client who finds the idea of abstinence unacceptable, in a final attempt to allow them to continue to consume the intoxicant in a controlled and nondestructive manner.

3. There is a subset of clients whose underlying motivations for their substance dependence and pattern of relapses appear closely linked to some causal motivation; for example, intense feelings of shame coupled with a profound inability to access anger. For these clients, attaining consistent sobriety seems impossible until they make some progress on their struggles with shame and anger.

4. More often, interpretations are relied on with clients who have recently relapsed after a lengthy period of sobriety, typically multiple years. Given that the fundamentals of 12-Step in these individuals are predominantly

strong (usually a relapse involves a resentment and questioning of powerlessness), it is possible to shift to an interpretative approach once they are sober for just a few months.

Another reason why practicing insight-oriented psychotherapy for substance abuse or dependence may not be the best initial approach: the vast majority of substance abusers assume an antisocial adaptation as a necessity for their substance use. This antisocial adaptation can greatly complicate interpretative and empathy-based approaches. Many a therapist has diligently pursued unconscious meanings in a substance dependent client, only to discover later that the work had little or no impact on the client's ultimate substance abuse; the therapist's tools of empathy and understanding were essentially tools that the client ultimately used to manipulate them.

As with any treatment, listening is a central function of the therapist. Along with all the other layers of meaning a therapist is attuned to hear, listen, and look through the worldview of 12-Steps. Consider the following client statement, "I saw this guy I used to get high with in the meeting last night. I wanted to say "hi", but I felt bad. I stole a lot of money from him once to get my drugs, but he did the same to me later on. I guess that would make us even." This statement can be understood using several Steps. First, his substance abuse caused him negative consequences that he still must face (Step One), but there is hope that he can resolve them or at least be at peace with them (Steps Two and Three). He also is having troubles seeing his contribution to his problems (Step Four), and has not attempted to take responsibility for his past behavior, especially with this person (Steps Eight and Nine).

All of these issues and conflicts are likely present to one degree or another. However, the key to listening is detecting which meaning is the most important, and responding to that meaning. For most clients, this is the Step that they are currently focusing on in their work. However, please be aware that not all Steps are equal for all clients. What is primary for a client at this moment may differ from where they were twenty minutes ago. Not every client also focuses on the Steps in a sequential manner. It is not uncommon for a client to struggle with more than one Step at a time, either due to their own unique experience or their current situation.

SUMMARY

Similar to the assessment process, therapists have a wide range of techniques they can employ when working with substance use. Whether in the prerecovery or early recovery phase, these techniques can be employed with a few differences. In the prerecovery stage, the clinician begins to lay the foundational work for early recovery by utilizing 12-Step concepts without the specific 12-Step language. Additionally, therapists have a wide range of roles they can employ in response to a client's denial or resistance to recovery. Therapeutic interventions do not stop with just the client. Support systems of all kinds, including sponsors, are apt to be pulled into a client's antisocial adaptive style of relating in order to produce or maintain enabling. It is recommended that clinicians consider these systems for intervention if clinically appropriate and do not prove a hindrance to the client's goal of sobriety.

QUESTIONS

1. What is motivational interviewing? Why is it an effective tool for a substance-using client seeking therapy?
2. Present the rationale for why recovery must always be at the forefront of therapy early on in the recovery process.
3. Name the role of defensive styles in active substance use. How are clinicians able to address these defensive styles in therapy?
4. In what areas do decisions of a sponsor trump that of a therapist? In what areas do decisions of a therapist trump that of a sponsor?
5. What is an intervention and name four factors that increase the likelihood of a positive outcome?
6. Name the difference between the therapist's roles as "recorder of events" versus "predictor of risks"? What about as a "Devil's advocate" and "expert advisor"?

Hitting Bottom

7

W hat exactly prompts a person into acknowledging that they have lost all control over their intoxicants? What causes people to revert back to intoxicant use after they get clean? Are there ways to detect substance use in therapy or signs that someone is contemplating relapsing? These are just some of the questions that are answered in this chapter while addressing the end point of using, and a relapse in sobriety. We begin by covering that event referred to as a "bottom" that often is the entry point of many into sobriety.

HITTING "BOTTOM" AND THE ENTRANCE INTO RECOVERY

What Is Meant by the Term Bottom and Is It Necessary to Reach Before Recovery?

There are many reasons why use happens. Sobriety, on the other hand, often occurs following a crisis of negative consequences. Consider a crisis point, commonly referred to as a "bottom," as one of the most common reasons for a person's entry into sobriety.

A bottom is a term employed to describe the end point of a person's using. Depending on the person, each crisis or bottommost point looks different, but generally it is the point at which the person decides that they have had enough of using by more realistically admitting the consequences of their using and deciding to try recovery. A bottom is often experienced as the lowest point of their lives brought on by the consequences of their addiction. Here are some common examples of the type of consequences (the resulting bottoms) created from using. These can involve either a single event or a combination of events:

- Health crisis (STD, stroke, heart attack, HIV diagnosis)
- Financial crisis (money exhausted, foreclosure, homelessness)
- Occupational crisis (job loss, final warning of job loss, loss of professional license)

- Legal crisis (possession charges, prostitution charges, indictment for embezzlement)
- Personal crisis (rape, sex work for drugs, harm to another, assault, psychosis, or severe depression)
- Relational crisis (relationship dissolution, divorce, loss of custody/court supervised custody of children, failure to care for dependents, and absent for important events like funerals, weddings, anniversaries, or birthdays)

However, it is important to note that not all clients need to experience a bottom to move into recovery. Some clients elect to receive help without professional assistance or even self-help groups. Many of these people realize that their substance abuse is spiraling out of control and respond appropriately. At this point, a variety of factors likely come into play, including a level of self-awareness, responsiveness of the person's support system, genetic factors, spiritual/existential factors, and even starting therapy. There are many factors that may protect a person from developing a substance abuse or dependence problem. Unfortunately, not all clients have adequate protective factors. For them, hitting bottom seems to be a necessity.

Involvement in group therapy (outpatient, intensive outpatient, or inpatient) may be a protective factor. Some of these attendees did not require hitting a personal bottom before committing to recovery, perhaps because they heard and witnessed others who hit bottom and decided they wished to avoid that fate. However, this example can have the opposite effect as well. Clients in group therapy can use those group members who are worse off as a comparative point to justify why their use is really not that bad. Using others as a comparative point is always a dangerous game in substance dependence. Unless you are dead, and then it is a moot point, it is always possible to find someone who is worse off. Encourage clients to use a more realistic comparative point to assess their use—themselves. In the Devil's advocate role, ask a series of questions designed to break down their denial:

"Gosh, it sounds like Joe-addict's life is really bad from using; what similarities are there to your life?"

"Tell me how your life has changed over the last three, six, twelve months?"

"We've talked a number of times about problems that have come from your using; do you think things have been getting better?"

"Help me to understand why you continue to talk about other people's use when we have yours to talk about? Help me to understand the connection between yours and theirs."

Managing a Client's "Search" for a Bottom

Generally, when a client's using increases there are substantially greater and greater consequences experienced by them that are painful to witness and can create a number of problem areas for clinicians. As you journey with your client toward their bottom, clinicians need to be aware of their own countertransference reactions; the most notable is the urge to save the client from their bottom. What do we mean by this? It is in a therapist's nature to want to stop self-destructive and self-harming thinking and behavior; to alleviate suffering. This often makes us clinicians feel better. We essentially helped to stop a building from burning down, and in the short-term that's precisely what we did. However, no matter how comforting, that effect doesn't match the long-term impacts on the client. Attempting to save the client from the pain and consequences of their using is described as enabling. Instead of helping the client bottom out, you are essentially protecting the client from the consequences of their destructive behavior, and ultimately furthering the descent into their dependence. (Note: it has been argued that it is this counter-transference reaction that often motivates the *inappropriate use* of harm reduction strategies.)

Clinicians should also be keenly aware that substance abusers can directly affect the treatment arrangement. In particular, several treatment issues arise when a client is descending toward their bottom or have hit their bottom. These include all of the therapy frame issues that we covered in Chapter 4. Exercise appropriate self-care and self-concern here by setting reasonable limits and adhering to them.

Therapists are emotionally impacted in other ways by a client's spiral down toward a bottom. Fear is one such emotion. Fear that the client will overdose and die, kill themselves and/or another while high or crashing, fear of permanent brain damage from using, and fear of the client leaving treatment and never knowing what happened to them. Then there is the sadness that comes from watching someone dance with self-destruction. The sadness witnessing a promising life spiral out of control, the unused talents, the suffering from physical and emotional injury caused by using, witnessing the increasing and debilitating depression and physical discomfort caused by withdrawal, and the mounting personal losses of the client. Anger is part of that emotional roller coaster as well. Anger at the disease slowly and inexorably snuffing out another life, of the client's failure to follow through, broken promises, missed appointments, wasted time, and the madness of the inability to stop an enabling system. Anger can lead a therapist to end therapy prematurely or punish the client by being overly (and sometimes cruelly) blunt, to the point of the intervention being nontherapeutic and borderline unethical (violating the "do no harm" oath of any doctor).

Feelings of failure and self-doubt also have the ability to creep in over time. These emotions are the most dangerous as they can motivate a therapist to further enable a client's using. The therapist's enabling thoughts or behaviors can lead to delaying the client from hitting bottom. By saving them from one consequence, it is inevitable that a harsher one is right around the corner. This can include thoughts like: "if I help him out one last time with his job," or "I know I need to recommend inpatient treatment, but what if he gets angry and leaves my practice." It may seem counterintuitive, but sometimes the most therapeutic intervention is to terminate treatment with a recommendation for a higher level of care. If you recognize that the client's use is beyond the management of individual once-a-week therapy, you are ethically obligated to refer that client to a higher level of care.

Clients, with rare exceptions, can always refuse to follow the referral recommendation, just as someone who is court-mandated to attend treatment has the option of not following that mandate. It is of vital importance that you clearly outline what conditions need to be met if they are to resume therapy with you. Is it inpatient treatment? Intensive outpatient? Sobriety time of 30 days? Residential treatment? Going to one meeting a day for three continuous months or 90 meetings in 90 days (in 12-Step lingo, this is referred to as "Doing a 90-and-90")? By doing so, your message to your client is that you are not ending therapy for punitive or rejecting reasons; you are suspending therapy so that more intensive work can take place in order to interrupt the addiction and allow recovery to take hold. These can be particularly troubling treatment decisions to consider. Seek out consultation from more experienced therapists when you are faced with these decisions, especially if these types of decisions are new to you. Despite our own extensive experience, we often still consult on these decisions ourselves.

Added to the above, most clients are not shocked by your treatment decision or referral. You might hear your client responding by saying "I wondered how long until this day came," or "Do you have an idea where I can go to get this help?" Clients are aware on some level, no matter how much denial they have, that their using and their lives are becoming unmanageable. Outwardly, the client's blame for the problem still might be externalized to other people, places, or things, but your proverbial ace-in-the-hole is the unmanageability of their life regardless of the disrupting factors.

Also, a quick word about the concept of bottoms as exemplified by two sayings within the 12-Step rooms: "underneath every bottom is a trap door" and "death is the ultimate bottom." These are two of our favorite sayings. It connotes two important concepts that those seeking recovery often do not think about. It is also what makes beginners' meetings so important to the sober individual. Bottoms are the low point in the active addict's life where the individual has suffered such mounting consequences from their use that they are forced to wrestle with the choice to stop. It may have been losing a job, divorce or break-up, becoming homeless, or crossing of boundaries (swearing to never inject drugs and doing just that).

What often becomes a risk in thinking that one has hit bottom is that this is as far as you can go in incurring losses from using. The bottom for a person does not equate to meaning that a person *must* stop for all time. The simple fact is that a person can hit a bottom yet still find a way to escape the obvious conclusion that they must stop using. Instead, they find a trap door and resume use. If a sober person relapses (or begins using), the losses may be far worse than the previous bottom. Addiction can lead to unimaginable losses. Just when you think that a client cannot possibly lose anymore, they relapse again, leading to more losses. For some, there is no bottom that will make them stop using. For them, the ultimate bottom is death. There is no greater loss than one's life.

Beginner meetings in 12-Steps are important to those with long-term sobriety because it reminds them what they were like when they entered the rooms: physically, emotionally, and mentally both run down and broken by their using. It is a powerful reminder of how far they have come since those early days in recovery and how much they stand to lose by venturing back out to using. It helps reestablish why they need to stay sober.

The statements of "underneath every bottom is a trap door" and "death is the ultimate bottom" hold important meanings for us as therapists: that addiction is a disease of relapse, that addiction has no cure, that addiction is profoundly destructive, and that people, through their continual choices to use, willingly engage in that self-destruction. If successful, recovery is a treatment that hinders the progression of the disease, and improves all-around functioning.

Returning to the notion of referring out a client, the best timing to talk about referral to more intensive treatment is at the point of the client's highest misery. This point is usually the day or up to three days after their last use ended. The withdrawal from the drugs or alcohol leaves the client acutely feeling the effects of their using, both in emotional and physical terms. Emotionally, the client may be feeling an overwhelming sense of guilt, shame, anxiety, fear, and depression. These emotions are spurred partly by their behavior, and partly from the physiological response that their supply of neurotransmitters (responsible for pleasant and happy feelings) is exhausted. Physically, the client may be feeling achy muscles and joints, feverish, stomach problems, headaches, run down, and generally pretty awful. The physical symptoms are partly caused by the effects of the additives in drugs; the effects on the central nervous system, and sometimes strain on the liver and kidney; and partly due to dehydration, poor nutrition, exhaustion, and exposure to transmittable diseases. As you can imagine, there is a whole world of hurt happening!

Aligning with your client in these moments of suffering and recognition of the unmanageability of their lives and addiction allows you to focus the client's desire to regain control by grasping at anything that alleviates their suffering, including recovery. It is at this time that you need to move quickly to capture the moment to spur the client into action toward recovery and/or treatment and overcome their remaining ambivalence. That means you better have all of your ducks in a row, be prepared for the discussion, and have the referral target equally prepared to act quickly with the client.

Bottom's Ahoy!

As stated, once the client's denial is broken through and they agree to enter into recovery, it is imperative that you have your referral options in line and ready to go. For this recommendation, as a first step therapists should refer to the ASAM criteria to best determine an appropriate level of care. This requires the therapist to be familiar with the different levels of care and different agencies that provide such treatment.

It is best to locate one or several agencies that specialize in addictions treatment, and offer free assessments. A good choice, if available, is a free-standing psychiatric hospital (a rarity these days), or a medical facility with psychiatric services (preferably one that has more than a single psychiatric unit). These facilities usually have a 24-hour emergency room that is open all year, including holidays. Medical hospitals with a single psychiatric unit can be problematic because the composition of the unit is often based on treatment for a hodgepodge of disorders; this makes it likely that in terms of treating the addiction, the generalist nature of the unit may be inadequate at best, and enabling at worst.

Because treatment can be so widely varied in terms of quality, you should tour the facility or facilities you are considering utilizing as a referral, and meet with the program directors and/or staff to assess the quality of treatment programming available. Some questions to ask are:

1. What types of addiction or drugs of choice do you treat most frequently?
2. Are you 12-Step based? Are you open to alternatives to 12-Step?
3. Do you assist the client in aftercare services and if so, what do you frequently recommend?
4. Do you assist the client in obtaining sober housing if necessary?
5. Do you provide family education and/or family therapy?
6. How am I alerted when the client is nearing completion of treatment?
7. What is your average waiting time in the emergency room? Are there some times or days that are less busy?
8. Do your psychiatrists have specializations and certifications in addiction treatment?
9. What does a typical day look like for a patient?
10. Do you offer or have referral suggestions for partial hospitalization or intensive outpatient services as a step-down to inpatient care?
11. What insurance do you accept? If my client has insurance that you do not accept, can I still refer them for an assessment knowing that you will refer them to an appropriate agency that does accept their insurance?

Basically, if you have a curiosity about the program or hospital, your client will too! So ask questions both as a provider and as someone who might be considering treatment for themselves or a loved one. Be sure to ask the agency if they have brochures for you to take that help explain their program.

If the therapist deems that a higher level of care is appropriate, the therapist should initiate the referral with the client present, and if at all possible arrange for the intake to place the client that day. Prior to this day, the therapist should be assessing for supports in the client's life (those people not supportive of the client's addiction) *who are likely to act,* if called on to help the client into recovery. It is at this time that the therapist encourages the client to call those supports who can assist with their entry into treatment, either by driving them there or meeting them at the referral agency.

If the client is still employed and actively working, this becomes one of the main excuses (legitimate or not) for not agreeing to the referral. Therapists can help the client objectively look at their likelihood of termination if the addiction goes unchecked. Conversely, the therapist can fill out Family Medical Leave Act (FMLA) paperwork that discloses minimum information for the need to seek treatment while guaranteeing the client's job, although not necessarily their position within the company. There are restrictions to FMLA, and you need to become familiar with this act in order to learn how to best utilize this tool to encourage clients to seek treatment. Employers can also approve short-term disability benefits for the client, although they may require the employee to first use up their remaining vacation and sick time.

For many clients, it is highly likely that if you only give a client a referral name and number to call after they leave your office, they will never make the call and instead go back out using or go home and crash. If the client goes home and crashes, it is likely that the moment to get the client into treatment has passed. It is amazing how a bit of nourishment and a few days rest reenergizes the client's brain to permit the welcome denial, full of fire and brimstone, to come stomping back into their heads to wreak "merry hell" on their resolve to find recovery. Specifically, this reemergence of denial has the substance-dependent person call into question their experiences of the bottom, thus minimizing the severity and need for treatment. Unfortunately, this leaves both the addicted person and the therapist waiting for another crisis.

If the therapist determines that the recovery can be managed by continuing in traditional once-weekly therapy, the therapist must clearly articulate his or her expectations to the client on the parameters of abstinence, attendance in therapy, involvement in 12-Steps or another recovery program, and the consequences for failing to follow through with agreement. The therapist must hold boundaries at this crucial point. If the client deviates from this plan and is unable to hold up their end of the bargain, the therapist is advised to not renegotiate or allow any failures to be classified as "minor" or "just a slip." All that does is to allow enabling to walk through the door, and the spiral of addiction continues.

SUMMARY

Although for all those addicted to substances, hitting bottom may not be necessary to end their using, it is often frequently the turning point where they seek help. Watching a client spiral toward their bottom can be an emotionally painful process, and therapists should seek their own consultation, supervision, or therapy during these times to manage the emotional fallout that can occur. Furthermore, clinicians need to be prepared to assist clients in accessing services when they eventually hit bottom by having systems in place for easy point-to-point referrals.

QUESTIONS

1. What is a "bottom"?
2. Name the ways in which a bottom can be both necessary and irrelevant for recovery?
3. What does the phrase "under every bottom is a trap door" mean?
4. Name four questions that help therapists assess the quality of a treatment center?
5. How can therapists be impacted by a client's spiral toward their bottom?

Substance Dependence—
A Relapsing Disease

8

So, you say you are interested in working with clients who want abstinence from substances as a treatment goal? Congratulations! We hope that this decision was made because you enjoy challenging work with *very* mixed results (spoiler alert!— many of your clients will relapse, and many of those who relapse will do so repeatedly). As soon as the treatment goal is abstinence, relapse is a very likely possibility. Far more of your clients will relapse than will not. This dynamic makes the work very challenging. If you are going to work with this population, please do not pin your professional satisfaction on clients in your care remaining abstinent. We fully support the notion of abstinence as a worthy treatment goal. However, if your work satisfaction is based on your client's sobriety, expect a high level of burnout and very strong countertransference reactions. Substance dependence is like any other chronic illness. There are periods where the disease is stronger than the current treatment regimen, which results in the disease itself creating symptoms. This process is termed *relapse*; the point where remission of the disease is temporarily or even permanently interrupted.

With substance dependence, by relapse we mean a return to intoxicant use. It's a recurrence of the primary symptom of substance dependence. There's a lot more to add to that definition and to the subject of relapse in general, which we cover below. For now, bear with us as we start with that definition.

Relapses as Learning Events for Recovery

To begin, we need to make one thing absolutely clear: Relapses can only occur once there has been a sustained period of sobriety or a break in the client's pattern of using. A client who uses on a cycle or a repeated pattern with some days of use and then other days in between not using is not relapsing. The substance use has never really stopped. This language is important in the prerecovery phase. Clients in active addiction refer to their repeated patterns of using as "relapses" although they have not had any sustained break in their pattern of use or any significant "clean" time. In these instances and for the reasons mentioned above, clients need to be informed that in fact their active use has never stopped. This type of intervention is sometimes the shock clients require to recognize that they are still engaged in active addiction and not recovery.

Relapse can be seen as ultimately either useful or nonuseful. A useful relapse is a relapse or a pattern of relapses that occur in such a way that the client is clinically progressing. The easiest examples to identify are a pattern of relapses that become increasingly shorter, or of less intensity, or are separated by increasingly longer periods of abstinence. Less easy to identify, but still a useful relapse, is when the pattern of relapses or abstinences remain consistent but each relapse deepens the client's commitment to sobriety work, or helps them become more aware of the changes they need to make, or why they need to make the changes. View these clients as people gathering strength, preparing to jump fully into recovery. Useful relapses result in growth. This growth or evolution can be necessary

> . . . because the client simply lacks sobriety skills or the skill set necessary to remain sober.

For these clients, the relapses are more like a stumble. The clients dust themselves off after the relapse, ready to address their deficits and gain stronger skills at remaining sober

> . . . because they need to readjust how they are working their 12-Step Program.

A 12-Step Program is a fairly lengthy and detailed program that suggests that the newly sober client make huge changes in their lives. For some addicts, they are so devastated after hitting their bottom that they will do everything and anything to remain sober. These clients surrender to the process and follow the full recovery prescription.

For others, they are not quite as convinced that they should make all the changes suggested by the Program (for the sake of full disclosure, we are often not entirely convinced either). These people did not choose the right elements of the Program for them to achieve long-term abstinence the first time they tried. The key for these people is that after relapse, they review their program and attempt to address what adjustments are needed to remain sober

> . . . because some are unwilling to give up some people, places, or things that are associated with their drinking and/or drugging. They will not embrace such a loss until they have proven to themselves that they must leave the person, place or thing in order to stay sober.

Some clients find that one or more of the aspects of their sobriety involve losses that are just too large to accept. This can include the example of an alcoholic having to leave their bartending career for a time, or perhaps a cocaine-dependent individual having to avoid spending time with family members because they also use cocaine, or perhaps having to end a romantic relationship with a substance-dependent partner. These clients try to find a workaround, a way to stay sober but also not have to lose something(s) they hold dear. Some attempt this workaround and successfully remain sober, but some do not. Eventually their relapses provide the proof that their only option is to embrace the loss in order to remain sober

. . . because they need one last hurrah.

Perhaps the most significant loss facing a chemical dependent person is the loss of intoxication and the lifestyle it represents. Let's face it: there is a whole lot of fun in intoxication and the shirking of responsibilities, cares, and worries that go along with it. The only reason that clients give this lifestyle up is because the negative consequences are too devastating to manage. When some clients face the necessity to give up getting intoxicated, they give themselves one final use, a last hurrah.

These relapses tend to be fairly intense, even spectacular events, but also fairly short-lived. Confusingly to clients, they may not even be aware, let alone able to articulate, that it was their last hurrah. Some indications that a client had a last hurrah are when clients suddenly become less resistant, make more investment in working their recovery program, or even adopt a different attitude toward their past abuse of substances.

Relapses as Activating Addiction

In contrast to the relapses that can effectuate growth, nonuseful relapses do not result in clinical progress. Often times they result in stagnation, an intensification of ambivalence, or a pattern of relapses that are longer, deeper, or more frequent. Clients who engage in this pattern often seem to express more antisocial adaptive traits than others. This makes sense as these clients are often psychologically closer to an active substance-dependent person than a sober one (or, in 12-Step terms, they are more wet than dry). These clients are some of the more challenging clients; rapidly vacillating between sobriety and active use requiring clinicians to quickly interchange between using the motivational-interviewing technique of prerecovery, to engaging in the powerlessness and unmanageability work of Step One. Complicating this, with these clients the therapist should expect testing of the rules and the therapeutic frame, which, in turn, can evoke strong countertransference reactions.

THE PROCESS OF RELAPSE

In addition to two general outcomes of relapses, there are two broad ways or processes used by clients to approach a relapse. One is an immediate process, and the other develops more slowly, often requiring multiple steps. Before we begin discussing immediate relapse, let's define what sets off a relapse: a trigger. *A trigger is anything (person, place, thing, or emotion) that, when it is encountered, sets the urge-compulsion-use loop into action.*

Relapse as a "Fast Burn"

The immediate relapse is a relapse process that starts and ends with intoxication almost immediately. It involves the person being rapidly flooded with urges to use of such powerful intensity that it overwhelms them. The sober person has no option or choice; they are *physically compelled* to use. This person simply turns to intoxication without forethought, consideration of the consequences, or even a conscious decision. The compelled person's substance use memory network is too strong, and their executive functioning is too weak. As a result, the threshold for triggering their urges to use is very low. It's almost as if they have a flash of temporary insanity. You often hear client's speak of this, "I don't know what happened, I saw my dealer and next thing I knew it was three days later and I was bottoming out all over again." This type of relapse commonly occurs during the initial phases of recovery. It is less common, but not unheard of, for it to occur after 6 to 12 months into recovery.

Relapse as a "Slow Burn"

The second way a relapse can develop is as the end stage of a longer and often much more convoluted route. Many of those with long-term sobriety talk about a relapse occurring long before the person consumes the intoxicant. In fact, you hear many clients admit that on some level they decided to use again *well before* they actually did use; they just weren't fully aware of making that choice (there's that denial thing again). There are many possible stages to the process of developing a relapse and, depending on the individual, the specific aspects to this development can vary quite a bit. Often this involves a series of thoughts, behaviors, and emotions that are discernible.

Thoughts

- Range of resistance to accepting feedback to outright denial demonstrated by taking unnecessary risks, such as
  - going to places where they used
  - seeing people who continue to use
  - lying about stored intoxicants or paraphernalia

These individuals become as secretive as if they were wet (i.e., using).

- Romanticizing or glorifying (remembering only the fun and pleasurable aspects) of using: yearning for the old days, while engaging in cognitive distortions (as discussed in this chapter, the client shifts from a sober, to ambivalent, to using position)
- Their focus is on how people are wronging them and/or not living up to their expectations: preoccupied with resentments, justifying a detachment from those around them
- Rationalization and justification of relapse behaviors and thoughts
- Obsessive thoughts of using: inability to change thinking to the benefits of recovery

Behaviors

- Any behavior that resembles their behavior while using, or regression, is a potential sign of this relapse process in action
- Compulsivity evidenced in other areas, such as eating, sex, Internet, work, computer games, gambling, pornography, and so on
- Failure to implement new coping skills
- Reintroduction of old using friends or associates back into their life
- Taking on too many things at once: ramping up affective states when the client has yet to learn effective coping and managing skills
- Reducing their recovery efforts (skipping meetings, not meeting with sponsor, etc.)
- Placing themselves in situations where they may be exposed to triggers (such as walking past bars, driving through known drug-dealing areas, etc.)
- Placing themselves in situations where their judgment or impulse control may become impaired (such as a cocaine-dependent person consuming several beers)
- Placing themselves in situations where their intoxicant of choice is present: rationalizing that just because it's there, doesn't mean they have to use

Emotions

- Gradual building up of anger and disappointment from resentments
- Gratitude for sobriety begins to erode
- Anxiety builds with realization that new coping skills do not help or have little effect at all
- A general sense that client's emotional life is becoming increasingly chaotic or dysregulated
- Client's disposition in session is serene and peaceful after weeks of struggling with powerful urges to use—may be an indication that client has made decision to go back out (conversely, it could signal that the client has surrendered once again and is reengaged in sobriety)
- Client is experiencing a natural "high" with life as things are going well—this may signal that the client is in danger of wanting that high to go that much higher through the route of their drug of choice

Again, these examples of relapse warning signs/processes are only the tip of the iceberg that a client can exhibit when recovery begins to falter and they may be considering shifting toward a potential relapse. However, each client usually has a core set of relapse thoughts, behaviors, and emotions that shift them toward using. Once these core factors are recognized and learned, they provide an early warning system that allows the therapist to attempt interruption of the cycle of relapse before it progresses beyond the scope of therapeutic intervention.

Over time, the therapist's ability to detect an oncoming relapse or at the least detect when one has occurred can have added benefits. In fact, it doesn't matter if the timing of a relapse can or cannot be predicted. What's more important is that treatment boundaries and limits are maintained and that the client believes that the therapist knows when they are headed toward relapse and especially when they are using. More than one client has told us "You knew I was using didn't you? I'd go back out there, and every time I knew that you knew that I was using. I felt like I couldn't get away with it; you'd know." We'd be lying if we said we knew every time our clients used, but that's not what's important here. The key here is that the client felt that they could no longer hide their abuse from us.

TRIGGERS

Before going into a deeper discussion of relapse and relapse prevention, a sidebar discussion is necessary about triggers or the stimuli that seem to set off the urge-compulsion-use loop, and techniques associated with them. The therapist and client need to discover these triggers, and how they work in relation to each other. This is not an exercise that is done just once. As the client moves through recovery, it is an exercise that continually needs to be examined and reexamined as an essential goal. As a person's triggers change, adapt, and reform over the lifetime of recovery, so does the risk of relapse. A person's risk of relapse tends to reduce as they gain continuing awareness and management of their triggers.

Trigger Identification

The first exercise is to identify people, places, and things that cause the client to think about using, or actually spur them into the action to use. Do not just note the triggers where the client ends up actually using the drug; take a more nuanced approach that looks at the level of risk versus absolutes. To start, have the client list out their triggers under the four headings: people, places, things, and emotions. After that is completed, have the client rank each trigger based on the likelihood the trigger results in a relapse. Once this list is completed, it is important to discuss the following points with the client

1. The risk of using is ever-present, even though you may feel very safe at the moment. Unforeseen things do happen: A dealer turns up in line behind the client at the grocery store, a person who wants to undermine the client's recovery shows up at their home claiming to be clean only to pull out their preferred intoxicant, or cousin Jed shows up to the family party buzzed and reminds them how fun it is to drink. Even the most careful planning and creation of sober spaces, relationships, and events can be interrupted by the introduction of intoxicants, whether through benign or malicious intent. This is an exercise in understanding the external manifestation of "cunning, baffling, powerful."

2. Conversely, no event is truly an absolute guarantee of using. There have been many people in early recovery who were exposed to their intoxicants with surprising results. This type of exposure was previously thought to be an absolute guarantee of using. However, the client was able to make it through because they were in the right sober frame of mind, utilized their new coping skills, and/or luckily had sober support with them.

3. When examining the list, the highest risk for the client is not those items listed on the fringes of the chart but those people, places, and things that make the client feel as if they have some control. The more they feel that they can resist the urge to use, the more danger that they fall into the trap of *underestimating the power of the trigger and overestimating their recovery skills.* It is highly recommended that clients, in even the safest of scenarios, develop emergency plans for support; for example, one technique that is especially helpful is the idea of "bookending" events. The client selects an activity that grounds them in recovery prior to entering into, and immediately after, a potentially triggering event. An additional measure is to have a recovery reminder on hand during the event, examples such as an anniversary chip from 12-Step, a copy of the serenity prayer, a copy of what they have gained back from sobriety, and/or what a relapse would cost them.

Following the creation of the trigger list, spend time with the client in examining each of the triggers. Work on how the client intends to avoid that trigger, and also what actions the client can take if they encounter that trigger. Listen for hesitation or uncertainty in the client's voice or body language that may counter what they are actually saying. These signs indicate that the plan is probably not going to be very effective if the client encounters the trigger. Often, the client gives answers that they think the therapist wants to hear, or answers they have heard from other people in recovery but have not fleshed out how that will work for them. If the client has to develop an overly complicated and elaborate plan to survive an event, reflect how the plan seems to reflect the concept of unmanageability and question if attending is actually a wise decision. Most often, clients recognize the high risk level and decide not to go (albeit with some minor harrumphing).

Influential Internal Triggers

You will hear the term "H.A.L.T." a lot in your work with substance use and especially in 12-Step. It signifies an easily identifiable cluster of feelings that can lead a person in recovery to mistake these sensations for an urge to use their intoxicant. H.A.L.T. stands for "Hunger," "Anger," "Loneliness," and "Tired." We believe that the acronym should be B.H.A.L.T. with the "B" being "Boredom." All of these emotions link to the experience of deprivation. That sense of deprivation can compel your client to try to fill the void the best way they know how—intoxicant use. Therefore, the use of B.H.A.L.T is a useful tool for a client to assess if they feel the urge to use. Is it really that they are having urges for their intoxicant, or are they misinterpreting the urge for another need as their intoxicant? You can also use it the other way around: if a client experiences a craving, they should pause and search for some unmet sense of deprivation via BHALT. When successful, this approach has the added benefit of allowing the client a sense of self-efficacy with cravings.

Hunger and sleep. The physical trigger of hunger makes a person vulnerable to relapse both by the sensation of deprivation and also the compelling urge to satiate created by the survival system in the brain. Think about going into your favorite restaurant after not eating for the past 12 hours. How likely are you to make healthy food selections and exercise good portion control? Not very. It is the reason behind the old saying to never go to the grocery store while hungry.

Sleep deprivation works along the same lines by sabotaging thinking and impulse control. Sleep deprivation impacts judgment, impulse control, and many other cognitive functions by steadily decreasing their functioning, the longer the sleep deprivation continues. Thus, the more a person in recovery is sleep deprived, the increased likelihood of them failing to see or respond effectively to an external trigger.

Boredom, anger, and loneliness. View these emotional states in terms of deprivation. Boredom is a deprivation of engagement, anger is a deprivation of understanding and love, and loneliness is a deprivation of inclusion. States of deprivation are worrisome times for any sober person because their drug of choice acts as a powerful weapon to fill up that space. Additionally, boredom brings up other feelings such as dissatisfaction and restlessness. Most people in early recovery have no idea of what constitutes sober fun, nor do the sober activities that they participate in begin to compare to the feelings they got while high.

Anger is another powerful motivator for relapse as it hits two birds with one stone. First, I get to feel great being high and don't have to feel my anger, but I get to hurt you through my act of relapse also. What the recovering person often needs to learn, prior to becoming angry and triggered, is that their using injures themselves more than their loved ones. Their loved one doesn't have to go through the physical and emotional withdrawal from the drug, or deal with the shame and guilt of using; only they will. This lesson is paired with social skill training on assertive communication in order to help the client decrease the likelihood that feelings of anger result in relapse (i.e., If I can talk about my anger and express my deprivation, my loved one has the opportunity to meet my needs).

Loneliness is an inevitable human event. It is the one feeling that newly sober people consistently express surprise at feeling, especially if they are well connected to fellowship and 12-Steps. Most clients are the least prepared to cope with this feeling. Couple the feelings of loneliness with substandard sober social skills and self-soothing techniques, and you can gather why this emotion usually ends with a client in tears or a relapse. Additionally, loneliness brings the risk of the recovering person going down the "woe is me" path; a very risky path to tread down. Once a person in early recovery begins lamenting the losses of their using world, recovery begins to feel difficult, unfulfilling (back to deprivation again), and replaceable by relapse.

Emotional dysregulation and low self-esteem. This discussion is not about the wild emotional swings of Bipolar Disorder, although that certainly could qualify. This references any emotional state, including "positive" emotions that are triggering to the client. For instance, the B.H.A.L.T. emotions may not trigger a person to use, if manageable under the threshold of their coping skills. Similarly happiness, if pushed over the threshold of coping skills, could trigger a person to want to experience greater degrees of pleasure than is humanly possible, thus moving the individual toward relapse. This determination of threshold tolerance needs to be monitored and adjusted as recovery progresses and life stressors emerge or decrease over time.

Low self-esteem is another internal trigger and one of those insidious worms that efficiently and effectively erode recovery efforts. How can you sustain recovery if, at your core, you feel that the misery and suffering of substance dependence is all deserved? The recovery slogan "fake it till you make it" is a handy tool to utilize with clients until healthy self-esteem develops through sustained recovery. It is the act of "acting as if . . ." that can help clients *act as if* they are worthy of love, recovery, respect, and inclusion until they *feel as if* they are worthy of those things.

For example, even though I don't feel like I belong in 12-Step—if I *act as if* I do by attending meetings, working with a sponsor, fellowshipping—then it may lead me to *feel and actually belong* in 12-Step. Low self-esteem doesn't always present at the beginning of recovery; sometimes quite the opposite. When clients begin to have to face the consequences of their addiction ("wreckage of the past" in 12-Step lingo), that is where the greatest risk lies. This is usually in conjunction with Step 4. This Step is highly triggering for most people in recovery. This topic is addressed in the next volume of this book, which specifically covers the middle phase of recovery associated with Steps 4 through 8 of the 12-Step Program.

Fear. People recovering from substance dependence have an uncanny ability to take the most innocuous and safe person, place, or thing and change it into a feared entity beyond measure. Most of the fear stems from low self-esteem and feelings of inadequacy, both real and imagined. It is strongly advised that the therapist examine the facts behind all perceived fears in order to help your clients dispel that fear or find their way safely through it. In contrast, people who are newly sober are able to look at the most dangerous and risky triggers and feel no fear at all. Grandiosity and an inflated sense of self are usually the defensive structure underneath this thinking. However, sometimes the facts of what a recovering person (during their active using days) has gone through, and survived, can give them a warped sense of danger and safety. Monitor risk at all times on both sides of the equation, and assist the person in recovery to learn to accurately assess risk and manage the emotion of fear effectively.

Influential External Triggers

External triggers are much more concrete and accessible to the client. They are the people, places, and things that are associated with a person's intoxicant or their lifestyle during intoxicant use. We broke down some of the more likely suspects for consideration in relapse prevention work.

People

- People with whom I have used intoxicants
- Dealers
- Family members who use intoxicants
- People who "look like" (do not have to be) intoxicant users
- Media figures who are intoxicant users
- Television shows, movies, Internet clips that show people using intoxicants

Places

- Bars, nightclubs, raves, circuit parties
- Liquor stores, grocery stores (that have liquor sections)
- Entire sections or neighborhoods of town or cities where I used to party
- Places both inside and outside my house where I have used (living rooms, back-yards, basements, bedrooms, etc.)
- Friends' or parents' homes
- Cars, airplanes, trains
- Alleys, fields, playgrounds
- Areas visited to obtain drugs

Things

- Intoxicants themselves
- Any paraphernalia associated with the drug of choice: alcohol bottles or glasses, pipes, matches/lighters, tin foil, plants, ashtrays, needles, pill bottles
- The chair or bar stool always used in favorite hangout
- Any sensation associated with use, such as the smell of burning marijuana or brandy

During the first three months of recovery, external triggers are examined on a weekly basis to ensure that risk for relapse is consistently assessed. Afterwards, evaluation on a biweekly or monthly basis is sufficient to note trends and catch new ones. Clients are recommended to keep an "active trigger chart" that over time shows them their progression in recovery by observing how once powerful triggers begin to drop off of the chart completely.

RESPONDING TO A RELAPSE: MEASURING THE IMPACT OF THE RELAPSE

Now that you have a better sense of triggers, the discussion can return to relapse. It is difficult to determine the long-term impact that relapse has on a client's recovery, let alone whether the effects are positive or negative. Just because the client relapses and resumes using for, say, ten months does not mean that the sobriety effort was a failure. Consider taking a broader view of what constitutes success in recovery. It certainly is not dependent on getting it right the first time (or even the eleventh). Often, clients seem to require relapses in order to make the changes necessary to achieve sobriety. Relapse is always a significant risk; once it occurs, it should be taken as an opportunity to refine a client's program. In other words, a relapse is typically a symptom of a client's ambivalence and/or a failure of their program. It is not a personal failure or a shaming moment. Instead, it is an opportunity to learn and improve.

In order to refine a person's program, it is necessary to enlist the client in assessing and responding to the factors that resulted in their relapse. Once a client's use is known, ask the following questions to determine the context of the relapse and recommendations for refining their program:

1. Was the relapse premeditated, impulsive, or unexpected?

This question helps evaluate which type of relapse, an immediate or a longer term one. If the relapse was impulsive, it means that the client's impulse control system is fairly compromised and therefore more stringent parameters may be needed to avoid triggers and to improve their chance of sustained recovery. Clients are also encouraged to review their day in the mornings with their sponsor or other recovery support (who has at least a year or more of clean time) in order to identify potential risks for triggers and safely plan for them. Clients at this stage are also encouraged to take recovery support with them if they have to go into triggering environments, which are sometimes unavoidable.

In recovery, unpredictable events can be treacherous but sadly often inevitable. Anyone can be ambushed by their triggers. No one plans to run into their dealer at the post office, or experience a (supposedly) solid recovery support person bringing drugs to their home, or come into a large sum of money suddenly (throwing the brain into a desire-to-use frenzy), or have a friend bring alcohol to a sober party, or suffer the surprise of a date's introduction of drugs right before engaging in sex. In these scenarios, evaluating whether the client was deliberate or impulsive in their reaction helps assess how therapy can be used to prevent the next unpredictable event from becoming another relapse.

If the relapse was the result of a longer process, you cannot be so prescriptive in your recommendations. There are many factors that may fundamentally underlie the relapse. Here are some areas to consider:

- Ambivalence over sobriety
- Incomplete work on earlier Steps, especially 1, 2, and 3, or a desire to avoid working on some aspect of a current or next Step
- Not adhering to the recovery plan as outlined by their sponsor and/or therapist
- Undetected and untreated psychological issues, especially diagnosable and severe disorders related to depression, anxiety, mania, trauma, or psychosis
- The environment not supporting the individual's sobriety (e.g., a family that subtly sabotages the client)
- Self-sabotaging, often related to shame
- Some previously undetected secondary addiction or abuse
- Incomplete identification and planning involving triggers

2. During the relapse, did the client use more, less, or about the same amount of their drug of choice than they used before?

The amount of drug is generally not a great indicator of anything in a relapse other than gaining a sense of whether the prerecovery use pattern has changed at all. Generally, the earlier the person is in recovery, the more likely it is that the use pattern does not change much. Generally, the longer sobriety is maintained does have an impact on the first relapse. This is due to the fact that the intoxicant likely has a more powerful effect on the brain since it has not been exposed to intoxicants for a long time and tolerance is therefore very low. When this occurs, the amount used could be less, because the drug is having a more powerful effect.

3. Was the amount of time the client was using during this relapse similar to the pattern before entering recovery? If a client is in a relapsing pattern, how long is the client out using compared to the client's clean or sober time?

Measurement of the time spent using offers insight into the cycle of relapse. For instance, if the client's time out using increases, it can be a sign that tolerance continues to build as they need to use for a longer period to have the same effect. It is also an indication that the substance dependence is cycling upward in intensity. Clients generally stay out for shorter periods of time in a relapse for several reasons, all of which usually boils down to recovery taking the fun out of the using. The awareness of the consequences of their using on themselves and their support system become the ultimate buzz-kill, halting using early.

If a client's use remains the same, generally it is an indication that the substance dependence pattern is fairly fixed. More clinical work needs to be done to ascertain triggers for the relapse, and what prevented the client from reentering recovery sooner. For example, is the client so overcome with shame and guilt at the relapse that intoxicant use is the only effective method of numbing those feelings? When the client returns to treatment, assessing these areas are helpful to further recovery efforts.

4. What interrupted the use? Was it the client's own initiative to reach out for help to stop, or did the addiction/use run its usual course?

These questions are a good barometer of several important factors for succeeding at remaining sober. If the client was able to interrupt the use through their own initiative, what was it that created the motivation to stop? Is it the client's ability to recognize the negative impact of the relapse while it is occurring, thus dispelling the fantasy of "missing out"? Was it looking at the other people they were using with and recognizing that their relationships in 12-Step are more fulfilling? Once this revelation occurred, were they able to interrupt their own using by reaching out for help, or stopping the use themselves? These answers provide a wonderful tool for the therapist to utilize as a motivational source for recovery.

Often, clients do not have the ability to stop their use by reaching out for help or interrupting it themselves. Knowing how the use ended helps to provide a record of both powerlessness and unmanageability that is useful when working through Step One. We review this type of example in greater detail in the next chapter.

5. What was the client's response to the relapse? Guilt and shame? Indifference? Denial? Excitement?

The client's emotional response to the relapse is seldom a surprise, and often it can be predicted based on their efforts in the recovery program. Those with ambivalent recovery programs often express guilt and shame, but they lack resolve to change. You can also detect undertones of excitement, relief, and pleasure. Often, those clients with firm recovery programs who relapse express shock, guilt, shame, and embarrassment for the relapse. This makes it difficult for the client to both reenter treatment and 12-Steps, regardless of the nonjudgmental efforts of both parties. We'll talk more about this later.

6. Is the client able to clearly articulate the trigger(s) for the relapse?

The client's ability to articulate the triggering person(s), place(s), thing(s), or emotion(s) is a solid measurement of the functioning level of denial still persistent in their assessment of their addiction. It also can be an indication of the client's willingness to stop using by consistently placing themselves in harm's way by downplaying the risk.

7. Is the client able to identify and utilize a coping skill that would have worked to prevent relapse given their cognitive, emotional, and/or behavioral limitations?

To a large degree, these questions assess both ability and willingness for sobriety. As we discussed previously, when clients with severely injured impulse control systems are confronted in early recovery by a trigger, no coping skill will stop a relapse from occurring. The brain's brakes are insufficient to overcome the addictive network when activated. This is where you hear your clients say, "I don't know what happened. I saw (trigger) and next thing I knew I was using." First, assess if the client actually had the behavioral controls that would even allow the potential use of a coping skill to avoid a relapse. The client's willingness (or ambivalence) is assessed next. If the client had sufficient impulse control, and encountered a trigger, did the client make *a conscious decision* to use (versus employ a counter-measure/coping skill to retain sobriety)? What determined that decision to use? In effect, what led to the client's choice to relapse? What benefit from using trumped the benefit of sobriety? Knowing this can help overcome ambivalence by either grieving the loss of that benefit derived from using, or finding its equivalent (or better) in sobriety.

8. Is the client willing to now avoid this identified trigger? If not, what prevents them from doing so, and what safeguards does the client advocate that will result in continued sobriety, if that same trigger presents itself again?

Both of these last measures come down to one final question that concisely evaluates a client's readiness to give recovery another shot. *Does the client make changes based on the above answers, or does the client choose to allow the risk(s) to remain?* If the answer is no to the first part and yes to the last, then the client is not willing to make changes, and it does not bode well for sustained sobriety. At this juncture, your best route is to fall back to a motivational-interviewing position, and reevaluate the client's goals for their intoxicant use.

This stance is consistent with research on relapse, specifically the Violation Effect and other explanations of relapse (Curry, Marlatt & Gordon, 1987). Part of this research suggests that if a person attributes their resumption of use as due to external factors, they are less likely to regress into a full-blown episode of abuse. However, if a person attributes their use to internal factors, then they are prone to feel responsible, guilty, and other negative emotions, which make a full-blown episode more likely. Likewise, a person is more likely to regress into a full-blown episode and give up recovery efforts if they believe themselves powerless over stable factors and attribute their use to these factors, such as "I have no control over my drug use." They are less likely to regress to a full-blown episode and remain invested in recovery if they attribute their use to forces which they can impact, such as "I need to avoid triggers." As a reminder, this is what is at the heart of 12-Step Programs: powerlessness occurs at the point of administering the intoxicant. Up to this point, 12-Step teaches that you are powerful to prevent that outcome by working the Steps and engaging in recovery.

For these and other reasons, it is possible to predict relapse at the start of every treatment involving substance dependency. Commonly, a therapist says something like, "To give you a heads up, it is very common for people to relapse or return to using for a time. Some people seem to be able to remain sober without ever relapsing but others cannot. Let's hope for the best and prepare for the worst. If you do relapse in the future, the best thing you can do at that point is to admit it as quickly as possible. That way, you and I can examine what happened in order to get a handle on what we need to change, and improve your program so that you're less likely to relapse again. Relapse is a sign that we need to reevaluate your recovery program."

THE POLITICS OF THE TERMS "RELAPSE" VERSUS "SLIP"

Clinicians invariably encounter a discussion about whether someone's venture back into using should be classified as a "slip" or "relapse." Both terms have no universally accepted definitions in the self-help or professional recovery world. Conventional wisdom suggests that relapse may be an intentional or unintentional one-time event, but one that could lead back into a repeated pattern of maladaptive behavior that re-engages the addiction. Sobriety date is therefore reset to the day of first nonuse. By comparison, a slip may be an intentional or unintentional one-time occurrence, and the person's sober date may or may not need to change.

If you are every bit as confused as we are, welcome to the show! The lack of consensus opens up a lot of room for interpretation and triangulation. Here are some of the most repeated arguments from clients when they want to classify the use as a slip:

- "Does it matter if I stayed out using just that one night? I didn't stay out all weekend the way I would before. I even went back to my meetings the next day."
- "It wasn't as if I planned to use. I even told my friend I wasn't using and they still offered me the joint. What was I to do, not use? I took a hit and then left as soon as I could."
- "Why do I have to change my sobriety date if I just had one sip of alcohol? I didn't know the punch was spiked, nobody told me."

What do you say to each of the above scenarios? How would you classify them? Relapse? Slip? Does it matter whether they planned to relapse? This is where context is everything. Resist the urge to engage in a power struggle with the client on the label of the behavior, unless doing so helps to highlight the denials or inconsistencies in the client's behavior or expectations. Rather, focus on the behavior and thoughts that occurred leading up to relapse, and what helped the client come back into sobriety. The determination of the sobriety date should be left to the *sole purview* of the client, sponsor, or home group.

Examine the recent use with the client, and mutually agree what to call any similar future using behavior, should it occur. Again, you need not nail down every possible scenario and detail. However, by reaching accord on the general definitions of relapse and slip, there is now a common language to measure and appropriately label future use.

THE AFTERMATH OF A RELAPSE

Recovering from a relapse is typically a dreadful experience for clients, even clients highly ambivalent about sobriety. First, there's the hangover and the potential withdrawal syndrome, which sometimes can require an inpatient admission. Within their 12-Step meetings, the client may feel like a disobedient child who must complete a walk of shame to resume attendance. They may have lost some respect from others in the room, especially if they have relapsed repeatedly. They may feel that others are viewing them as not serious about recovery; sometimes these suspicions are correct and sometimes they are not. They may find that they have to earn back respect and trust from some individuals in the room. Simultaneously, they should be reminded that almost everyone in the room knows what it is like to attempt to stop using and not be immediately successful. Almost everyone in the room has relapsed and is willing to give clients another chance to reinvent themselves.

COUNTERTRANSFERENCE ISSUES WITH RELAPSING CLIENTS

For practitioners, relapsing clients bring varied emotional reactions to the forefront. These countertransference reactions are very informative for the therapist, if they are attuned to them and seek appropriate guidance. When treating clients in addiction and recovery, consultation and supervision are effective tools in remaining aware of your different countertransference reactions. Therapists may be attracted to working with addicted people due to their own familial or personal history with addiction, setting the stage for their countertransference to interfere with valuable clinical work. Therapists are encouraged to examine their common countertransference reactions to relapse, and seek consultation to find effective strategies to ensure that those reactions inform their clinical work in a safe and positive direction.

Although a client may seem to be doing "all the right things" in their recovery work, therapists can begin to feel emotionally detached from the client, generally without awareness as to the reason for the detachment. Therapists report feeling that they still like the client, or are engaged with the client's work, but feel an absence of emotional connection. Indeed, often new clinicians report emotionally being aware of an impending client's relapse before being able to cognitively recognize it through the client's behavior or thinking.

There are two reasons that come up most often in our clinical supervision work on the function of emotional detachment. The first is that the therapist is unconsciously and emotionally aware of the client's movement toward relapse, even though they are not cognitively able to understand how they know this. As such, the emotional distance serves as an early warning sign that stretches beyond the client's verbal assurances. At the same time, the client may be moving emotionally away from the therapist, unconsciously knowing that they are moving toward a necessary detachment in order to leave the therapist and return to using. The client—aware of disappointment, shame, and guilt as products of relapse—moves to create an emotional barrier with the therapist, in effect to ease the emotional impact for both of them by their choice to return to using.

Anger and frustration are also common countertransference reactions when working with addiction, especially in newer clinicians. Anger and frustration typically result from the therapist placing too much emphasis on the client's success in recovery as a reflection of their own worth and effectiveness. Each time the client tests their recovery and then relapses, the therapist takes the relapse personally. Therapists may express their anger or frustration by verbally punishing the client with sarcastic or shaming statements. Additionally, therapists can express their anger or frustration by overcompensating for their own feelings of ineffectiveness by setting extremely unrealistic expectations on the client, or by making sly remarks to the client to foster feelings of guilt for using.

The therapist's hopeless and helpless feelings are all indications of their knowledge that a client has not yet hit bottom, and/or an indication that the client may not be ready to stop using. Usually these emotions stem from the therapist owning the client's recovery; that the therapist is working much harder at trying to sustain a client's sobriety than is the client. Hopeless and helpless feelings may also indicate that the therapist is nearing compassion fatigue or burnout and is in need of a temporary separation from clinical work (e.g., a vacation) or clinical supervision.

The desire to save the client from their addiction or help alleviate the fallout from their using is a good indication that the therapist has fallen into an enabling role and is in a codependent relationship with the client. Therapists demonstrate this quality by being in denial with the client about the severity and impact of the addiction. This occurs most often with therapists who enter addictions work with a family history of unresolved or active addiction. Therapists should consider attending Al-Anon or Codependents Anonymous (CODA) and therapy to resolve those outstanding issues.

Finally, feeling confused in therapy is usually an indication that the client is throwing a bunch of red herrings the therapist's way in order to distract from relapse thoughts and behaviors. Frequently, the client comes into session with several stories of drama that are intellectually and emotionally enticing to the therapist. The therapist can feel flooded with information and be uncertain which story or topic should hold focus. Remember that most addicts, through the very nature of their addiction, and in order to keep themselves functional with their using, are master manipulators. During these moments of confusion, therapists are encouraged to internally pause and assess how much of the session has focused on recovery. If the answer is little to none, then it is best if the therapist asks the client to explain how each story relates to their efforts in recovery.

CLINICAL INTERVENTIONS WITH RELAPSE

Once a client forms a therapeutic contract based on sobriety as a goal, a relapse can be viewed as a setback. After a relapse occurs, join with your clients and empathize with their shame and disappointment. Yet, at the same time, also attempt to identify the components of their recovery program that are in need of fine-tuning or overhaul. Your options include:

Do Nothing, and Mean It

This choice is often the best case when the client seems to be working a good recovery program, and the relapse seems to be the result of a freak occurrence (such as the client lost their job and that same day bumped into their dealer at the unemployment office). You and the client agree that nothing needs to change.

Do Nothing, and Don't Mean It

Sometimes the client believes their recovery program is working hunky-dory, but you disagree. Despite exploring and processing your concerns, the client remains adamant that nothing should change. In this case, take the stance that the client makes the final decision. However, the client's behavior is ultimately the barometer. Should the client again relapse, then the therapist's fears are confirmed and the client's recovery program is in need of change. Should the client remain sober, then no change was necessary and the client was correct. This approach allows you to maintain the therapeutic relationship regardless of the outcome.

Skills Training

In this case, you and the client see a need for targeted skill development that, if in place, would have helped the client avoid relapse. Assertiveness training, mindfulness, trigger chart, or some other skill deficit seems to be the culprit and demands further attention.

Improved Trigger Management

The client lacks a complete understanding of their triggers, or a comprehensive plan to avoid or cope with them, when and if they appear. This response typically results when the relationship between triggers is very complex and difficult to identify. It may take several relapses before a client and therapist can understand the interplay of triggers and how to interrupt those factors that lead to relapse. This can involve reviewing and adjusting a cross section of trigger identifiers and the skills-training development listed above.

Address a Co-Occurring Disorder or Symptoms

During the first year of sobriety, it is preferable if clients do not work on underlying emotional issues. However, sometimes circumstances intervene and clients do not afford us this luxury of time. Depression, mania, anxiety, intrusive thoughts, and hallucinations are all impossible to therapeutically avoid. Indeed, if avoidance is attempted the results often provoke relapses. At these times, refer the client for psychiatric evaluation.

Take Relapse and the Goal of Sobriety More Seriously

Clients, especially those who are first getting sober, are prone to view sobriety as a simple decision that they need to execute. Now for some clients, this is correct. They decide to stop using, and without much effort never use again. More commonly, your client's sobriety is fragile in early recovery, and their risk of relapse is significant and ongoing. The overconfident client may only partially invest in recovery efforts, expose themselves to triggers, and unwittingly sabotage their sobriety. Relapse can be an unwelcome eye opener for these individuals, resulting in a large scale change in their investment and approach to sobriety.

Acceptance of Some Aspects of the Program

This option can involve accepting a variety of options from their 12-Step Program. Often, this occurs when the client rejects some aspect of the Program and is now forced to reconsider elements after relapse. This change may require:

- Attending more meetings
- Finding a sponsor, changing sponsors, or working more closely with their sponsor
- Changing which meetings or 12-Step programs they attend
- Reworking an earlier Step or moving forward to the next Step
- Becoming more invested in fellowship

This change can also include other parts of their recovery efforts that are not 12-Step related, such as avoiding triggers, improving sober support, and so forth. They do not necessarily need to make the massive changes of an over-confident person; they just need to readjust some components of their recovery program.

Face the Loss

Earlier in this chapter, we spoke of this outcome. This illustration is the client who has a partner, family, job, or even a life goal that they value. However, as recovery progresses, it becomes clearer and clearer that this element serves as a sabotaging agent in their recovery efforts. If a client is unwilling to make the difficult choice to lose something or someone of significant value, work with them to find a work-around solution, if possible. Sobriety is the test of the effectiveness of those efforts. If relapses persist, yet sobriety is valued by the client, it may eventually signal that they have to sacrifice something they hold dear for the safety of their recovery.

Treatment Intensification

A relapse or pattern of relapses sometimes suggests that the client is simply unable to remain sober given their current situation and/or treatment modality. The client just may be too prone to become overwhelmed by urges to use, no matter how much relapse prevention efforts are implemented. Alternately, they may be homeless or living in a family residence where others get high. In either case, they are incapable of avoiding or managing triggers. A treatment alternative is to increase the level of care for these clients for a time until circumstances or skills are optimal to meet their challenges. Some of these options include:

- See the client more frequently than once per week
- Arrange for the client to live in a sober residence/halfway house
- Have the client complete multiple weeks or months of a partial hospitalization program or an intensive outpatient program
- Admit the client to an inpatient program immediately after a relapse

SUMMARY

Frequently, an episode of relapse can require the need for several of the above outcomes. Clients may need to invest more in their recovery program, make some significant changes, and/or enhance or gain some skill sets. We should also add that this development requires more ability than simply making an assessment and recommendations. Instead, it becomes a process over time of exploration, negotiation, and trying out different alternatives; this frequently necessitates the incorporation of many of the prior skills and therapeutic roles previously discussed. For some clients, this cycle needs to be repeated multiple times, with the therapist reframing setbacks not as failures but as opportunities to improve recovery efforts and ultimately sobriety time.

Up to this point, the chapters of this book have constructed the framework and context for the remaining focus of the book: examining Steps One through Three. These remaining chapters discuss specifics of the Program in an effort to reveal a comprehensive approach to therapy that successfully blends psychotherapy with clients involved in a 12-Step Program.

QUESTIONS

1. How can relapses serve as learning events for recovery?
2. What are some reasons that relapses occur?
3. Give a definition of a trigger.
4. What does H.A.L.T. stand for, and how does this acronym refer to triggers?
5. Name four external triggers for each category:

    a. People
    b. Places
    c. Things

6. Name three factors, not related to triggers, which may be responsible for a client's relapse?
7. What is the difference between a relapse and a slip?
8. Name three clinical interventions for working with relapses in therapy.

Step One, the Journey Begins

9

All of the previous chapters focused on the various tools and concepts inherent in substance abuse therapy and a 12-Step Program. The next three chapters integrate that knowledge and techniques with each Step, providing a road-map for clinicians in their efforts to merge these two philosophies. Each chapter follows a similar format. We first cover general considerations at this stage in the recovery process and then talk about the key concepts within each Step, therapeutic issues and interventions to address those concepts, and finally warning signs and prevention strategies for relapse.

Step One ushers in the beginning work of recovery starting with the first day of sobriety. In actuality, Step One most likely began in the moments that led up to the client's decision to give sobriety a shot. As therapists, the work would be a whole lot easier if it solely entailed attending to the processing and enacting of Step One with your clients. But who said being a therapist was easy? Recovery begins a long journey that starts with the pressing of one gigantic "reset button" for your clients. To be fair, not only is it "reset," but also "rework," "relearn," "release," "revive," and "reengage." These changes are no more vividly displayed than in the beginning months of recovery.

GENERAL THERAPEUTIC CONSIDERATIONS

How Personality, Executive, and Memory Functioning Confound Assessment

If you recall back in Chapter 3, we talked about how chemical dependence essentially evokes an antisocial adaptation. A surprising amount of the 12-Step work, and ultimately the work in treatment, focuses on these dynamics. This is not the field for those who are easily manipulated.

Also, you want to remember that these individuals have impaired executive functioning. This impairment can be quite severe, making it very difficult for these individuals to cope with cravings during the initial stages of recovery. In addition, expect a high level of impairment in problem solving, in particular, difficulties breaking desires and needs into manageable, measurable, and achievable subgoals. As a result, many tasks can quickly become insurmountable to a client. This includes homework and any set goals. Associated with this, it is very common for individuals to display impairments in their memory functioning, especially short-term memory. As such, clients require notes, written homework, and a variety of reminders to help them recall the material discussed in session.

Finally, assessment is a very complicated procedure in early recovery. The problem is that the targets to be measured are often unstable. For instance, it is almost universal for clients to appear in exceedingly high levels of distress during the first week of abstinence. Three weeks later, their level of distress may be significantly reduced. On more than one occasion, during their third week of abstinence we assessed a client as displaying a certain personality organization, only to review this assessment six months later and find that it no longer applied. Remember, these are clients who are making tremendous transitions in many areas of their lives. As a result, at any given time, assessments can be correct but show far less temporal stability than is typical for other clients. Emotional, social, personality, and neuro-psychological results can show large shifts during the first year of sobriety.

The Impact of Post-Acute Withdrawal Syndrome (PAWS)

In addition to the issues described above, the therapy process and recovery itself are continually challenged by the presence of PAWS. Depending on the client's preferred intoxicant, PAWS can last for a couple of weeks and up to a couple of years. PAWS can fade away only to reemerge seemingly out of nowhere and without provocation. A few common features of PAWS are problematic short-term memory; problems thinking clearly, including poor concentration and focusing ability; difficulty regulating emotions; insomnia or hypersomnia; overreactivity to stress; and problems with coordination.

As mentioned in previous chapters, these symptoms are compounded if they continue to prompt your client to relapse. Seek medical intervention and employ cognitive-behavioral and relaxation/mindfulness techniques as needed to help prevent the cycle of these symptoms from becoming a motivator for substance use. Additionally, remember during these periods that 12-Step meetings have the ability to act as an emotional container for the client while the collective wisdom of the group can also act as a de facto brain for them. You need to be vigilant in monitoring your client's phasing in and out of PAWS, and help to normalize the client's experiences as a part of the recovery process. Educate your clients about the potential of developing some of the symptoms of PAWS at the start of their recovery, which helps them understand and anticipate the process of recovery. This also helps to normalize some of their heightened emotional responses during 12-Step meetings.

Get the Client's Self-Care Groove On

Another part of the challenge in early sobriety is getting into the life habits of "normies" (12-Step label for those never experiencing addiction). For most addicted, living a life of substance abuse or dependence throws self-care out the window. Many areas of personal maintenance are often neglected, including nutrition and hydration, sleep, hygiene, exercise, medication adherence, meeting financial obligations, maintaining a clean living environment, and healthy sober socialization. Therapists should not automatically assume that their clients new to recovery understand what healthy self-care behavior looks like or even the rationale for it. However, successful implementation of self-care begins a new tangible affirmation of the client's self-worth and can not only serve as motivation for recovery, but also help to mitigate some of the PAWS symptoms and physical damage suffered from intoxicant abuse. Some specific self-care issues to observe and discuss:

Hygiene

Not surprisingly, a client's hygiene takes a major hit on a global scale during binges or sustained periods of using. Clients do not always shower, brush teeth, shave, wash clothes, do the dishes, clean the house, pay the rent, stock the refrigerator, and so forth. A client's hygiene maintenance varies greatly. Several factors that may influence a client's hygiene are their social support system, severity of their intoxicant use, frequency of use, and the element of children residing in the home. When necessary, conduct an initial assessment of these hygiene factors at the beginning of treatment, instruct on them, and monitor periodically along the way. If hygiene slips, and notably in a dramatic way, it can be a sign that a relapse is about to occur or has occurred. Prior to the onset of recovery, hygiene level has the potential to be an evolving example of the progression of the use, which can be helpful in breaking through denial.

Exercise

20 minutes of moderate-intensity exercise has the equivalent benefit of antidepressant medications. Therefore, it should come as no surprise that exercise is a great alleviator of PAWS symptoms. Exercise releases endorphins, which are our natural "feel-good" chemical in the brain. Exercise also aids in improving health outcomes on blood pressure, circulation, respiratory function, weight reduction, and muscle growth. Most importantly, as it relates to PAWS, is its ability to reduce and/or release anxiety and emotion in general. All in all, exercise is highly recommended for those in early recovery as one of the tools for emotion management and physical recovery.

However, be warned that no exercise program should be started without the client undergoing a full physical examination, including heart, respiratory, kidney, and liver function tests. Knowing the documented and damaging effects that using has on these and other systems in the body, therapists would be remiss in recommending starting an exercise program without first referring for a medical evaluation of the client.

Nutrition

There is never a more inappropriate time to start a diet than early in the recovery process. As the body and brain have been beaten and abused by alcohol and drug use, healthy eating in line with, or better than, the food pyramid recommendations is essential. The body and brain need the nutrients of protein, healthy carbohydrates, fruits, vegetables, and healthy fat (think avocado) in order to begin and sustain the healing process. It is a common misconception that all addicts are emaciated at the time of their bottoming out. While physical wasting occurs in some addicts and alcoholics, some come into treatment on the obese range of weight after eating nothing but high calorie/high fat diets from fast food or junk food, since these are the cheapest options after blowing all one's money on drugs or alcohol.

Regardless, advocating for balanced nutrition is essential, and any referrals or information sources you can provide are often helpful. Additionally, clients usually don't eat on any type of schedule. Evaluate eating patterns and nutritional knowledge of your clients, and when appropriate work with them to develop a schedule for meals and meal planning. Food journals are a helpful tool. Please make certain that you are practicing within your scope of competence and expertise. If a client has health conditions complicating a simple meal plan, refer the client to a registered dietician or their primary care physician for follow-up care.

Sleep

The use of intoxicants has profound effects on the ability (or lack thereof) to sleep. Hypersomnia and insomnia are common side effects of any substance use. As one comes down off a high from alcohol or another substance (notably stimulants), people often desperately wish to sleep but are unable to actually fall asleep. Using intoxicants commonly occurs at night, although this is not a foregone conclusion (remember the Golden Rule: always ask). As such, healthy sleep routines are often a mystery to clients in recovery, with prior routines lost in the insane using schedule. To complicate matters, some clients never learned a sleep routine, even as a child.

While some of us were blessed to have parents that put us to bed at the same time every night and woke us at the same time every morning, this is generally not the experience of clients with addictive disorders. Considering that there is a genetic component attached to addiction, chances are if you have an addiction, one if not both of your parents may too. Given that tidbit of information, it's a pretty safe guess that some clients may not have had the best teachers of sleep routines, or were ever taught healthy sleep hygiene.

So what is meant by sleep hygiene? Here are recommendations for clients in early recovery:

- *Go to bed at the same time every night.* This includes weekends until a sleep pattern has been formed and maintained (usually 1—2 months).
- *Go to bed, even though you may not feel tired.* Eventually your body and brain adjust and release melatonin around the same time every night to help you feel sleepy.
- *Get up at the same time every morning.* Again, weekends are included until a sleep pattern has been formed and maintained (usually 1—2 months).
- *Get up, even though you may have slept poorly the previous night and are tired.*
- *Avoid napping during the day as much as possible.* If necessary, take one 15 to 20 minute power nap only.

- *No caffeine or energy drinks 8 hours before bedtime.* 12-Step meetings are notorious for having ample supplies of coffee available. Educate the client that even decaffeinated products have caffeine in them. Suggest water as a healthier option.

- *No sugar products 4 hours before bedtime.* For example, no ice cream, pastries of any kind, candy, or juice drink that is high in sugar.

- *No large meals 3 hours before bedtime.* Although many clients claim this helps them fall asleep, it does nothing for them in terms of a sound sleep. Eating a large meal before bedtime results in all of that energy releasing itself in restless sleep.

- *Stop drinking liquids about an hour before bedtime.* A full bladder equals interrupted sleep.

- *No smoking at least an hour before bedtime.* Nicotine raises blood pressure and heart rate—not the best thing when you are trying to slow down for sleep.

- *No heavy exercise 4 hours before bedtime.* Exercise gets the body (and brain) moving long after the workout ends. Stretching is a good bedtime exercise to do to release tension and unwind. Yoga and meditation—even better.

- *No computer, television, or video games an hour before bedtime.* Although the history channel may provide restful subjects, commercials are notorious for loud sounds, flashing scenes, and pressured voices. Explore activities that do not entail high stimulation—such as easy crossword puzzles or word searches, journaling, reading, playing solitaire (with cards, not computer), sketching, and coloring.

- *Mind your medicine.* A thorough review of the client's medications may reveal that they are hampering the sleep cycle. For example, some HIV drugs are notorious for causing vivid dreams and restless sleep. If appropriate, and if there exists a sharp interference with sleep, some physicians will move medications from a nighttime to daytime administration schedule. If a client is prescribed medicine for sleep, instruct clients to take the sleep medication at the same time every night. It is best to start anywhere between a half hour and an hour before bedtime. Once they know how quickly the medicine takes hold and when they can expect the onset of drowsiness, together you can plan the best time for bed.

- *Sleep medications.* Physicians and psychiatrists not familiar with substance abuse often prescribe clients medications for sleep that are addictive or cause rebound insomnia once they are stopped. Some clients ask for these sleep medications as they know that they can create an effect like a drug high. If utilized on a short-term basis and the client takes the medication as prescribed, this may not pose any long-term problems. However, frequently they are prescribed on a longer-term basis without good instruction for their use. A good addictionologist will have alternative choices for sleep medications besides those which pose abuse or dependency risks.

- *Make certain that the room is dark.* If the client is unable to get a sufficient level of darkness, suggest wearing an eye mask.

- *Make certain the house is quiet.* Assess whether it is feasible for those living with your client to have a set time when the house quiets and darkens.

- *Stop all activities in bed beside sleep and sex.* The bed should be used only for those two purposes. In doing so, the brain and body gets trained to know that only two things happen there and begins to respond accordingly.

- *Remove the television from the bedroom.* If someone needs noise to fall asleep, have them get a noise machine with a timer. Our brains are processing information when we sleep, whether we are conscious of it or not. Our ears still hear, our eyes still notice the light fluctuations, and our mind notices it all.
- *Keep the temperature cooler rather than warmer.* Most say 65 to 68 degrees is a good temperature range for sleep. Your body heats up when it sleeps so keeping the room cool aids sleep.

Those entering an inpatient detoxification or treatment unit are fortunate. Those treatment settings have structures in place that allow clients to get a jump start on resetting these self-care behaviors. Sleep times, meals, medication distribution, and exercise are all scheduled to be at or around the same time every day. This is done so that when the client is discharged from inpatient treatment, these early habits have already been thoroughly practiced with the hope that their body and brain is sufficiently conditioned to follow the same schedule at home.

THE BATTLE BEGINS FOR CLIENTS AS THEY ENTER RECOVERY

The first year of sobriety is often the most challenging for those recovering from substance dependence. When considering everything involved in resetting a way of life, this makes perfect sense. However, most of the general public believe that recovery is as simple as a person not using their preferred intoxicant(s). "Just stop. Why is that so hard?" "All you have to do is not drink. Everyone and their mother can do that; why can't you?" The client's support network is often unaware of the reality that we are not just asking them to stop using. We are asking the substance dependent to think and behave in ways that are completely foreign to what has become *the norm* for them. Although we have reviewed some of these essential changes in previous chapters, it is necessary to review them again *as a whole,* in order to accurately paint the picture to show where the majority of clients first begin their path to sobriety.

Sever Contact with All Using People, Places, and Things

Clients need to avoid triggers, especially during the earliest phase of treatment. Could you leave your friends behind and never speak to them again? Leave your neighborhood and home? Avoid the areas of town you enjoy the most? Change jobs? Sever contact with your family? Never again participate in your stress-relieving fun activities? Remember when we flipped the script and asked you to envision plunging into the world of substance dependence? How to obtain the drugs? Use the drugs? Where to go and what to do? Know the social norms of substance dependent people? This is the equally strange world that your client faces when they take their first steps into sobriety. Most definitely, they are a fish out of water.

We ask our clients to remove themselves from everything that they know, and then ask them to successfully function and operate in a world without the requisite skills. It is a wonder that people with substance dependent histories achieve sobriety at all! It also underscores why so many of our clients "fail" to leave behind drugs and alcohol on their first attempt. Just as we would have difficulty abandoning our world with all of its familiarity and support, and attempt to function in a community that we know nothing about—so our clients are faced with the same struggle.

Form New Sober Support System (Without Sober Social Skills)

In the cutthroat world of substance dependence, you are only as good as the amount of cash or intoxicants you have. The addictive lifestyle is rife with the mentality of "what can you do for me?" Social skills are skewed toward the antisocial. Remember, this does not mean that the client has antisocial personality disorder; rather, they have adapted coping skills for surviving addiction. For instance, there is very little interest in sharing intoxicants, unless there is a corresponding trade-off: sex, companionship, ability to get the drug later when they run out, and sabotaging a person's recovery, to name a few. In order to keep sober people involved in their lives from finding out about their using, clients learn to be deceitful. Some only know how to be the life of the party when their intoxicant has lowered their inhibitions and, without intoxication, they live in isolation. In the world of the convoluted reality produced by the intoxicants, connection with another is meaningful only as it relates to the use itself.

Not many of these social skills work very well when trying to form friendships and relationships in a sober environment. In order to work, sober relationships often require a mutual exchange, honesty, vulnerability, and meaningful communication. All these wonderful qualities have a difficult time emerging if there is not a strong core self that can weather rejection and hurt. Substance use has its roots in adolescence, the key time to form identity and further development of social skills. Intoxicant use interrupts this process and slows down this developmental stage, shifting behaviors toward the antisocial spectrum. Later, when individuals become sober, many come to realize that their development more or less stopped at the point that they developed their dependence. Newly sober, this individual is faced with progressing through the developmental stages, sometimes with a 10 or 20 year delay.

Think and Behave Opposite to Their Usual Practice

So much of the thinking and behavior of the substance dependent mind is centered on one thing: ensuring the likelihood of using again. This often entails a lot of impulsive, compulsive, and manipulative behavior. When someone has overlearned addictive networks in the brain that are the size of a redwood tree, and their learned recovery network is the size of a sapling, changing thought and behavior patterns is difficult. This is why it is difficult for clients to alter, and why a therapist can repeatedly feel frustrated when patients consistently turn back to old behaviors and thought patterns.

Again, remember that it is often exasperating for us to change the simplest of our habits or to establish a new routine. For example, even changing our bedtime by an hour at daylight savings time can take a couple of days or weeks to adjust to the new sleep schedule. This same difficulty applies for eating habits, exercise routines, positive thinking, or basically any change at all. What we wish to create takes energy, and forcing ourselves to fight against the impulse to return to our old ways can be exhausting. Now imagine that clients are asked to change on a *global scale* on entering into sobriety. They do not have the luxury of changing one thing at a time.

Experience Feelings from Consequences of Using (with No or Few Emotional Management Skills)

It is a terrible day when you wake up stone cold sober and begin to face the damage you wrought both to yourself and others during your using days. These feelings are further magnified by the affective instability brought on by chronic using and a general lack of coping skills. Now that you are hyperaware and in the midst of experiencing the pain, guilt, shame, sadness, disappointment, anxiety, and despair, the one proven method you know to remove these feelings (using) is unavailable.

Most newly recovering people have a very limited emotional vocabulary. There are several emotions that they readily identify: anxiety, anger, fear, and happiness. What you find is that most newly sober people lump a lot of other emotions into those four listed. Using good questioning and reframing techniques, you can help them expand their emotional vocabulary to better understand their experience. It is helpful to have pictures of emotive faces with emotions listed underneath either in the room or as a handout.

Another task during this period is helping these newly sober clients experience this array of emotions *without doing anything about them except to feel them*. It is magical to watch a person accustomed to medicating their emotions through using experience emotions by tolerating, feeling, and talking about them.

Experience Reality as It Is (Without Distorting It)

One of the main rationales for making substance use permissible is to deny that it is having any impact on you and the systems you are involved with, such as family and work. The ability to warp reality to fit the picture you need in order to continue using is a powerful weapon. So powerful in fact that you can lose a job, half of your body weight, your family, all of your possessions, and still convince yourself that your using is not as bad as everyone else makes it out to be. This is where sober support and therapy play a crucial role—that of an external brain for the recovering person to check the cognitive distortions and introduce more accurate reality testing in perception, judgment, reasoning, and planning for action.

Function as a Rational Person (with Broken Emotion Regulation, Impulse Control, and Anxiety Suppression Systems)

It is easy to forget that you are working with individuals who have sustained some brain injury from using. It is easier still to fall into the trap of translating continued addictive thinking and behaviors as resistance, not wanting recovery enough, not taking recovery seriously, and/or being antisocial. Although this may be a part of the equation, it is rarely the entire formula.

Most of what we see may have a component of ambivalence about recovery, but it has been our experience that more often than not we witness thinking and behavior resulting from an injured brain. Most intoxicants damage parts of the brain responsible for regulating our emotional states, helping us to pause and consider consequences prior to thinking or acting, creating or storing short-term memories, and helping us make sense of the world.

Engage in Sober Fun and Recreation (with a Damaged Pleasure Sensing and Seeking System and a Highly Skewed Experience of What is Pleasurable and Exciting)

From their using, a number of clients are accustomed to the social environment of a bar, rave, nightclub, house party, sex party, or some other high stimulation environment. Going to a meeting, or worse yet, a sober party, is going to feel like we sat them down in an empty room with chopsticks as the only form of stimulation. It should come as no surprise that your recovery clients are going to have a highly skewed sense of what "exciting" is to them. This makes finding enjoyable recreation or social activities a challenge.

On the other side of the equation are clients who spent their using time isolated and alone. Their pleasure was often derived solely from the using and therefore an empty room with chopsticks is going to feel like a wild nightclub. Finding enjoyable activities are challenging for the opposite reasons, in the latter case titrating the client up slowly to the tolerance of stimulation. Clients are at particular risk of skewed pleasure if their isolation at home entailed online sexual activities (mobile apps, web-based chat rooms, sex sites, pornography sites, etc.). Sobriety is often challenged by the memory of these behaviors and activities as they have the potential to trigger using thoughts.

Piecing Together the Harsh Reality of Recovery

In order to achieve sobriety, we ask clients to give up everyone associated with their using (friends, family, romantic partners) or risk being triggered. We ask them to give up everywhere that they went to use their substance (parties, bars, parks, their homes, family homes). We ask them to give up activities and things associated with their using (paraphernalia, glassware, furniture, web chat/Internet sites). We ask them to give up the incredible feeling of being high. We ask them to take on all of the responsibilities they have been avoiding with their use. We ask them to interact and survive in a sober world with social skills suited for the world of addiction. We ask them to think, feel, and behave in a measured and controlled fashion with a malfunctioning brain. We ask them to embrace a world of ordinary living, with their old world of excitement and thrill a moment's notice away. We ask them to do this while they are lost, confused, beaten down, scared, and suffering from the physical and psychological effects of withdrawal. Is it any wonder at all why clients relapse?

The first year of therapy must ultimately have in its sights at all times one thing: sobriety. As your alcohol-consuming clients hear in AA meetings: "The only thing you need to do right now is not have that first drink." Upon entering sobriety, the client's life is generally a mess. That lifestyle of drama is addictive, even if painful; an exciting alternative to the "boring" world of recovery. It is no surprise then that clients toss many interesting and mouth-watering bones for us to fetch in therapy. While important, the enticing tidbits of information about past trauma, psychological distress, dysfunctional relationships, most recent family drama, and so forth, are often an effort to avoid talking about the steps they need to take in order for recovery to succeed. It is not so exciting to talk about planning structure into an upcoming weekend, identifying triggers, creating a budget or financial restitution plan, or one of the many other methodical topics on the mechanics of recovery.

Beware the red herrings! "I know you [the therapist] want to talk about this party I want to go to this weekend, but first I have been having lots of thoughts of abuse by my father." "That's not alcohol on my breath; I just used mouthwash prior to coming here. Speaking of which, I have been so badly depressed this week that I felt suicidal!" "I know I used again, but you'll understand once I tell you what they did to me at work. It was unbelievable!" These are all actual comments made by clients in therapy. After falling for the bait innumerable times, we learned that clients are best served by keeping our eyes on the prize—sobriety.

12-Steps and its attendant Program (i.e., sponsors, meetings, and fellowship) and designed as a step-wise guide to change, embedded in an environment to support and assist the individual to discover and embrace that change. Therapists and counselors can play a key role in helping the client as they progress through that process. You may have set the stage in prerecovery, but the real work begins with the Program's Step One.

STEP ONE: WE ADMITTED WE WERE POWERLESS OVER (INSERT INTOXICANT)—THAT OUR LIVES HAD BECOME UNMANAGEABLE

Key Concepts

There is a lot of misconception about what Step One means (and does not mean), especially for people being introduced to 12-Steps for the first time. The most common belief is that the concept of powerlessness means that they are helpless people who are unable to take care of themselves in any fashion. That is not what Step One means. Quite the contrary, there is a great deal of empowerment in this Step. For a 12-Step program, powerlessness is the point where a person dependent on substances becomes powerless over their intoxicant(s)—at the point of ingestion/administration. When that ingestion/administration occurs, the phenomenon of craving begins. No amount of ingesting/administering feels like enough, and the end point of the use is unpredictable. The interruption of the use is usually through outside forces, not the person's own willpower. Therefore, what Step One is saying is that until you have the first sip or hit, you remain powerful in your choice to not pick the intoxicant for use at all.

The concept of powerlessness has a second facet to it. Namely, once you have crossed that threshold of powerlessness due to the phenomenon of craving, you can never again regain that ability to regulate your using for any sustainable time. As an example, a substance-dependent person may begin using their intoxicant again after a period of sobriety. To their surprise, initially they are able to regulate their use even though they feel that craving to use become increasingly powerful. Whether quickly or gradually, the person eventually loses the ability to stop their using and they have a moment when their resolve slips. The craving for more is too powerful to overcome. Step One says that the person cannot control their use. The only power they have over their addiction is to not use.

That leads us to the second part of Step One: the unmanageability of their lives while engaged in active substance dependence. How an individual describes or experiences unmanageability due to their addiction varies from person to person. Each person has a different threshold of when their lives feel out of control and unmanageable. Unmanageability often comes into awareness when the addiction begins to move into areas of a person's life that they desperately tried to keep separate from their use. Work, family, spouses/partners, children, money short-ages, and run-ins with the law are some of the areas that tend to raise awareness that the person is losing control, despite attempts to reassert control. The user tries everything to stop the slide into unmanageability, including the implementation of antisocial behavior and even efforts to cut back or stop the use. However, due to the phenomenon of craving and the inability to regulate the use once started, unmanageability is always around the corner. Attempts to manage their use fail. Efforts to avoid consequences fail.

Although it doesn't formally appear anywhere in the Steps, the final concept within Step One concerns the concept of surrender. There is a great deal of misunderstand-ing about the meaning of surrender. Surrendering is not about ceding your power or control—it is about redirecting it. Instead of pouring all of your energy and efforts into controlling your intoxicant use once started—that very thing that you are power-less over—you can surrender that fight. It is the very measure needed to break denial; the idea and belief that I choose to surrender the hope that I will one day be able to use intoxicants successfully. In essence, it is the admission of the need for help. Once I realize that all of my energy and efforts will fail in controlling my use, I can redirect my energy and efforts toward stopping myself from having my first hit or sip of my intoxicant of choice. This is where I have immense control and ability to change. I can also move outside of the isolation of my using and ask for help. In effect, the clients have to surrender to the idea that they can, in fact, control their lives.

A client summed it up nicely many years ago. He said, "I love heroin. I love how it makes me feel. What it does isn't the problem. The problem is that once I start I can't stop. I'll slam it until my life is empty. No friends, no family, no work, no health, no me."

Key "Bumper Sticker" Sayings

The Program relies on multiple sayings or "bumper stickers" that sum up impor-tant aspects of the Steps. These often simplify complex concepts in ways that are easier for a recovering individual to retain and apply. Here is a selection of some of the sayings that are key to the first Step:

"Under Every Bottom Is a Trap Door." A powerful reminder to not be compla-cent about recovery; you can always sink lower, lose more, and ultimately reach death with every use.

"Easy Does It." This is a reminder for clients to be gentle with themselves during their early days in recovery. They are making the best of a very challenging situation. Similar to Rome, their recovery won't be built in a day.

"One Day at a Time." The quintessential saying at Step One; similar to that of "Easy Does It." Out of all the bumper stickers, this is perhaps the most central con-cept of all at this point in the recovery process. It reminds clients that all they need to focus on in their recovery is keeping sober just for today. Tomorrow's stressors, challenges, and triggers will be waiting tomorrow; no need to bring them into today when you cannot do anything about them.

"It Works if You Work It." It is a reminder that recovery doesn't happen unless you actively practice recovery itself. The sentiment is that if you are not feeling that 12-Steps is working for you, you probably are not working the Program.

"Keep Coming Back." Many want instant results for anything and everything. This can make the initial phases of recovery difficult to sustain. "Keep coming back" is an encouragement and a promise that if the person sticks with recovery, they will see and feel results.

"We Are Only as Sick as Our Secrets." Next to "One Day at a Time," nothing is more applicable to the principle of recovery and 12-Steps as rigorous honesty. It is a warning to all; the secrets you keep move you closer to standing over that trapdoor.

"Walk Slowly and Carry a Big Book." The slogan speaks for itself. Similar to "Easy Does It," it reminds newly sober people to pace their recovery, and never leave home without your recovery sources of strength.

"Sick and Tired of Being Sick and Tired." This saying reminds members of a key reason many chose sobriety: the exhaustion of the lifestyle of substance use or any other routine/pattern that causes distress.

A.B.C. (Accept, Begin, Continue). A simple slogan to remind the newly recovered the simple steps to overcoming a problem. You have to accept something is wrong, in order to begin work, which then, beyond starting it, has to continue for it to be successful.

B.A.T.H. (Behavior, Attitude, Thinking, Habits). The core components in need of change for recovery to happen. Also a quick assessment for daily living to ensure each area is progressing toward sobriety versus the old antisocial adaption.

C.H.A.N.G.E.D. (Choosing Honesty Allows New Growth Each Day). Remaining honest with your intentions helps guide you to working on the vulnerable areas in your recovery program. It also pairs up with the slogans "telling on my addiction (or disease)," and "we are only as sick as our secrets."

I.S.M.'s (I Sabotage Myself). A clever saying that has been pronounced "eye-sms" rather that "isms" in an effort to remind people that it isn't the outside forces (like isms—racism, sexism, etc.) that create relapse, it's your own.

N.O.W. (No Other Way). A reminder that they are in 12-Steps for a very specific reason; they tried "every which way and Sunday" to control their using and failed. The only other way is go back to using.

S.O.B.E.R. (Staying Off Booze, Enjoying Recovery—or—Son Of a Bitch, Everything's Real). Two very different takes on sobriety. Usually, members enter 12-Steps with the latter feelings about being sober, yet as time progresses in their sobriety the former takes hold.

W.I.S.D.O.M. (When Into Self, Discover Our Motives). This is the belief that egocentricity erupts for nefarious reasons, often to go back out using. If you are able to pause and reflect why you are defensive or egocentric at that moment by analyzing your vulnerability through your motives, you have the ability to correct it and ultimately avoid relapse.

Therapeutic Issues Within Step One

Admitting powerlessness taps into the emotions of fear, loss, and vulnerability for the client. Acceptance of powerlessness requires that they dispel their illusion of predictability and control over intoxicant use. It requires a client to admit that their multiple master plans of controlled using, the plans that they over and over staked their life on, have done nothing more than keep the status quo at best or degenerated their life at worst. It creates feelings of defeat, dejection, and loss. It requires them to have to admit that what they claimed was cleverness and righteous indignation was actually stubbornness and manipulation. In arriving at these conclusions, they admit that they are out of answers, and have to open themselves up to ask for and receive help. Perhaps even more profoundly, they admit that the battle to control their using is truly lost. The only sane choice is to stop using.

"We admitted we were powerless over (insert intoxicant)."

One of the most frequent events that occur in first-time attempts at sobriety is relapse. There are many determinants that influence the probability of relapse, but we find one uncannily frequent reason trumps them all. That one factor, towering over all others, is that *people in early recovery frequently overestimate their recovery skills and underestimate the power and influence of their triggers or their ability to effective manage them.* This leads to their taking unnecessary risks with their recovery while also not adequately preparing or knowing how to cope with those risks. It is like a knight going into battle with only some armor or weapons. Sure, skill may help dodge swings and land blows, but the less armored the knight or the weaker the weapons, the less likely the knight will come out of the battle unscathed. Clients can be very poorly prepared to cope with triggers and cravings, especially when these are so strong that relapse occurs immediately and without forethought.

Kira, a 22-year-old college student, was 2 months into her recovery for prescription opiate (pain-killer) dependence. She was attending 12-Step meetings daily, spoke twice a day with her sponsor, and was working actively on Steps 1, 2, and 3. She created a comprehensive list of triggering people, places, and things, and was active in avoiding them all, and implementing new support networks. She was particularly successful in making new friends on her campus. In effect, she was following a very strong formula for maintaining sobriety.

One night, Kira went to study in the apartment of a new classmate in her biology class. She was having a sinus headache and asked for ibuprofen to help. Her roommate told her there was some in the medicine cabinet, and to help herself. When she opened up the cabinet, a bottle of Vicodin greeted her. "I don't know what happened. I saw the bottle, and the last thing I knew I was popping a handful into my mouth. I was like 'Noooooo!' but I couldn't stop myself. I didn't even think about it, I just did it, I swallowed them. I stuffed some more in my pocket and made an excuse that I had to go and left. I was lucky that I didn't take the whole bottle. After I used all of the pills, I felt so guilty and ashamed. I called my sponsor and we met at a meeting. I want to be clean, that just caught me totally off-guard." The therapist responded, "I am glad that you are back giving sobriety another try. It is important that we learn from this event, and it sounds like it is safer to not go into people's medicine cabinets, even if they give you permission. I know this differs from 12-Step, but for you it sounds like some triggers right now are too powerful for you to resist. You are powerless against them, at least for now." Kira replied, "Yeah, I know you warned me about this but I didn't believe you. Okay, I'm adding medicine cabinets to my trigger list. How do I go into bathrooms now without checking them for pills?"

As important as it is to keep in alignment with 12-Steps about the concept of powerlessness, it is equally important to provide education to your client about the potential of their addictive neuro-circuitry overriding their sober willpower (thus becoming powerless), if they encounter a trigger. Clients at this phase are highly vulnerable to these fast-burn relapses. However, it is not a foregone conclusion that if a client encounters a trigger that they will relapse. But, the earlier the client is in sobriety the more vulnerable they are to this automatic reaction to a trigger. Again, this is due to their diminished internal and external resources and skills for sobriety.

Unfortunately, we do not know precisely why some clients are able to take more risks in early recovery and not relapse. Generally, the more cautious a client is in exposing themselves to their triggers in early recovery, the larger the likelihood of avoiding relapses. This often seems to relate back to how fully a client has accepted the concepts of unmanageability and powerlessness. As clients more completely accept that use is intolerable and uncontrollable for them, they seem more willing to make the extreme sacrifices that increase the chances for them to remain sober. (Notice how relative this statement is. There are no absolutes and no way to predict what changes a specific client needs to make to guarantee that they remain sober. Our knowledge here is very incomplete. If nothing else, this reality should remind therapists of their own need for humility.)

Another obstacle to accepting that one is powerless is the denial defense, which we covered in previous chapters. The focus was primarily on how denial operates at the end stage of using, prior to the decision of recovery. Not surprisingly, the defense of denial does not just go away once the client determines they are ready to give sobriety a chance. Denial in sobriety can operate stronger than when the client was in active addiction. One form of denial that challenges the premise of Step One is the selective recall of only good times while using. Gone are the memories of the horrible emotional and physical crash from their last use, or their overwhelming feelings of guilt, shame, and embarrassment at where their addiction took them. If not constructed early on to include healthy experiences of fun and adventure, life in recovery can seem awfully dull compared to the thrills and spills of addiction. This is a powerful motivator to rationalize giving using another try because, "this time I know how to stop."

We recommend that the therapist combat denial and its related cognitive distortions by exploring with the client the many ways the client demonstrated both powerlessness over their using and the unmanageability that was the result. In this route, the therapist adopts the Recorder of Events role to remind the client how their life prior to sobriety was the epitome of Step One. We find it very useful to also utilize the technique of "playing the tape through," in order to have the client examine the result of returning to using. In these cases, the client often wants to put their best foot forward in deducing the outcome. We recommend then moving into the Devil's Advocate role to break through the denial by outlining a worst case scenario. Let's look at a clinical exchange of these techniques with Step One integrated into the example:

> Martin, a 42-year-old self-employed man, had smoked marijuana since he was 16 years old. His use pattern evolved from monthly in his teens, to weekly use in his 20s and into his mid-30s, and finally to nonstop use. Martin, now four months clean, has been involved with Marijuana Anonymous, attending meetings four times a week, and working with a sponsor. The therapist noted that in the past two weeks, Martin's stories in therapy predominantly centered on a theme of discontentment and dissatisfaction. Martin opened the session.

Martin: "I was reading on the Internet that pot isn't addictive. The more I thought about it . . . I guess, I question whether I just bought into the 'just say no' hype I heard when I was a kid. I mean pot's not that bad, and it really made me relax and have a ton of fun with my friends. I know we agreed on me staying clean for six months, but sorry Doc, I don't think I would have a problem if I started smoking again."

Therapist: "I see. You're right, you did have a lot of laughs with your friends watching movies and hanging out. It did sound like a lot of fun. But if I recall correctly, that was a long time ago (beginning Recorder of Events role). The past several years, you *haven't been able to exert enough willpower to stop using* (powerless) at all, even for a day. Your use was completely *unpredictable as to when it would end* (powerless), and it was rarely your choice when it did. I may be wrong, but I thought your use ended when you either *ran out of pot, your wife threatened to leave you, or your sales at your company went down so low it threatened your ability to pay your mortgage* (unmanageable)."

Martin: "Sure, it caused some problems back then, but I think I can handle it now. I'm not as depressed or anxious. You taught me those breathing techniques and relaxation. I don't think I will need it as much. I just want to have fun again."

Therapist: "I know that recovery has been a lot of work for you. It hasn't been easy assuming all of the responsibilities your wife and employees turned back over to you. I also want to acknowledge your efforts to take up basketball again to try to regain that sense of fun in your life, and I am sorry it hasn't lived up to your expectations."

Martin: "Thanks for recognizing that."

Therapist: "Of course. Let's run an exercise for a moment. You already gave the best case scenario of what would happen if you started again. Tell me what the worst case scenario looks like." (Devil's Advocate role and "playing the tape through").

Martin: "Um, well, I suppose it would look like it did when I first came to see you."

Therapist: "And what was that like?" (Devil's Advocate)

Martin: "Well, *my wife was threatening divorce. I couldn't make payroll nor did we have enough to pay the mortgage. Over time, I burnt through all of our savings on drugs. I was depressed and hopeless. I would hit a panic, if I was running low and couldn't reach my dealer (unmanageable).*"

Therapist: "Yes, that sounds accurate (Recorder of Events). I also remember that you were pulled over by the police while high. Even though they didn't recognize that you were high and released you, that scared you so much you decided to stop using. Martin, I understand your desire to want to use again and be successful at it. My question to you is, what if you're wrong? How much are you willing to lose if you find out you are still powerless over your ability to stop using once you start?" (Devil's Advocate)

It is certainly a struggle for Martin, as well as many other substance dependent people, to admit that they are not in control of their using. This is especially true for those who never hit a bottom, or the pain of their last withdrawal or detox has faded. The memory of those experiences where they did have control of their using can be a powerful lure back. It is a strange phenomenon, the power of substance dependence. To have such a compelling pull on people is remarkable and terrifying; to be able to lure them back to using time and time again, while systematically dismantling their life.

It is often the testing and retesting of their powerlessness that eventually brings active substance abusers to finally admit, through sheer failure, that they are unable to control their using. That is not to say that the wonderment of controlled using goes away, and the underlying premise of Step One is something that therapists need to consistently readdress in therapy. The flirtation of the idea of controlled using can provide enough fodder for even the most solid of recovery programs to falter.

This does provide a difficult place for therapists to stand. None of us have the power or ability to decisively identify whether or not clients may or may not be able to go back and use successfully after a period of sobriety. As it is today, there is no psychological test or medical verification tool that says "You are an addict." This conclusion is determined by the clinician's best judgment based on the current diagnostic criteria and the client's behavior. In addition, 12-Step's belief of "once an addict, always an addict" has not proved to be true for everyone. This conundrum places therapists in a position to make a judgment call to either support a client's experiment to go back out and try to control their using, or not. Both positions carry risk for the client and the therapeutic relationship.

If a therapist supports a client's effort to go out and try using again and the client fails, the therapist's credibility on addiction expertise can be called into question by the client and the client's support system. If the therapist does not support a client's choice to go out and try using again, and the client does so and succeeds, the therapist's credibility again is called into question. Additionally, the client may view the therapist as having a "12-Step agenda" or be biased against drug and alcohol use. If a therapist does not support a client's choice to go out and try using again and the client does so and fails, the client may be too ashamed or humiliated to come back to the therapist and admit failure.

You can resolve this dilemma by letting the client decide. It is not your place to make the decisions for the consumer and it would take great hubris to argue that you should make such choices for a client. No, the job of a therapist is to help the client view their lives with as much clarity as possible, allowing the clients themselves to make the best informed decisions. This includes allowing clients to make decisions that run counter to what you might think or know is the better choice. However, that doesn't mean your work ends there. From this perspective, the discussion with Martin could go in a very different direction. After a lengthy discussion of his prior powerlessness and unmanageability, Martin could arrive at a conclusion to return again to using. If that is his decision, then alter your treatment position to reflect one more consistent with a client in prerecovery instead of one focusing on sobriety.

A final challenge to the concept of powerlessness in therapy is when the client identifies being out of control with one substance, but not others. This is heard most often with drug users and their relationship to alcohol. "But Doc, I never got out of control with drinking!" The rumination to explore alternative intoxicant use generally indicates a failure to fully accept Step One. It continues the client's fantasy to still have all of the pleasures from an intoxicant without the costs. Regardless, the therapist should assess the function of the alternative intoxicant in order to evaluate whether there is a skill set that is absent and in need of development. Is the desire to use again due to feeling anxious and insecure at social events? Are they bored and need recreational activities or new hobbies? Is it a method to cover up anger or resentment at home?

Once you are able to work out the client's intention or the desired outcome behind the wish for the alternative intoxicant, then you can present the client with an acceptable substitution. For instance, this type of intervention might go something like this:

"I understand your desire to want to drink when you are out with your coworkers. I also hear, and believe, that you previously had no problem managing drinking, before you became dependent on cocaine. I'm not convinced that you will be successful in your attempt to moderate your drinking, and it seems like an awfully big risk to take. You've already had some struggles with urges to use, it'll be a lot harder to resist them if you've had a drink or two and they turn into full-blown cravings. Let me run something by you and see what you think. It seems from your description that you feel very self-conscious of your coworker's reaction to your not drinking, so how about we strategize some ways to help you cope during these events first? If they still don't seem to alleviate the problem, we can talk further about introducing alcohol. Sound like a deal?"

It has been our experience that most clients turn to alternative intoxicants due to a skill deficit that is left unaddressed. Addressing the problem by robustly building up coping skills usually resolves the issue. However, there are those who simply desire to use an alternative intoxicant that they once used successfully.

Individuals may accept powerlessness over one class of substances (sedative vs. stimulant vs. hallucinogen, etc.) but not another. Finding out whether this powerlessness is truly demonstrated, however, presents challenges on multiple fronts. There are two very large risks to consider. First, does the use of the alternative intoxicant become out of control? Second, once under the influence of the alternative intoxicant, does the loss of judgment and impulse control lead them back to their intoxicant of choice?

These risks need to be carefully weighed with the client prior to the initiation of experimentation of the alternative intoxicant. It is often helpful to remind the client that their controlled use of the alternative intoxicant was prior to their developing dependence on their intoxicant of choice. In short, the addictive networks in their brain may preclude sustained controlled use of the alternative intoxicant, even if it is a different class of intoxicant. Also, the alternative intoxicant may bring about old associations of people, places, and things making them more susceptible to falling back into their old using patterns. If the experiment fails, welcome to the second half of Step One.

"—That our lives had become unmanageable"

We addressed the concept of powerlessness as evidenced in Step One. Now, we turn our attention to the latter half of the Step; the recognition and acceptance of unmanageability. In exploring this facet of Step One, once again denial has an uncanny way of initially blocking, and then gradually creeping back into a newly sober person's awareness of the full extent of the unmanageability in their lives. "After all, it wasn't that bad was it?" Thus, without acknowledging the full impact of their substance use and with the denial ever present, people in early recovery have ample rationale to go back to their intoxicant.

In addressing unmanageability, the therapist adopts several roles to help the client recognize the need for sobriety based on the wreckage accumulated through using; wreckage that impacted both themselves and their support systems. It is imperative to remember that this is *not* the appropriate time to process the wreckage or encourage the client to begin making amends or atonements for it. First, from a clinical perspective, most newly recovered people have few and poorly developed coping skills, insufficient emotional regulation, and poor impulse control to effectively manage major emotional turmoil. Second, the work in Step One is solely to bring about an understanding for the need to be sober. Later Steps are designed for the systematic process in which people in recovery accept responsibility for that wreckage and make amends. In exploring this facet of Step One, denial remains the main culprit in successfully completing this work. It is important to reiterate this point; denial has an uncanny way of both blocking, and gradually creeping back into a newly sober person's awareness of the full extent of the unmanageability in their lives.

During their early recovery days, most people who attempt sobriety do so for no other reason than that disrupted areas of their life became impossible to ignore any longer. Economic problems, strained family relationships, poor work performance, failing health, skirmishes with the law, and increased risk-taking behaviors are often easily rattled off as problem areas where unmanageability is acutely felt. Rarely is the reason to stop because they hate feeling high! However, even with this awareness there may be more sensitive areas that the client is attempting to deny. There may be a good reason for this denial, and requires careful evaluation from you about the best timing to expose this material to a client's awareness.

One of the litmus tests to use is the question, "Does the event, if left unaddressed in the immediate future, provide the client with a compelling rationale to resume using?" This question is mainly used to assess whether the denial or minimization of impact grants the person in recovery the luxury of keeping a path to relapse open. Here is a case example to highlight this test:

> Miguel, a 62-year-old alcoholic, first entered into recovery after 35 years of drinking. During that time, he was divorced four times, lost 15 jobs, had strained relationships with his seven children, and was nearly losing his current job, despite having only three years left until retirement. He completed a medical detoxification from alcohol through an inpatient stay, and was referred for outpatient therapy and 12-Step involvement. Miguel, now three weeks sober, was attending daily morning meetings of 12-Step before work and was working on Step One with his sponsor.

> Miguel was readily able to acknowledge how drinking placed severe stress on his employment. He spoke openly about his wanting to be a better coworker and employee. Additionally, he was able to talk about his current wife's strain of keeping their household together while he was out drinking. Miguel was tearful during his talking about the impact his drinking had on his wife. The therapist responded, "There is a lot of sadness associated with the impact your

using has had on your wife. I can see how reflecting on this is painful. Does thinking about this, or feeling this level of sadness, trigger you to want to use alcohol?" Miguel replied, "No, it's okay. We've been talking about it a lot lately."

The therapist observed that Miguel did not mention the influence his alcohol use had on the strained relationships with his children. "Miguel, you have talked about your wife a great deal, but I haven't heard anything about your children other than that your relationship with them is strained. Is this because of your drinking as well?" Upon inquiring about this, Miguel became defensive, "It has no relationship whatsoever. My ex-wives are to blame for that. They're the ones who poisoned their minds against me." The therapist noticed the anger in his voice, and reflected on what was contained in his chart records, which noted that relapses into drinking were commonly triggered by his drinking routine after work with friends and after attempts to contact his estranged adult children.

The therapist determined that, at this time, it was countertherapeutic to introduce discussion of the impact of his drinking on his relationship with his adult children. If this area was addressed immediately, the client was highly affected, possessed few coping skills, and based on past history at risk for relapse. Instead, the therapist refocused efforts on working with the acceptable examples of unmanageability, such as work and his relationship with his spouse to reaffirm his commitment to sobriety. The therapist concurrently charted a treatment plan to build emotional management skills for anger and sadness, in order to incorporate discussion in the near future of these strained relationships as a product of his using.

Another pertinent question that is highlighted in the case of Miguel is, "If this event is brought to the client's awareness, does he have the emotional fortitude and coping skills necessary to manage the associated feelings (guilt, shame, etc.) without relapsing?" As you saw with Miguel, pressing forward and bringing more awareness about how his drinking negatively impacted the relationships with his children was ill-advised. Miguel was not even three week's sober at this point and still too emotionally labile from the Post-Acute Withdrawal Syndrome to address his anger. Additionally, Miguel is already struggling with threats of loss from his current wife and employer and those are sufficient enough to engage him in recovery. This allows for a titration of losses to evolve in therapy to coincide with the building of coping skills and the healing to the injured parts of Miguel's brain brought about through using. Overloading a client with all of the impact of their using without having solid coping skills only places the client at greater risk for relapse. These secondary areas become more important as clients develop more coping and emotional regulation skills. Again, the therapist must judge the client's ability to tolerate the effect versus the risk of relapse, if the denial is not worked through.

Another aspect of denial related to Step One is the ability of a client to monitor themselves, their program, and their future risk of relapse. This likely relates back to deficits with executive functioning. These clients typically have difficulties anticipating the consequences of their behavior and evaluating or monitoring themselves. For instance, most clients have a difficult time, especially early in recovery, monitoring the adequacy of their program and signs that they are entering into an area of higher risk. When phrasing this intervention, use the technique of the expert in recovery. For instance, you may say something like, "I notice you're attending fewer meetings lately, you're sleeping less, and you're telling me that you feel more cranky than usual. For some, that means their program is slipping and they're at higher risk of relapse. Does that fit for you?" Clients frequently respond to comments like this with concern, if they begin to see such a self-sabotaging pattern that was previously invisible to them.

Work on Step One does not end once a client shifts to working on the next Step. Instead, Step One tends to be an ongoing process that is best reinforced over and over again as the client moves through sobriety. For those in a 12-Step program, sobriety is achieved and maintained because of the key concepts of Step One: a client cannot control their use; their only choice is total abstinence; and if they return to use, their lives will be unmanageable. Reinforcement of these foundational concepts is a reason that 12-Step meetings focusing on Step One are universally one of the most popular meetings, even among those with long-term sobriety. This is a lesson that those in recovery must hold onto to remain sober.

Toward that end, as clients move forward in treatment, the therapist needs to keep Step One constantly in mind. Always filter the client's material through the lens of each Step, but especially the first. Then reflect back on material that mirrors aspects of Step One, framing it as a process of providing more clarity. During times of crisis and regression, this reframing can be a crucial component to preventing a relapse. Remember, regardless of their stage of recovery, substance dependence is viewed as incurable from within this model. Instead, it requires a recovery process that the person engages with for their lifetime.

Chloe found it a struggle to quit crack. However, after multiple treatments, untold consequences, and many failed starts, she finally seemed to settle into a formula that worked for her. She found a sponsor with whom she bonded. She attended frequent NA (Narcotics Anonymous) meetings and weekly individual counseling. Initially, her treatment focused on her struggles accepting that she had to avoid everything even vaguely connected to her prior use.

At multiple points, her therapist and sponsor struggled with her to help her fully articulate and accept that her drug use was unmanageable and that if she did not avoid all use she would destroy her life. Initially, it was as if every negative consequence of her use was acknowledged with a resistance bordering on resentment. She was ambivalent over leaving her using life and sorely wished she could somehow have found a way to control her crack use. Simultaneously, she did not want to deal with the weight of shame her past life brought to her, and she would be blindsided by seemingly random attacks of cravings that she could not predict. However, with more meetings and Step work she learned to admit to this shame, her cravings became less frequent, and she acknowledged that there was hope for her after all.

As she more fully owned her past life and its attendant shame, the therapist occasionally responded to a poignant admission by reflecting on the extent of the toxic consequences her use brought to her, despite her efforts to somehow control her drug use. Years after she became abstinent, Chloe felt more confident in her sobriety. She had made amends to many individuals that she hurt, sometimes bringing these experiences back into treatment. As before, the therapist again reflected on just how out of control her crack use was and how it ravaged her life. Chloe's response showed none of the resistance that she initially displayed; instead she smiled at the therapist and responded "we both know it."

Although not directly stated in Step One, there are several companion concepts that are rooted in a 12-Step philosophy and ever-present in the meeting rooms. We are going to address these companion concepts for Step One, and you will be referred back to these same concepts when we address Steps Two and Three. These are actionable concepts that make the Steps live.

Willingness: The Key to Success in 12-Steps and Recovery?

The assessment of a 12-Step member's willingness to change is a critical component at each Step and is talked about often in 12-Step meetings. Sponsors and 12-Step members alike assert that willingness is the lodestone of recovery. Recognition of powerlessness or unmanageability is useless unless there is a willingness to do something about it. We agree that willingness has to be a major assessment area and treatment focus in recovery work. Ambivalence about willingness to change is rife in the prerecovery stage, and remains the salient feature in detecting relapse. When clients begin to reject suggestions from sponsors or therapists, it may be an indication that the client is reconsidering their belief in their ability to regulate their use.

A lack of willingness can also indicate a resistance to the oppressive orderliness of recovery and a desire for a return to the more familiar chaotic environment experienced in their substance use lifestyle. A fair number of clinicians have misinterpreted a client's unease with the orderly and accountable lifestyle of recovery as outright resistance. You discover that when you explore a client's unwillingness to follow suggestions, often it is not the suggestions themselves under question but the client's own ambivalence about their ability to succeed and/or the pressure and anxiety they feel from their mounting obligations. Therapists in these instances should focus on skill-building with the client in areas such as anxiety management, time management, and asserting boundaries. Often addressing these areas provides the client with the skills they need to complete their obligations.

Despite what is suggested above, never *prescribe* such things to an unwilling client. You might suggest and assist the client to more fully appreciate their behavior, its consequences, and the underlying motivations for it; but the decision is the client's. Despite a therapist's best efforts, sometimes clients make decisions in opposition to a 12-Step approach—decisions that seem to place them in danger of failing. Many years ago, one of the authors was told, "Sometimes clients are hardheaded. 12-Step Program tells a person how to recover, and sometimes they're just not ready to accept it. They have to write their own program. You have to let those clients try and fail. A lot of them figure out that their way doesn't work and they return to the rooms, now knowing that there's only one way to recovery." We're not ready to invest in such a demanding approach to recovery, but you should be aware that there are many therapists and people in the 12-Step rooms who hold to this philosophy. Simply put, some clients respond to this approach and some do not.

Humility and Ego: The Most Misunderstood and Misused Words in Recovery

At that surrender point, the point of recognizing powerlessness and unmanage-ability, most people come to sobriety with the recognition (however tenuous) that what they have been doing is not working. Their drug of choice has left them with a mess to clean up and no clear way to do it. At this juncture, the person in the midst of pain and suffering is open to learning anything they can in order to allevi-ate that discomfort and misery. This is what is meant when the term "humility" is talked about in 12-Step rooms. Simply put, humility is the willingness to learn. It is a shift away from an egocentric view of oneself and one's world. As recovery progresses and the client begins to feel better, their openness to learning decreases. Their desire to reassert control over their lives, and to feel empowered, shuts down even the most previously open mind. This is the challenge of ego versus humility.

The first hurdle to overcome is the preconception of what is meant by the term "humility." What do you think when you hear this word? Is it a positive associa-tion? Chances are, probably not. Most of us confuse humility with humiliation. The words couldn't be further apart in meaning, but alas, most people associate humilia-tion with humility. You hear this struggle in all sorts of complaints, such as "I don't want to have to grovel to anyone!" "Am I supposed to do whatever my sponsor wants? Where is my say in this?" and "I'm not going to be controlled by anyone." It is important to educate the client on the misinterpretation of humility, and stress that it merely suggests being open to learning and trying new and different things. Once clients are able to understand that they are not ceding any of their power or control (after all, they can refuse anything they wish, whether their therapist or sponsor likes it or not), rather they are empowering themselves in their decision making by considering all alternatives.

How can you know when your client is stuck in their own ego versus humility conflict? Some examples are:

- Being closed off to recovery messages in meetings.
- Claiming they know exactly how to stay clean/sober.
- Stating that they do not need anyone's direct help. Wanting people to support their decisions without question.
- Rejecting outright a sponsor or therapist's suggestions.
- Stating a continued desire to test their recovery by actively seeking triggering people, places, and things.
- Seeing themselves and their problem as somehow special, making them the victim of a unique illness/problem.
- Seeing themselves as better than other addicts/alcoholics.

The last point is one that is particularly prevalent in the prerecovery stage, and also in early recovery as observed when attending a 12-Step meeting. As we discussed in the last chapter, there is a strategic comparative technique employed by those mired in ego, to compare themselves to everyone who is *worse off* than them. Notably absent from their observations is the desire to find people in the rooms who are doing *better than* they are in recovery. This focus allows justification for their substance use to continue, although it is like comparing apples to asphalt. The only true comparative measure that has any accuracy is for the person to compare themselves *to themselves.*

Also discussed in the preceding chapter, no matter how severe the consequences get with a person's addiction, they can always find someone worse off than them, thus justifying that their life is really not all that bad, even though it is ebbing away. We find that once a client directs the comparison inwards to themselves, the desire to maintain the moral high ground gives way. It is not easy for clients to remain in denial and egoism when they have to face their own decline without anyone else to point to in order to make them feel better or superior. This therapeutic moment is to be treated with the utmost care. Rarely is there any efficacy at this point in going for the proverbial jugular. Rather, empathizing with the clients' losses and suffering, and noting the difficulty in honestly putting forth the reality of their situation allows that vulnerability (humility) to be safeguarded. It provides a structure for therapy that demonstrates to the client that the therapy space does not need to be filled with ego and the false/addicted self, and that you do not exploit their honesty or vulnerability. It is helpful to label this for what it is: humility—the openness to learning.

Facilitating Understanding of "Cunning, Baffling, Powerful"

The phrase "cunning, baffling, and powerful" in 12-Step refers to the many ways in which the disease of addiction can subtly move an individual toward the use of their intoxicants, or in the ways that life brings about unexpected temptations and inducements for a person to return to using. This phrase and the manner in which some people in 12-Step speak of addiction is almost by metamorphosing the word: addiction is thought of as an entity separate from the person. In reality, what is being perceived as a separate entity is in fact just the addictive networks in the brain, all of that learned thinking and behavior and altered reward pathways.

As such, therapists need to assist clients to understand that their addiction is simply their own cluster of thoughts and behaviors. There is no separate entity that is creating their urges to use or their obsessive/compulsive thinking. It is only their brain, which given time, sobriety, and their efforts in recovery hopefully repairs and restructures to healthier ways. For those therapists who follow mindfulness approaches, especially third wave behavioral approaches, this perspective is well known.

Relapse and Step One

Step One's Role in Relapse Prevention

Preventing powerlessness. As previously described, understanding powerlessness and practicing it is like understanding what each piece in a chess set does, and believing that knowledge makes you an expert chess player. Conceptually understanding the nature and power of triggers, and yet being willing to give them up, leads to complications in recovery. Therapy should focus on the following areas in the hopes of preventing that first administration of an intoxicant that kicks that powerlessness into high gear. In that vein, it is unrealistic to expect that new sober clients have a comprehensive understanding of what puts their recovery at risk. There are many models for building recovery skills, but the Matrix Model has the best overall structure. It is simple yet comprehensive enough to build a solid foundation (Matrix Institute on Addictions, 2005). That said, we extensively covered triggers in the previous chapter and, not surprisingly, triggers are at the top of the list in this model.

Trigger identification. As we reviewed in the relapse chapter, the first exercise is to identify any people, places, and things that cause the client to think about using, craving use, or actually spur them into action to use. As addiction encourages all-or-nothing thinking, do not just note the triggers that caused actual use. Rather, encourage a more nuanced approach that looks at the level of risks versus absolutes. To start, have the client list their triggers under the four headings: people, places, things, and emotions. After that is completed, have the client rank each trigger based on the likelihood that the trigger results in a relapse. Once completed, it is important that together you create, rank, and plan responses to these triggers. This may be some of the most important work you can accomplish during the very early phases of treatment. Also, remember that this is a living document and it is very worthwhile to periodically review and update it with the client.

To review from Chapter 8, clinicians are encouraged to work actively with the client to begin to systematically eliminate triggers and their attendant risk for relapse. This includes:

- Getting rid of all drug and alcohol paraphernalia, including pipes, ashtrays, mirrors, razor blades, favorite drinking glasses or mugs, matches, lighters, and so forth.
- Avoiding mixers for drinks (including staying away from beverages they would normally mix with the alcohol).
- If the client used in their house, have them rearrange their furniture or repaint a room to break the associations of using in their place.
- If there is a specific piece of furniture that was central in their using, such as a computer desk or favorite chair, encourage them to either get rid of the furniture if they have the means to do so, put the furniture in storage for the time being, or move it into another room where it cannot be used in the same manner.
- A ceremony, spiritual or not, can also be a useful way for a client to move beyond the past and redefine a future meaning for a living space. Clients reported burning smudge sticks, asking for clergy blessings, and planning simple gatherings of other sober people as methods to help disassociate a space with using.

To accomplish these goals first requires the client to reenter their homes. Returning home after their initial decision to become sober can be an especially risky event. Consider the following vignette.

Ivana, who was dependent on a combination of alcohol and amphetamine, most commonly Ritalin, had worked as a retail store manager for ten years. She enjoyed her work and was hoping to work her way up the ladder. One day her district manager made a visit to her store after a night where she had snorted Ritalin and drank alcohol until the early hours of the morning. Her manager commented that she smelled of alcohol, "looked like hell," and this was not the first time she had appeared that way. She was told to either deal with the problem or her manager would.

Ivana was terrified of losing her job. A woman of action, she immediately arranged for a leave from work, flew to the city where her family lived, and admitted herself into a detoxification program. Once she had completed that, Ivana spent the next month at her family's vacation home where she attended a few 12-Step meetings and had several sessions with a substance abuse counselor.

Ivana made a plan to return home, resume work, and to set her life on a new course. Ivana flew back home and arrived back at her apartment.

Upon opening the door, Ivana smelled the alcohol. Looking around her apartment, she immediately spotted a half-consumed liter of vodka, a bottle of Ritalin, a mortar and pestle, a mirror, and a razor blade. Before she was aware of anything, Ivana was inundated by urges to use. She sat down, began drinking the vodka and crushing up a pill. Years later, she would say that it wasn't even a conscious choice. She simply resumed her use.

Homes are commonly filled with an overwhelming number of triggers for the newly recovered. For this reason, clients should not return and clean out their home alone. Most sponsors, even temporary sponsors, are very willing to accompany clients on this task. They are often particularly good at the task because they can think of many more hiding places than the now sober client.

Warn clients that it is common for them to discover some left-over paraphernalia or even drugs/alcohol after they have cleaned the house. Possibly, these items were hidden when the client was very intoxicated or in a blackout and the client cannot even remember hiding them; nor were they discovered during the house cleaning. The item can sit, like a ticking time bomb, waiting to be inadvertently discovered and trigger the client. Such discoveries frequently occur when the client is packing up to move to a new home or when they do a major house cleaning, requiring them to go poking about in the dark corners of their home. Also, warn clients of the potential risk of these discoveries and make plans for how to respond to these discoveries. Often, the best plan is for the client to immediately leave the room or even the home and then for them to call their sponsor or therapist.

Phone numbers and contact lists. When it comes to phone numbers, advocate for the client to completely erase their contact lists and syncing programs. It is not uncommon for clients to delete the numbers of their using friends and dealers only to have them replaced by their backup systems. This removal is best done with a person who is supportive of the client's recovery, in case the client is tempted to make a call while going through and deleting numbers. If necessary, the therapist should spend whole sessions on this process by going through the name of each person, inquiring about their relationship to the client's using, and having the client decide and then delete the number. This becomes a person-by-person assessment of how strongly the client feels triggered by each individual.

Considering the risk, strongly encourage clients to also completely change any phone number(s) that was previously used in the pursuit of their addiction. Clients generally prefer to stop at deleting numbers from their phone. However, this leaves the door wide open for relapse, and directly places the control of recovery in the hands of the dealer and/or using friends. There are very few dealers (although there have been some) who are supportive of the recovery efforts of their former clients and therefore might be induced to not call. More often, though, it is the using friends who miss their compatriot in addiction and work to undermine recovery in order to gain back their using partner. As the 12-Step saying goes, "misery loves miserable company." It is not uncommon for clients to receive texts, phone calls, and phone messages from dealers and using buddies. These can occur weeks, months, and even years after the client became sober. These reminders of their past lives can be especially triggering if they occur when the client is simultaneously struggling with other triggers, cravings, or ambivalence over sobriety.

Few clients welcome the suggestion to change telephone and cell phone numbers. The recommendation is an ordeal (often a very large one) for the client. However, phones play a significant role in the events that can lead many new sober individuals to relapse. Communicate this risk to your clients. Although inadvertent, a client's agreement to take these steps with their phone, and to embrace the ordeal of changing their phone, can be a good barometer of their willingness for recovery.

Changing online relationships and activity. In a similar way to telephones, a person's online activity can become triggering. It may be that the client's online activity was primarily to locate drugs or other users. Or, it may be that when the client got high, they spent time online. Or, maybe the client found sexual partners online and then got high with them. Or, maybe the computer simply became the vehicle that a client used to isolate from others. For these reasons, assess what, if any, connections the clients have between computer use and substance abuse. In effect, what triggering value does the computer hold for the client?

Some computer-based triggers are obvious: chat programs with friend lists where the client stayed connected with dealers or others with whom they used, sex sites where the client found sexual partners to use with, and sex sites where a client masturbated while intoxicated. Recommend that if the computer was in any way involved with their substance use that the client end that form of computer use. For some, this means avoiding all chat programs, sex sites, and so forth. Some clients feel especially vulnerable to triggers from the computer. Some clients enlist their sponsors to place child monitoring programs on their computer, such as Net Nanny, and give out the password control to the sponsor and not to themselves. A few clients decide that their best option is to remove all computers from their home until they have a great deal more recovery time under their belt.

Letting go of using friends. One of the great struggles for clients is letting go of people in their lives who continue to use. Not surprisingly, this can involve family members, romantic partners, coworkers (and jobs), long-term and short-term friendships, and even adult children. This can be especially difficult for those addicts from cultures that support, if not all but demand, tightly woven families and/or friends. The struggles over these losses can be mitigated by suggesting that those who support using or used with the client might be permanently or only temporarily removed from the client's life. Others can be permanently removed if they have no meaningful relationship with the client outside of the using. Think "bar buddies" as an example; the only time the client socializes with them is at the bar and only the bar. Temporary removal is usually recommended for the people identified as important to the client because of an emotional and significant relationship, but with whom the client is likely to continue using intoxicants if they are around. Clients do understand the need for removing people from their lives who put them at risk for using, but often are reluctant to do so for a myriad of reasons. Careful assessment is key to determining the client's willingness to let go of some of these people.

If the client is unwilling to temporarily remove from their lives a person who is a trigger or, for some reason, is prohibited to do so, then therapists need to help the client manage the risk by limiting exposure and bookending encounters with the high-risk person. Limiting exposure can mean, when possible, only engaging with the person when the triggering person is sober. It may also mean going to bed or doing other activities in the house (or ideally outside of the house, such as going to a meeting) once the person begins using. If a couple has children, this is often more restricting as the sober parent cannot just up and leave the children in the home with the using parent. However, with the plethora of resources online, sometimes a meeting is just a few mouse clicks away. As you can see, limiting exposure is dependent on the circumstances of the relationship, and the availability of resources to the recovery person.

Utilizing unmanageability as an assessment tool. Like powerlessness, the client's experience with unmanageability is a great tool for assessing different components of their sober life, whether or not these are actually remnants of their substance dependent world. The points below highlight the most obvious areas where this presents itself. Comparing how each component is similar to and different from what it was during substance dependence is an approach to determine where change is needed.

"One day at a time." This concept can be a very powerful one for clients, especially those who have difficulty breaking goals into manageable steps and feel overwhelmed. Related questions include "What do you need to do today?" and "What do you need to do now?" Finally, this concept can be directly related to coping with cravings and sobriety. Clients are prone to become overwhelmed with these tasks and can find it helpful for therapists to remind them that they only have to stay sober for now, that they only have to tolerate the craving for right now.

Managing sexuality. For some clients, drug and alcohol abuse became so closely tied to sex that one triggers the others. Most troubling is when sexual activity directly results in urges to use. Sex is a strong trigger for these individuals. At this point, the client is left with few options. For some, they can mitigate the triggering effects of sex by altering some aspects of the act. Perhaps sex isn't triggering with their significant other, or maybe they can tolerate the trigger if their sexual partner is also in recovery, or maybe only anonymous sex serves as a trigger. For these individuals, managing sex effectively prevents activating their intoxicant triggers. However, if this is not possible, recommend that the client abstain from sex for at least the first year of sobriety. This is not welcome news to most sexually active clients. Many come to accept this recommendation, albeit typically reluctantly, only after multiple attempts to be sexually active either resulted in relapses or close calls. If the client, after multiple relapses with sex and drugs, still rejects the notion of sexual sobriety, fall back to the Motivational Interviewing mode and assess goals. We recommend that you also assess any social skill deficits and implement harm reduction techniques as appropriate.

Like moths to flames: The replication of unhealthy relationships in sobriety. For decades, therapists have remarked that almost all clients have an almost supernatural ability to repeat difficult or problematic relationships. It's uncanny how clients can repeat dysfunctional relationships and how they do this without even being aware of how they're doing it or even that they are doing it at all. Those who struggle with a lack of love continue to find partners who are incapable of love. Clients who had a series of abusive partners are truly surprised when their current one becomes abusive. As one client remarked "It doesn't matter where I am. I can be in a room full of strangers and within a few minutes, I find myself attracted to one person. Later, I'll find out that they were the worst person in the room for me. Try as I might, I end up back where I started."

This pattern exists for substance-dependent individuals as well, and they are usually just as unaware of it as your other clients. Without intending to, most newly recovering individuals find themselves attracted to others who somehow reengage their cravings. One particularly self-aware and recovering cocaine dependent client put it best, "I can walk into a bar, look around the room, and without even trying I can identify all the addicts in the room. I can even tell you who's carrying drugs on them. If I don't stay aware of it, I find myself interested in those people and start talking to them. It's like a predator in a slaughterhouse. I don't even have to try. I can smell where the meat is and I'm drawn to it."

This dynamic likely results because the memory networks of these individuals are running on autopilot. Without even being aware of it, these clients set themselves up for failure. To varying extents, these clients cannot trust their gut instincts and many of their decisions. Part of their recovery process involves reevaluating the reliability of their judgments. They can compensate for this by relying on external reality checks, such as at meetings, or with their sponsor, and their counselors. As previously discussed, they begin to rely on others to act as auxiliary egos. As therapists, one of your goals is to help clients become aware of their issues with judgment and how to respond.

Managing urges to use. Urges to use are a biological phenomenon that commonly lasts 10 to 15 seconds, about the same time as three deep breaths. The mindfulness techniques of deep breathing, combined with an accepting approach of allowing the experience of the urge while not trying to control the experience, and not acting on the urge, can be an effective short-term technique to try to cope. If the urge lasts longer, commonly the person is still being triggered or is fueling the urge with their ambivalence over abstinence. As the person gains more sober time over the course of weeks and a few months, the intensity and frequency of their urges should diminish. If they do not, it may be appropriate to reevaluate the client to determine what is disrupting this process.

Managing boredom. There is an adage, "idle hands are the Devil's workshop," and it is difficult to find a more applicable population for this saying. Unstructured downtime can be very risky for the newly sober, especially if the person feels bored. Left to themselves, this population is prone to turn inward and activate their memory networks. Clients then fill the time worrying, thinking about craving, thinking about when they used, or focusing on a myriad of topics that risk engaging a craving or relapse. To combat this, it can be useful to explore a client's weekly schedule, monitoring their amount of activity, and avoiding prolonged periods of unstructured time.

Other Relapse Prevention Efforts During the First Through Third Months of Recovery

Weighing 12-Step Program suggestions with clients in therapy. In addition to the work of processing through the underlying issues present in Step One, there are a number of other tasks important to the client's recovery that clinicians need to track. You, as the therapist, are often just one piece of an accountability puzzle in the client's recovery program. Ideally, a sponsor, other 12-Step supports, family, friends, work, partners/spouses, physicians, psychiatrists, and therapists are all working separately but together to support the newly recovering person. Let's look at a number of areas where therapists can best be of assistance to the process of recovery.

To "90 and 90" or not. Most clients start out their recovery with a healthy amount of enthusiasm and hopefulness in their first 30 days of sobriety. A great deal of this is due to several factors: feeling the support of people rallying aid in their efforts, mentally and physically healing from the haze of intoxicants, and the newness of learning about recovery and connecting to people who share their struggle, to name a few. We have all initiated a new self-improvement strategy such as weight loss, gone to the gym, or engaged in a new financial discipline. We begin these initiatives charged up with the ideas of what these changes mean for us. But as we all know, ambivalence about letting go of our old habits or routines often throw wrenches into our new gears. Motivation and perseverance are difficult to maintain, especially without support and accountability. This process is no different when initiating a recovery program with the exception that the stakes are higher for failure.

12-Step recognizes the enthusiasm gap that occurs in early recovery and recommends that newcomers do a "90 and 90." As we mentioned previously, "90 and 90" means attending a minimum of ninety 12-Step meetings in 90 consecutive days, or more simply put, one meeting a day for three months. It is intended to help establish the habit of going to a meeting everyday as part of the maintenance of your recovery program. So, no matter how busy your life gets, whether you feel like going or not, travel destinations, or whatever reasons come up to distract your attention from your recovery, you make your recovery a priority through the practice of taking time out for a meeting.

This is a challenging task for any one of us. However, due to their use, this is especially true for our newly recovering clients who did not have consistency or accountability as part of their lives for a long time. It comes as a shock to some that recovery is not a passive process that just happens, and that sustaining it requires a great deal of effort. Reminding clients, in a nonjudgmental manner, about the effort they expended to get drunk or high is an effective technique to aid in this process. Indeed, many braved severe weather, dangerous neighborhoods, physical deterioration and poor health, sleep deprivation, and going out at the wee hours of the night and early morning in pursuit of their intoxicants. The reality is that the reward for those efforts of seeking their intoxicant was the experience of a high or relief from their withdrawal. In sobriety, the reward is not so tangible or immediate. Helping the client to identify the positive effects that the meetings have on their recovery is an effective strategy to assist in completing a "90 and 90."

When meetings feel dissatisfying. If a client in unable to list a positive effect of a meeting, it may be that the meeting is not carrying a message that is resonating with the client. For instance, is the meeting only focusing on the struggles of recovery, and if so where is the message about experience, strength, or hope in moving beyond that struggle? In previous chapters, we purposely made the recommendation for therapists to attend 12-Step meetings: to understand and observe the messages, sobriety time, and attendees in order to help make a more accurate referral for your clients. When running an outpatient program, one of the authors regularly asked clients about the meetings they attended and compiled a spreadsheet of meetings that he handed out to clients new to 12-Step. The list gave all of the pertinent information about a meeting, including what parts clients liked and didn't like about the meeting. This guide was helpful for clients to select meaningful meetings for them. Additionally, a client's needs in terms of message content or level of support differ as their recovery progresses. The meetings that worked for them in their first month of recovery may drastically change as their needs may also change in the subsequent months completed in recovery. In short, assess, assess, assess!

Specific to Step One and based on your client's meeting complaints, you also should carefully gauge the client's belief in their powerlessness and unmanageability. If no message is resonating with them, or they reject messages that hit at the heart of their vulnerability for relapse, it is helpful to bring this to the client's attention again in a nonjudgmental fashion. This is especially true when clients are attending meetings in which members there had worse bottoms than the client. In hearing these stories, their substance-dependent judgment and reasoning can cause doubt to sneak in, grab hold, and what had been a firm belief in their powerlessness and unmanageability now is open for interpretation. A sure recipe for relapse if there ever was one. It should come as no surprise then that therapists are encouraged to assist clients in exploring how meetings can be beneficial to them. In building awareness of their needs to maintain recovery, a better selection of meetings and realistic expectations often ensure a more valuable experience.

Sponsorship. Sponsorship is another area in need of monitoring for compatibility and compliance. Also, there is usually a need to help the person in recovery learn how to manage that relationship. A great deal has been covered in previous chapters about the sponsor-sponsee relationship, so it is not readdressed here. Suffice it to say that it is most important at the Step One stage to urge and often guide the client to select a temporary sponsor and then a longer-term sponsor quickly after a client engages with the 12-Step program.

Holding onto hope. This highlighted population is easily discouraged. Meetings can counteract much of this, but the therapist can also play a role. It is very useful to simply tell clients that it does get better after one month, three months, and one year; that they do begin to experience fewer cravings, and that they are more likely to achieve long-term sobriety.

Pushback from the client's support system. A final point to add in this section of building recovery skills is the reminder of the "pushback" that can come from various support systems in the recovering person's life. Often, the pushback is not for malicious reasons; quite the contrary, most support systems want the person in recovery to succeed. The resistance is often due to misunderstanding the need for 12-Step involvement, and more importantly feeling left out of the process. Helping your client share the importance of the Program, *and how the Program is keeping them sober,* is a critical component. Additionally, having the client articulate to their nonrecovery support system how they can help in their recovery process is a surefire way to include them in supporting their efforts. Let's highlight an example through a case:

Ian has been in recovery from crack cocaine for 40 days. His partner, Chesterton, was very happy when Ian decided to get clean, and was supportive of his recovery efforts, including going into an intensive outpatient program for three weeks. However, now Chesterton feels that Ian is engaged with 12-Step too much. Chesterton complains to Ian that he barely saw him when he was using crack cocaine, and now feels that he sees Ian even less with his recovery program. Chesterton badgers Ian every time Ian comes home from fellowship after the meetings asking "Why can't you just go to the meeting and come home? I miss you so much. Don't I mean more to you?" In order to keep the peace at home, Ian stops going to fellowship after the meetings, and begins to lose some of the recovery support due to his absence and failure to participate in the fellowship aspect of the meetings.

Lately, Chesterton is complaining about the time Ian spends on the phone with his sponsor. Chesterton frequently interrupts their calls asking "When will you be done?" and "Are you almost finished with that call?" Gradually, Ian's calls to his sponsor become more sporadic as he feels that he does not have the emotional energy necessary to deal with Chesterton's reactions. On their last call, his sponsor expresses concern about their lack of contact, and Ian's distance from his fellowship support. Three days later, Ian runs into his dealer at the grocery store and is triggered to use. He phones Chesterton and confides to him that he feels like using. Chesterton begins to panic, peppering Ian with questions and anxiety that only serve to raise Ian's own anxiety level, thus driving up his desire to use. While waiting for Chesterton to pick him up, Ian goes to the alley behind the grocery store and uses crack cocaine with his dealer.

As you can see from this example, support has to be knowledgeable about addiction and recovery. If not, support given with the best intentions can backfire. To be clear, Chesterton did not cause Ian to use. Ian made several choices that led him to relapse; namely stopping fellowship, reducing communications with his recovery support, becoming sporadic with his calls to his sponsor, and not encouraging Chesterton to go to Al-Anon or helping to educate Chesterton on his recovery. The relapse still lies squarely on Ian's shoulders, even though the anxious feelings after the call with Chesterton put him over the edge.

How Step One Can be Utilized to Process Relapse When Relapse Occurs

The first year of recovery can feel like a big game of Chutes and Ladders™. How do you address relapse as a product of failing to practice Step One? How can clinicians assist the client to begin the recovery process by utilizing Step One again? At this point, in order to proceed, the therapist has to first acknowledge the client's condition if and when he walks through your door: this is a client in acute or post-acute withdrawal, including all of the resulting physical and psychological manifestations of that condition, often coupled with feelings of bewilderment, shame, guilt, and frustration. The client may express this best in their agitation, guardedness, proverbial self-flagellation, and hopelessness at the prospect of sustained recovery. Get ready for a wild ride.

We discussed earlier in the chapter about all of the therapeutic issues underlying this Step, and that the act of a relapse is the physical manifestation of this struggle of ambivalence. After a client relapses and reenters therapy, clinicians are encouraged to step into their roles of Cheerleader, Recorder of Events, and the All-Knowing/Impossible-to-Deceive Parent. In addition to addressing the questions and areas of focus outlined in the preceding chapter, the therapist begins to evaluate and compare the client's beliefs about their control over their intoxicant use, and consider ways to ensure that this event can be used in future times of ambivalence to root the client back into recovery and Step One. Let's examine a clinical interaction to highlight this technique:

Taio, a 49-year-old executive, had struggled for 4 years with cocaine use after being introduced to it by another executive colleague. He used alcohol occasionally without abuse up until his introduction to cocaine. In fact, he used alcohol only at corporate social events, and then only a glass of wine as he felt that alcohol "slowed me down too much." His cocaine use started in middle age after he began to feel himself slowing down and unable to meet the demands of his job, which involved traveling 18 days out of every month to China. His use quickly escalated and became problematic as it increasingly interfered with his work performance, resulting in posting a substantial quarterly loss for him for the first time in his entire career.

He refused to go to any formal treatment program for fear of having to use his company insurance plan. He opted to come directly to outpatient therapy, and paid cash. He agreed to participate in 12-Step therapy, although ambivalent about the quality of anonymity in the groups. With the help of the therapist, they located several "professional's meetings," and he has attended them when he is in town. Taio has not sought a sponsor, finding the concept unappealing.

He remained clean for five weeks. He was successfully managing his schedule and work obligations, but recently began to notice he was not performing to the level he desired. Despite multiple conversations attempting to address his unrealistic expectations of his performance level, Taio instead chose to initiate using over-the-counter products such as energy drinks to boost his energy level. He quickly tripled the amount of energy drinks he consumed per sitting.

The therapist noted how his behavior was identical to that of using cocaine, in that his life continued to be planned around the effects of the energy products. Taio denied that this was an issue, as he was "certain this isn't going to make me go back to cocaine." The therapist inquired, "So how do you feel on the energy drinks?" Taio replied, "Great! I have tons of energy, and I feel incredible and confident." The therapist noted that this was how he previously described feeling on cocaine. Taio blew off the suggestion, noting they are "two totally different things." Taio rather rapidly fell into the same behavior pattern he displayed with his cocaine abuse, and after 2–1/2 weeks of energy drink use, he relapsed on cocaine. He continued using for a week until he became so scattered that he missed an important meeting with a board member. He reentered treatment.

Taio:	"So I relapsed. I don't know how it happened. Everything was under control."
Therapist:	"Well, first I want to congratulate you on coming back. It takes bravery to admit that you lost control. Where do you see yourself in terms of sobriety? Do you still feel you can use cocaine successfully?"
Taio:	"No! Are you kidding me, this was a disaster! I spoke to my sponsor two days ago and went with him to a meeting. I'm two days clean now."
Therapist:	"Again, I want to congratulate you on your two days. I imagine you aren't feeling so good right now. You look pale, your face is drawn, and you have dark circles under your eyes."
Taio:	"No, it's the typical withdrawal stuff. I feel sad, guilty, depressed, ashamed. I know it will pass but I just feel like going to sleep. I just have to make it through tomorrow and then I can rest this weekend."
Therapist:	"Yes, rest is needed. Also make sure you practice those self-care techniques we enacted when you first came to treatment. You need to do some work to physically recover from the relapse. What about the energy drinks? Do you plan on continuing them?"
Taio:	"Hell, yes. Those weren't the problem the cocaine is. I was able to control those without a problem."
Therapist:	"I'm not sure I agree. It seems the two are directly related. Correct me if I'm wrong, but you were getting buzzed on them, your life began to be planned around them, you were drinking them from the moment you woke up until right before bed, and you described the high in the same terms as you did the high from cocaine."
Taio:	Sits silently looking at the floor.
Therapist:	"What's going on for you right now?"

Taio:	"Well, I'm pissed that you remember this shit."
Therapist:	"It can't be easy to hear, especially when you want what you want."
Taio:	"Ugh, my sponsor said the same thing. 'I want what I want when I want it.' I know, I know. Yes, so what?!?! Is that so bad? Why can't I take the energy drinks? It's not cocaine."
Therapist:	"You're right, it's not cocaine. It is however another stimulant and stimulants are your problem, not specifically the cocaine and not specifically the energy drinks. I bet that if we tried prescription stimulants or methamphetamine, the result would be the same. Would you agree with that?"
Taio:	"Yes. Fuck! What the fuck am I going to do? I can't do it anymore. I can't travel like I have been and do it without stimulants, okay?! What do I do?"
Therapist:	"First, welcome back to living Step One. I am not saying that your upcoming choices or efforts are going to be easy, but I have full confidence in you. We need to put your executive skills to good use, and tackle this problem using your best qualities. Would you agree?"
Taio:	"Huh. I never thought about applying my business skills to recovery. Okay, where do we start?"

This was not the last time that Taio relapsed. There were several more: a new energy drink that he felt wasn't as potent as the others, not exerting more control in his schedule for it to become more manageable, and hooking up with a woman at the bar who pulled out cocaine when they got to his hotel. Each relapse brought us back to examining Step One. What factored into his wavering on the belief that he could not control his stimulant use? What were the signs he missed that indicated his thoughts and behavior were becoming more chaotic (unmanageable)? What techniques from 12-Step did he fail to utilize when his powerlessness was active (reaching out, praying the serenity prayer, reading the Cocaine Anonymous text, etc.)? Despite the reasons for relapse, the therapy focused on understanding where he was in Step One prior to the relapse occurring, and also what needed to be implemented in his recovery program this time to ensure success.

Two points about Taio. First, the issue may be far deeper than it initially appears, and second, he seems to be striving to put together a way to stay sober. Let's first address what may be his deeper issues. Specifically, it would not be at all surprising if Taio was struggling with basic life goals other than simply staying sober. For instance, his job requires him to be away from home for a great deal of time. While his work might fulfill some of his needs (perhaps success, high income, and authority) it may be throwing his life severely out of balance by causing him to neglect some other needs that are important to him (perhaps those related to obtaining close relationships, love, and family). In effect, he is in a conflict between competing needs. If that is the case, he may find it very difficult to achieve long-term sobriety. Given the option, it is better for him to achieve sobriety before he identifies and resolves this underlying goal conflict. However, if this interferes too much and prevents sobriety, then it may be impossible to delay exploring and resolving the conflict.

Taio may also be attempting to write his own program to achieve sobriety, by determining what changes and what parts of a 12-Step Program he needs to follow. Specifically, he is unwilling to accept the recommendations of those around him in regard to his energy drinks. Although this led to a relapse for Taio, it won't necessarily for every client. The key issue for clients is: Do they pick and choose the correct mix of program components to achieve long-term sobriety? For Taio, the answer to this question was a resounding "no."

As a therapist, you can often predict what behaviors are risky, but you cannot say with certainly which will ultimately lead to failure. For this reason, hold onto the idea that recovery is an experiment, and in this vein a relapse is a sign that the client's behavior needs to be retooled. Also, hold onto the notion that relapses, while often involving a sense of shame and defeat for the client, should be viewed as an opportunity to learn and a way to better fine-tune a client's recovery strategy.

QUESTIONS

1. What self-care behaviors need monitoring in early recovery?
2. Name four major changes clients are asked to make in their early sobriety. What is the rationale for recommending these changes?
3. Recite Step One, and list the key concepts in that Step.
4. Name two "bumper sticker" sayings appropriate to Step One.
5. Name two therapeutic issues in Step One, and corresponding clinical interventions to address those issues.
6. How is Step One helpful in preventing relapse? What are some behaviors clients can engage in following adoption of Step One?
7. How can Step One be utilized in therapy to process relapse?

Step Two, the Journey Continues

10

Typically, most clients at this early phase in treatment and recovery are decidedly uncomfortable. They often have to acknowledge and cope with the losses associated with their use; their sobriety allows them to experience the difficult emotions associated with these losses at full volume. This commonly occurs at a time where their brain is just beginning to recover from the damage associated with their dependence, making them particularly vulnerable to both internal and external stressors. The character Suzanne from the movie *Postcards from the Edge* may have said it best, "Thank GOD I got sober now, so I can be hyperconscious for this series of humiliations."

Simultaneously, the vast majority of clients at this point struggle with urges. For some these are quite strong and frequent, while for others they are weak and sporadic. These urges may be fueled by ongoing ambivalence over becoming sober, but they are ultimately triggered by a wide variety of stimuli that the client is still struggling to identify and manage. Added to all this, the client may be struggling with basic components of the Program, creating a great deal of frustration that can also be fuel for the urges. Most commonly, this includes avoiding the people, places, and things they associated with using, attending frequent meetings, building social connections within the meetings, and taking things one step at a time.

Transitioning from Step One to Step Two

As they begin Step Two, clients can be expected to have wrestled and come to terms (to a greater or lesser degree) with admitting that they are powerless over their intoxicant(s) and acknowledge that their use has made their lives unmanageable. This means that clients should be acknowledging and taking some responsibility for at least a portion of the wreckage they created in their lives. This often leads clients to feeling that both their life and they personally are a train wreck. Added to that, many have learned that their addiction is cunning, baffling, and powerful. To one extent or another, they cannot truly trust themselves or their choices.

Correcting the Antisocial Adaption

We have talked extensively on the antisocial adaption that substance abuse and dependence can create as a product of continuation of the use. As such, the vast majority of clients still retain, and may even rely on these using or antisocial personality characteristics, despite the ending of their substance use. In particular, clients can display varying degrees of these antisocial tendencies: self-focused and egocentric; prone to fix, manage, or control situations; a predisposition toward denial; and the avoidance of taking responsibility. As a consequence, it is recommended that therapists continue to provide a treatment approach that parallels some of the treatments of antisocial personality disorder.

The Confounding Influence of PAWS

Due to the lingering effects of PAWS, clients can continue to have problems focusing and retaining the work they do in therapy, within 12-Step meetings, and with others in recovery. Due to this variable, it is important for the therapists to consider and titrate (measure and monitor) the speed of the work consistent with client functioning levels. This also helps the client not feel emotionally overwhelmed. To accomplish this balance, an effective method is to keep a high level of therapeutic interaction on the part of the therapist, which requires that the client frequently respond. Concurrently, also remember that clients continue to struggle with breaking goals down into manageable chunks. As such, they may require multiple cues and gentle reminders that feelings of emotional upheaval can be triggered by taking on too big of a goal at once.

Conducting therapy at this stage is often about repeating and reframing issues for clients, especially with issues they have learned but not internalized. Managing triggers and urges, taking things one day at a time, practicing skills and reinforcing the meaning of Step One can preoccupy much of the therapeutic time. Reinforce all of the techniques and skills that the client learned in Step One, and also help them to apply those skills on a broader level. Clients continue to need assistance in monitoring self-care and self-regulation; connecting disruptions in their daily functioning to their self-care efforts. Do this by commonly drawing attention to their self-care efforts when clients report emotional upset, increased urges, or even irritability during a session.

THE BATTLE RAGES ON

For most clients, completing Step One is an achievement. Indeed, it is the foundation of the client's sobriety. That said, they are also a long way from achieving sustained recovery or creating stability in their internal or external lives. As we said before, Rome was not built in a day, and neither is recovery. Clients at the onset of Step Two should be evaluated for further work on the general therapeutic considerations outlined in the Step One chapter, in addition to introducing the following new and ongoing challenges.

Hopelessness

Many clients end Step One struggling with feelings of hopelessness. This often stems from several sources. First, many clients at this point are now hyperaware of the devastation that substance dependence has on their lives, their careers, relationships, family, finances, and/or health. Many simply feel overwhelmed by the challenges presented in their lives, and do not feel that they have the resources to face these demands. Couple this fact with the reality of forsaking many of the most familiar people, places, and things in order to avoid relapsing. Those support systems still remaining in your client's life may feel that, now that the initial crisis is over, they can begin expressing their anger and resentment over the client's prior mistreatment of them. At this point, your client has to begin to face the negative consequences of their addiction, without experiencing many of the positive outcomes of abstinence and recovery. Given all of this, it is little wonder that these individuals are prone to hopelessness.

12-Step meetings are a great source of comfort to some clients struggling with hopelessness. The client may not be able to experience hope in their own lives, but some can take a measure of comfort in hearing how others further along in recovery created hope and happiness in their now sober lives. Socializing during fellowship with these individuals outside of meetings also provides connection and optimism. The Big Book and the Promises can offer a ray of sunshine too. Taken from the Big Book (2001), the Promises are the promised benefits of being in recovery:

> If we are painstaking about this phase of our development, we will be amazed before we are half way through. We are going to know a new freedom and a new happiness. We will not regret the past nor wish to shut the door on it. We will comprehend the word serenity and we will know peace. No matter how far down the scale we have gone, we will see how our experience can benefit others. That feeling of uselessness and self-pity will disappear. We will lose interest in selfish things and gain interest in our fellows. Self-seeking will slip away. Our whole attitude and outlook on life will change. Fear of people and of economic insecurity will leave us. We will intuitively know how to handle situations which used to baffle us. We will suddenly realize that God is doing for us what we could not do for ourselves. (pp. 83–84)

Mood Swings

Affective instability remains a consistent trouble spot for most clients at this stage in recovery. They are prone to mood swings, often composed of depression, anger, irritability, or anxiety. This dysregulation may still be fueled by both PAWS and a general lack of developed alternative coping mechanisms. Coping skills taught during Step One are still at their infancy stage, and usually are not yet strong enough to serve as fully effective countermeasures. These mood swings can be very impairing for some clients, making life miserable not just for them but for those around them.

Additionally, fueling this mood instability is the fact that newly sober individuals commonly struggle with problem solving and conflict resolution. As these problems feel insurmountable, clients tend to "spin out" emotionally, which results in a pattern of worry, anxiety, and frustration that can lead to feeling triggered to use. Simply helping clients break these problem areas into small and achievable steps can go far to stabilizing their moods.

Finally, it can be very useful to identify the precipitant, or trigger, to a client's mood swing. Clients who are in early recovery often do not see how events in their lives contribute to their emotional states. They may not see how their antisocial adaption is still working and disrupting their sober life. Alternatively, enabling or dysfunctional jobs, relationships, friendships, and other systems in the client's life that may have been tolerable when they were out using intoxicants can become increasingly intolerable the longer the client is sober. At its root, the mood instability may simply be caused by a lack of congruence between their addiction and their efforts to function in the sober world. Working with clients to articulate and problem solve these relationships can sometimes supply the calmness or tranquility that they lack.

Monitor these mood swings, and pursue medication if the client's sobriety is at risk. The therapist should frame the need for medication as a temporary measure while the client's brain is healing, and attach a commitment to reevaluate the need for medication after a stipulated time. Encourage the continuation of mindfulness, meditation, and relaxation instruction and practice to help ease the distress from the mood swings, and advocate that the client get some exercise every day—if only a 10 to 20 minute walk.

Egocentricity

By this point, clients often begin to tone down their egocentricity and self-centeredness. However, efforts to fix, manage, or control their worlds often emerge into the foreground. Examples of this can sometimes be quite subtle. Clients may struggle with being honest; sometimes finding they are lying about fairly inconsequential things in their day-to-day lives. For some clients, they may be prone to various forms of egocentric anxiety and worry. These worries can take on the form of simple ruminations while others may have an all but incessant effort to plan responses to behaviors or sentiments of others. It's as if the client is playing an ongoing chess game, attempting to play out multiple moves in the future.

Shame and Guilt

It is almost impossible to meet a client in early recovery who does not struggle with the feelings of shame and guilt. Few are portrayed in the media as more shameful than a junkie or a drunk. Unfortunately, add to this the fact that almost all clients have had many abhorrent, humiliating, degrading, and/or abusive experiences or behaviors while they were using. Lying, cheating, and manipulating became their stock in trade. It should therefore come as little surprise that these clients struggle with shame and guilt. These are powerful feelings that can lead the client to feel unlovable, unworthy, and inconsolable. Therapeutically, it can be very useful for therapists to remain highly sensitive to these feelings by labeling and interpreting them to see how they can fuel a client to detach and punish themselves, especially through self-sabotage. Meetings can also help clients cope with these feelings, for who best to show someone that they are not entirely broken than another person who has worked through the same experience?

Social Skill Deficits

In the Step One chapter, we discussed the many social skill deficits that clients possess when they enter into recovery. Suffice it to say, social skills continue as an area of deficit during the first year of sobriety, although with therapeutic attention they steadily improve. In particular, conflict resolution and assertiveness skills may be especially weak. Continuing family conflicts or families undermining recovery, problems getting needs met with the sponsor, or inability to articulate needs to loved ones are all examples of the continuing social skill deficits that need to be addressed at this stage. We refer you back to those sections in the book that address working with families in recovery and social skills training.

Additionally, clients typically attend from 5 to 7 meetings a week at this point in their recovery. Some even attend more, perhaps as many as 2 or 3 meetings on a difficult day. As such, it is very common for clients to make social missteps within the rooms of 12-Step. Fortunately, people in 12-Steps generally expect that a newly recovering individual will make social skill missteps. They often find these social errors, such as lying or embellishment, more tolerable than a client who attempts to manipulate and refuse suggestions. Sponsors can be especially helpful at this point and often help guide a client through these problems.

As usual, there is much to attend to by both clinicians and clients in the therapy sessions in early recovery. However, the Steps are helpful tools in therapy to not only address the recovery concept being taught by the Step, but also as a tool for these other areas of recovery as well. With that in mind, let's venture into the world of Step Two.

STEP TWO: CAME TO BELIEVE THAT A POWER GREATER THAN OURSELVES COULD RESTORE US TO SANITY

Key Concepts

Step One focuses on the full recognition of the insanity and chaos created by the substance dependent's attempt to predict and control their use, the damage it caused, as well as the people it touched. It is through the recognition of this hopeless struggle and the state of insanity caused by the substance use that the awareness of change emerges. Step Two then directs the person to build hope for themselves and their lives.

Step Two restores hope by asking the question, "now that you recognize that an insane mind cannot heal itself, to whom do you turn for guidance on healing?" This is critically important as most people in the depths of their addiction talk about how alone they feel; that no one anywhere can help them or understand the level of their struggle. Nowhere does Step Two say you have to move anything into action; that is the work of Step Three. The work of Step Two is finding *and believing* that the source you select returns your sanity back to you. Sanity, of course, being a euphemism for sobriety and recovery.

This Step describes a type of self-defined spirituality that resolves to have the individual consider extending themselves to accept help. This path rests on the notion of a Power Greater than Ourselves, or what is commonly referred to as a Higher Power. A Higher Power is simply something greater than the client can ever be by themselves. The Higher Power is defined solely by the sober person. For many, but not all, in the United States, this translates to some version of God. However, clients have chosen the Earth Mother, the Spirit of Man, and even the teachings of Oprah Winfrey as their Higher Power.

Clients also choose more than one Higher Power. Some may opt for a more tangible version of a Higher Power, in addition to, or instead of, an ethereal being. Thus, anytime a client is with another person who supports their sobriety, they are considered Higher Powers. Some choose to elect their sponsors, home groups, or any 12-Step meeting they go to as a Higher Power. Yet others choose the Big Book as that entity. The specifics of the Higher Power are unimportant, as long as the client believes that this power has the ability to help them stay sober. Step Two attempts to begin the journey to hope and it does so through the development of a form of faith.

Key "Bumper Sticker" Sayings

Before charging into the bumper sticker sayings, let's introduce the Serenity Prayer. The Serenity Prayer cited in some 12-Step meetings is, "God grant me the serenity to accept the things I cannot change, the courage to change the things I can, and the wisdom to know the difference." The Serenity Prayer's origins have been attributed to Reinhold Niebuhr, but whether this was his creation or adapted from another source remains an unanswered question (Shapiro, 2008).

Although the Serenity Prayer is more in line with the work of Step Three (we cover it more extensively there), it can serve as a useful tool at the Step Two level. This prayer or meditation essentially focuses the client on the cessation of worry. It helps to provide skills to allow the client to think about, or be granted the wisdom, to know what the client is able to change or not. In effect, there is no reason to worry about something over which you have no power or control. Usually this involves a refocusing of energy back toward the individual. If I cannot change something out of my control, the one thing I always have the ability to change is me.

Some of the other bumper sticker sayings that are effective for this Step are:

"Easy does it." Take it slow and do everything in moderation. Don't take on too much, don't think too much, and don't get yourself too worked up. From this stance, often the best response is leavened with lots of calmness.

"Experience, strength, and hope." Nothing signifies the philosophy of learning in 12-Steps more than this phrase. Learning does not occur through telling people what to do, or berating them for their choices. Learning occurs when you can share your own experiences and their influence in your recovery.

"Keep it simple." This is essentially a response to a tendency of many to over-think a situation or become obsessive about it. It is a commentary on a 12-Step Program itself (i.e., it's a difficult but simple program).

"Stick with the winners." A 12-Step Program places great emphasis on fellowship and forming relationships with others in the room. However, water tends to seek its own level. Likewise, the newly sober client feels drawn to other newcomers in the room. This is not the goal of fellowship. Instead, newcomers are urged to include those with long-term sobriety in their fellowship. In this way both parties benefit. The newcomer gets the wisdom of those who have been successful in sobriety, and the old-timers get reminders of where relapse would take them.

"Take what works, leave the rest" or "Take what you need, leave the rest." This essentially encourages the person to take whatever they find useful in a meeting or from the Program and to ignore the rest. This slogan helps reduce the tendency of this population to become drawn into conflict. It essentially says, "You only have to do what you want to do." Not everything in the Program, and especially not everything said at any one meeting, is meant to apply to everyone in the room.

Other useful 12-Step acronyms related to Step Two:

A.N.G.E.R. (A Negative Grudge Endangers Recovery). A simple reminder of the power that anger and its partner, resentment, have in rationalizing for you why you are entitled to relapse or use relapse as an emotional weapon.

F.E.A.R. (False Events Appearing Real or Forgetting Everything's All Right). Nothing can derail a recovery program like the inaccurate perceptions of someone in early recovery. This slogan helps remind those new in recovery to check in with their Higher Powers on the accuracy of those perceptions.

H.O.P.E. (Having Optimistic Perspective Everyday). Step Two enables the installation of hope, and this slogan helps clients to become aware that their attitude has a large impact on their ability to experience gratitude and hope.

P.R.I.D.E. (Personal Recovery Involves Deflating Ego). A carryover from Step One, this slogan keeps the focus on having the newly sober individual remain teachable for the work of Step Two.

S.O.L.U.T.I.O.N.S. (Saving Our Lives Using The Inspiration Of Necessary Steps). This slogan rests on the Program's foundational belief that ideas of recovery are successful when experience, strength, and hope are shared by another alcoholic or addict. This is especially true when they see how far others have come to understand that there is a power greater than themselves.

S.T.E.P.S. (Solutions Through Each Positive Step). Wins the "obvious award" for its meaning: negativity and inaction lead to further misery and/or stagnation.

S.W.A.T. (Surrender, Willingness, Action, Trust). This is a slogan that is for both Step Two and Step Three. Surrender and Willingness are related to the process of the installation of hope in Step Two, and Action and Trust are the epitome of Step Three.

T.H.I.N.K. (Thank Heavens I Now Know). Pun aside, this is a reminder that the pain of the struggle of discovery is worth the knowledge in the end.

W.A.S.P. (Worry. Anger. Self-Pity). Just like the insect it's named for, these emotions can sting your recovery and ultimately fuel you for relapse.

Y.A.N.A. (You Are Not Alone). This connects to the idea that a Power Greater than Ourselves can be anyone or anything, and that your struggle has been felt and overcome many times by others who are willing to aid you in your efforts.

Therapeutic Issues Within Step Two

Recognition of "Fix, Manage, Control"

One of the hallmark struggles for clients in early recovery and at Step Two is the letting go of their ingrained behavior to fix, manage, and control. There is no better example of insanity than the lengths that active users will go to allow their use to continue. Unfortunately, like so many other antisocial adaptations created by addiction, this skill set does not go away simply by the decision to be sober. Instead, this technique is often used as a distraction from their own recovery in order to ramp up their emotions beyond a tolerable level and thus justify relapse. Step Two addresses this antisocial adaption by creating a vessel from which the client is able to seek wisdom and guidance. The actual act or process of seeking wisdom is the function of Step Three.

Step Two involves clients becoming aware of their needs and efforts to fix, manage, and control their world, including the therapist. Therapists can assist in this process by advancing a client's awareness of this dynamic, exploring it with the notion of making it increasingly egodystonic. This does not mean that the client easily becomes aware of these dynamics and can consciously control them. No, few clients are so lucky. Instead, this means that clients become more open to having these dynamics identified by others, join in efforts to become more aware of them, as therapists and sponsors and others call attention to the client's efforts to change things that are not in their control.

Seeking an Understanding of Their Power Greater Than Themselves

The main task of the client in Step Two is to define a Power Greater than Themselves, or a Higher Power. It is about finding that Higher Power that restores your sanity (i.e., keeps you sober). Most people automatically connect their Higher Power to their concept of god without much thought of how god will help them stay sober. Clients should be encouraged to talk out how their concept and belief of god can aid in their efforts in recovery. Will their god aid them through prayer, religious or spiritual writings, divine inspiration, sermons through religious leaders, or another means? It is important for clinicians to understand how the client envisions their spiritual system aiding in the recovery tasks we outlined in previous chapters.

By no means are we encouraging clinicians to challenge a client's belief systems or concept of a Higher Power. If their concept of a Higher Power does not meet the litmus test of being able to *restore* their sanity (sobriety), probe to see if there is an openness to having an adjunct Higher Power that will fit the bill. Surprisingly, very few clients consider that they can have more than one Higher Power. It is almost as if having another is somehow cheating on god. Describe this situation to clients as god serving as your spouse/partner, and the adjunct Higher Powers as your good friends.

So what makes a good adjunct Higher Power? Advocate that clients become comfortable with the concept of tangible Higher Powers by helping them to understand that they themselves plus, *insert sober resource here,* are a Higher Power. Although Higher Powers may be ethereal beings, there are plenty of powers greater than ourselves able to restore sanity (sobriety). Consider the following examples:

- A meeting with a sponsor
- A 12-Step meeting
- Reading recovery literature
- A sober support
- A group of recovery people hanging out
- Watching an inspirational film or hearing a song about the trials of addiction
- Any medium that connotes the values of 12-Step
- Guided Meditation
- Yoga

This list could fill up the entire book. Always advocate for clients to build as wide a grouping of Higher Powers as they are comfortable with or that their spirituality allows. Do not pressure clients to adopt this view. Encourage it only as a means of finding hope in many places.

However, it is common for clients to struggle with the concept of god or a Higher Power. This is often a sticking point when the client is an atheist or when local meetings tend to espouse a faith tradition that the client is uncomfortable or unfamiliar with, or outright opposes. Certain groups tend to have more difficulty with the application of a Higher Power. It is commonly believed that sexual orientation minorities have a difficult time with religion and spirituality given the opposition of most major religions to any form of sexual orientation outside of heterosexuality. Additionally, there are differences within the diverse groups under the sexual orientation rainbow that have stronger affiliations with both religion and spirituality than others. For instance, many sexual orientation minority clients who are White and in an urban setting tend to struggle with religion and spirituality. Conversely, many sexual minority clients who are non-White and in an urban setting tend to have more intact and connected religious and spiritual lives. White privilege may afford the ability of Whites to discard religion as a primary coping mechanism against heterosexism in a way that non-White sexual orientation minorities do not, given its buffering effects against racism and connection to community.

The notion of a Higher Power, whatever the client's vision, is often crucial at this point. In fact, for many clients their specific articulation of Higher Power isn't important. It is the process of discovery and exploration that is at issue.

Vernon had struggled for weeks to identify his Higher Power. All of his life he had rejected the notion of a God, and the concept of a Higher Power simply seemed impossible for him. Finally, he settled on the notion of evolution. His Higher Power became the process of all systems to evolve and develop in order to become more successful. Years later, Vernon joked that his Higher Power allowed him no choice but to go back and use. He would either evolve into a successful sober individual or he would be selected for extinction. This belief helped to firm up his resolve about his sobriety. It was the threat of extinction that helped to restore his sanity (sobriety) and to remove any doubt about going back out and using. In fact, his growth was inevitable given his Higher Power.

Processing Spiritual/Religious Experiences in 12-Step

Remember that clients at this early stage in their recovery have difficulty containing emotions once stirred, and nothing stirs emotions like religion and spirituality. For some clients, it is difficult to hear talk in the meetings about Higher Powers that they find offensive or against their personal beliefs. In most instances, the discussion that is emotionally stirring is one that has navigated toward an actual deity or religious figure (Jesus, Allah, Moses, Buddha). If the client does not belong to this faith system, they can experience feelings of rejection, ostracization, exclusion, or simply feel distanced by this language. This can be very problematic for someone new to 12-Step.

It is helpful to process these reactions in therapy. At this juncture in Step Two, clients are encouraged to explore their spiritual selves in an effort to find something that works—not necessarily what they have been brought up to believe. There can be an all-or-nothing approach to looking at religion, spirituality, and Higher Powers. Advocate for a broader interpretation when appropriate. For some a rigid belief system is what works for them in their lives and in their efforts to stay sober. For these clients, they can be equally emotionally stirred when conversations in meetings stray outside of their belief system.

For those who become emotionally stirred by differing views on spirituality or religion, apply some bumper sticker sayings to help them process their negative responses. For example the saying, "take what works (or take what you need) and leave the rest" is the most useful for this exploration. Ask clients to examine their negative reactions to a discussed spirituality and explore what about those beliefs run counter to their now emerging moral code. Rather than adopting that spiritual system or religious belief, look to see if there is a helpful belief, slogan, philosophy, or example that fits within the client's own concept of spirituality to utilize for their recovery. In this way, begin to pull the client away from that antisocial adaption of self-centeredness; the belief that it's my way of experiencing spirituality or the highway.

In some cases, the history of negative experiences with certain religions or spiritual concepts is much too deep and painful to tolerate in early recovery. If the client is simply too stirred and unable or unwilling to resolve those differences, recommend that they attend a different meeting. If a pattern of this emerges, and the client chooses to shift to different meetings, beware as this behavior can signal more concerns about ambivalence in recovery than a spiritual struggle. Religion and spirituality is one of the easiest areas to grasp and justify in order to explain why 12-Steps won't work for someone. While this is a real factor for some clients, especially atheists, sometimes it is beginning of a retreat from recovery.

Speaking of atheists and agnostics, their experiences with religion and spirituality vary across the spectrum. Some atheists are able to compartmentalize the talk of religion and spirituality; some are able to separate the philosophy from the spirituality; and others go ballistic whenever there is a discussion about religion, spirituality, or the Higher Power as an etheric being. Apply the same techniques that you would with any other spiritual person. After all, atheism is a spiritual belief! True agnostics tend to be the most adaptable with spirituality and religion in meetings. We use the word "true," because we have had many clients enter into recovery claiming to be agnostic; however in reality they had a pretty solid belief system, but were injured by organized religion in some way. For these individuals, it is helpful to process the negative religious experiences, unless doing so emotionally stirs them past their coping skills or tolerance levels and places them at risk for relapse.

Combating a Different Form of Dogma

Step Two is just as much about the installation of belief and hope as it is about the journey to find a Higher Power. What clients often confuse is that this is not about believing in dogma, including some dogmatic beliefs about 12-Step programs! There are hardcore believers in 12-Step who behave in a fashion similar to the most ardent religious zealots. They tolerate no dissent or deviation of the Program, and they attempt to discredit other recovery programs that are non-spiritually based. However, if that approach is working for the client do not interfere, even if you disagree with the approach. For those clients who are not this hard core about the Program, it can be equally as challenging as any religious discussion. This is especially true if the client is working a blended program such as SMART (Self-Management and Recovery Training) with a 12-Step program. Even if clients are not working a blended recovery program, such a dogmatic approach can create an aversion to 12-Step, which if left unprocessed can have a lasting negative impression that hinders involvement over the long-term.

If your area of service has the luxury of having a wide number of meetings available, this is a fairly easy fix simply by suggesting that the client select other meetings to attend. Again, this is where your firsthand knowledge of meetings is crucial. If there are a limited number of meetings to choose from and they follow a similar dogmatic format, then help the client to contextualize the experience. You can do this by having them observe who that approach might work for, and if there is anything useful that can be included in their own recovery program. Sometimes, therapy is simply a place for the client to vent their frustration with the dogma in order to remain involved in 12-Steps.

Installation of Hope

The beginning words of Step Two, "came to believe" are the cornerstone of instilling hope that there is something out there that can help relieve the insanity wrought by the substance dependence. It is the action of believing in hope, and sometimes even in just the existence or possibility of hope, that emboldens clients to begin the process of reinventing their lives away from their intoxicants and all the accompanying madness.

It is hoped that they get better, that they find serenity, and that they find happiness. This can be harder than it sounds, especially for someone who struggles with chronic feelings of shame, defectiveness, or resentment; the hallmark of addiction. Substance dependence breeds hopelessness. Remember that by the time clients reach your office, they have already achieved limited success attempting to cut back or stop their use on their own. From the first failed attempt to control their using, hopelessness begins to root.

At these junctures, adopting the role of the Cheerleader is an effective tool to help the client recognize hope. Nothing instills hope like being grateful for what you have, and gratitude is another of those massive cornerstones in the foundation of recovery. Helping the client recognize the small ways in which their sanity and sobriety is showing itself daily is impactful as a representation that things are indeed getting better. The client can keep a tangible record of the benefits of their recovery by creating "gratitude lists." For some, this list becomes their Higher Power steering the client's thinking and perception away from deprivation (the relapse instigator), and toward fulfillment. This change is a powerful preventer of relapse, but a difficult skill to master.

At this phase, addressing the hopelessness in order to help the client instill belief in sanity and sobriety mirrors the rest of your treatment. It is preferable to use here-and-now work, and concrete interventions that do not involve deep insights or interpretations. Sometimes gratitude is hard to find, and it feels empty; sometimes it takes tragedy to change perspective. Consider the following:

Sara was raised in a particularly abusive home. Her mother, who was a very fragile narcissistic individual, emotionally and physically abused her in profound ways. Sara's only way to cope was to disavow herself and take on a rigid obsessive-compulsive and passive personality where she allowed herself little if any assertive expression of her wants, needs, or frustrations. She became a person with few desires, feelings, or a voice. She found alcohol to be an almost magical elixir. It allowed her to express her needs and feelings, especially those associated with anger, by melting away her self-control, guilt, and shame.

Over time, this developed into alcoholism, which made a shambles of her life. She walked into psychotherapy and 12-Step meetings because she had no other choice. Highly analytical, Sara quickly saw the wisdom of the first Step and embraced it only to find the second Step was a wall for her. She believed in a God, but her conception of a God held no warmth, no hope for her. Her conception of God was as a cold and harsh judge who doled out punishment without empathy or concern. She could acknowledge the idea of a loving, hope-filled God, but she could not experience one. In many ways, her concept of her God appeared to mirror her experience with her mother and the hopelessness of her youth.

The therapist and Sara had multiple discussions of her concept of God, increasingly drawing parallels to her experience as a youth, and the mood in the sessions became more sad and hopeless. Sara's progress on finding a God that would instill hope was stalled. Then one evening, Sara was in a serious car accident. She was driving on a back road, flipped her car, lost consciousness, and awoke upside down in the total dark. She became terrified, worried that she was going to die, that her car was going to catch on fire or blow up, or that she would simply hang there until she died alone. After several minutes of this, she heard a siren that quickly became louder and louder. She found her fears diminishing and hope rising as the siren became louder. The fire department was arriving and they rescued her out of the vehicle. Although the car was totaled, Sara was essentially unharmed.

The next day, Sara returned to the scene of the accident to retrieve some possessions out of the car, which had since been flipped back onto its wheels. The car was a disaster, and viewing it brought back all the worry of the night before. In the midst of this, she looked up and there in a nearby tree was one of her headlights, looking essentially unharmed and pristine. This reminded her of the siren and the calmness and hope it brought to her as she hung upside down in the dark. She took a picture of that headlight and then retrieved it.

This experience marked a significant turning point in Sara's life and in her recovery. That picture became the symbol of the hope that she could experience. To this day she carries that picture in her wallet. A copy of it sits on her desk at work and at home. She only needs to look at it to help her find the hope within. And years later, as she more deeply processed the rage and hopelessness of her childhood, she again turned to that picture when she felt the most sad or hopeless.

It is preferable if no one ever needs to face this type of life-threatening experience in order to help them define their Higher Power, but Sara did. As a comparative point, bringing clients back to their experience of their bottom is another method of finding faith in the belief that sobriety is possible and that a Higher Power is in motion for them. At their bottommost point, the client likely experienced life as harshly intolerable as they ever will. Invariably, some outside influence provided the means to recognize the hazard of their substance-dependent life, and usually exploring this event helps the client begin the process of defining their higher power.

Easing of Shame

As you saw in the example of Sara, the client's ability to commit to hope rests on the acceptance of themselves as a person worthy of help. Clients go through unbelievable events of humiliation during their using career. It is not uncommon for us to hear stories of rape or sexual humiliation, homelessness, being disowned by family, constant verbal berating or physical abuse for their use, begging for money or food, having people on the street pull their kids away from them, and other horrific events. During using, clients learn that they are only as worthy to another substance user as the intoxicants or resources they can provide. It is every client's struggle to accept love, compassion, and help in early recovery.

Clients, like Sara, also have histories that are fraught with messages of their low worth to others; it is often what drives them to use in the first place. Discovering a Higher Power that makes the client able to feel, at minimum, that they are worthy of help is the entry point. It is fairly unrealistic to expect that clients will feel a sense of worthiness of love, compassion, or empathy in the beginning of their recovery. Step Two begins this process by increasing a client's sense of self-worth and opening up their belief that they are a lovable person.

Relapse and Step Two

Most clients begin working on Step Two within the first three months of their sobriety. Statistically, they remain at high risk for relapse due to their ambivalence about their sobriety and involvement in 12-Steps. In the following sections, we examine how Step Two can aid in the prevention efforts of relapse. We then discuss the impact relapse has on the acceptance and adoption of Step Two.

Step Two's Role in Relapse Prevention

Step Two can be a powerful motivator for recovery if the exploration process is successful. To assist in the prevention of relapse, clinicians are encouraged to utilize gratitude lists, revisiting the client's experience of their bottom, what spurred their entry into recovery, and the exploration and discovery of themselves as spiritual and moral beings. All of these techniques are aimed at combating feelings of deprivation, discouragement, and resentment.

Countering Deprivation. Remember, deprivation can take on many emotional and physical forms, and gratitude is the most effective tool in your therapeutic arsenal to make certain that those feelings do not lead to relapse. Focusing on gratitude, either through daily gratitude lists or in conversation in therapy, begins to flip the script on how the client perceives and responds to their states of deprivation. Take the sensation of hunger. If a client is feeling hungry, the client can shift their focus from "I'm starving!" to "I'm not starving, that is not possible since I just ate a few hours ago. I am hungry, but I am not someone who is starving. I have food available for me to eat, which I wouldn't have if I was still out using and blowing all my money on drugs."

This shift in thinking usually does not happen quickly or easily. Once at the stage of Step Three, the client is normally able to utilize the technique of "turning it over" to their Higher Power for relief. Alas for now, the client needs to make do with the therapist, their gratitude list, or help from other recovery supports to assist with developing a positive outlook. In this way, everyone in that support system becomes a Higher Power for the client.

Countering Discouragement. Clients in early recovery have a tremendous capacity to berate themselves for not progressing at an unrealistic pace. Demonstrating their progress in recovery is crucial to continued motivation toward sobriety. This involves "keeping hope alive." Clients often view any setback in recovery as a blaring indictment that they don't belong in the world of sobriety. Helping clients to reframe their slipups, struggles, setbacks, and challenges as part of the normal process of recovery begins to contextualize their progress beyond an either/or mentality. 12-Step meetings are an absolute gold mine for the clients to see that they are not alone in their struggle for sobriety. However, remember that clients can also take an opposite view in the rooms; finding themselves as not progressing quickly enough compared to others. Patiently work with your client as they move from their focus on deficits to strengths.

Countering Resentment. Nothing produces feelings of justification for relapse more than the building up of resentments. Resentments are particularly dangerous as they combine both discouragement and deprivation. It also brings to the surface feelings of entitlement, inferiority, and anger; these are certainly not experiences that can coexist with a healthy expression of gratitude. Resentment breeds the ugly side of gratitude by focusing the expression of gratitude on your "rightness" or ego versus your "openness to learn" or humility. Resentments are all about how someone or something has caused you insult or injury. You perceive yourself as the victim, void of any personal responsibility in that injury. In effect, it grounds the client back into their antisocial adaption, pulling the client further away from the hope of sanity and sobriety.

You can generally combat this progression back toward antisocial adaption by playing the role of Devil's Advocate in order to have the client begin to accept responsibility. By doing so, you encourage the client to take responsibility when appropriate and also teach them to have empathy and compassion for others. It is also helpful to have them evaluate the event that created the resentment, in order to help the client redefine the moral compass. Are the actions that the client perceives as injurious, the actions that they would use toward another? How are they different?

The typical goal in confronting these three risks (deprivation, discouragement, and resentment) is not necessarily to gain insight; rather the goal is for the client to remain sober. At this point, utilize support combined with concrete approaches such as cognitive-behavioral or skill training interventions that are symptom focused. Remember the example of Sara, an exploration of the underlying meaning of her hopelessness was only started after other interventions, more concrete ones, had failed. Then, once she discovered hope through the accident, the therapist withdrew from this deeper exploration for the time being because it was very difficult and troubling for her. If possible, avoid this level of emotional upset until a client has much stronger recovery skills.

Other Relapse Prevention Concerns During the Third Through Sixth Months of Sobriety

Relapse is a common risk especially during the first year of sobriety. Constantly evaluate this risk while working through the concepts of the Steps. The most common occurrence at this stage is the relitigating of Step One; ambivalence of powerlessness and reemergence of denial in recognizing the unmanageability of their life during substance use. Regardless of which Step the client is processing, it is absolutely appropriate in your work with the current Step to return to further discuss and resolve any lingering doubts about the preceding Step. In effect, the treatment alliance built around the goal of sobriety is challenged if the client begins to turn away from a belief in Step One. At this point, return to a more neutral stance akin to Motivational Interviewing to assess and process those concerns. For example, does the client still wish to work toward sobriety? What does the client want? What is best for them as they see it?

As with Step One, you want to continue to frequently review a client's triggers and how well they are coping with them. Around Step Two, it is typical for clients to experience a reduction in the rapid fire urges experienced through Step One. Continue to monitor your client's urges to use in order to identify what triggers them and how long they last. Over time, a client's urges should reduce in intensity and frequency. If they do not, a closer inspection is warranted.

It is also helpful to begin attending to the client's fellowship efforts at this time. Do not be surprised if sponsors begin to do the same thing. Clients often do best if they begin forming closer social bonds with those at the meetings. By this point, the client should be attending multiple meetings consistently from week to week so their face and presence becomes more familiar in these meetings, and vice versa. Arriving a bit early to set up the room or staying a bit late to set the room to rights can be a great way for newcomers to break the ice. It is also common for newcomers to be invited to coffee or a meal, either before or after a meeting. Strongly support clients engaging in these behaviors and building meeting relationships. However, remember that this population is liable to display a broad range of social deficits and difficulties. This is part of the reason for the slogan "stick with the winners." Checking in around fellowship activities and offering some guidance or skill training can be invaluable to moving this process along.

The most severe consequence of a relapse at this stage of recovery is the demoralization that comes with a relapse for a client. Relapses have the ability to seriously throw a major wrench in the client's belief in their ability to break the cycle of using, and become a prosocial person. Additionally, all of the feelings of guilt and shame that had been processed and eased through the discovery of a Higher Power reemerge stronger than ever.

How Step Two Can be Utilized to Process Relapse When Relapse Occurs

The most impactful effect of a relapse when it occurs in Step Two is the doubt it recreates, not only in a Higher Power, but a Higher Power's ability to help sustain recovery. After a relapse, clients often displace their feelings of anger, disappointment, and frustration on their Higher Power as a means of avoiding confronting those feelings about themselves.

One method to realign the client with their newly discovered Higher Power is to reflect back to the hopeful outcomes that the client believes were the result of hitting bottom. Through this frame, the client is generally able to look at relapse as a lesson rather than a failure. In accepting the relapse as a lesson, the client reasserts their belief in the concept of restoring sanity (sobriety).

Additionally, take the liberty to look at the client's selection of their Higher Power and examine more closely how the Higher Power is either restoring sanity or the client's willingness to be guided by their Higher Power to further recovery.

QUESTIONS

1. Name three psychological challenges to recovery and therapeutic techniques to use to help process these challenges. What role does a 12-Step program have in helping to process these same challenges?
2. Recite Step Two, and list the key concepts in that Step.
3. Name two "bumper sticker" sayings appropriate to Step Two.
4. Name two therapeutic issues in Step Two, and corresponding clinical interventions to address those issues.
5. How is Step Two helpful in preventing relapse? What are some behaviors clients can engage in following adoption of Step Two?
6. How can Step Two be utilized in therapy to process relapse?

Step Three, the Journey Becomes Purposeful

11

Our work with clients in 12-Steps has revealed a pretty consistent pattern of pacing in working the Steps. Specifically, Steps One through Three are tackled in the first year of recovery at a slow pace, allowing each Step to be thoroughly worked and then reworked as subsequent Steps are negotiated. Sometimes Steps One through Three are worked in conjunction with each other at a client's entrance into recovery, and then worked concurrently together through the first year of sobriety. Regardless of the actual pacing and plan with a sponsor, the first year of sobriety offers fertile ground for therapeutic work in the context of the first three Steps. Additionally, any relapse is thoroughly processed, hopefully resulting in a more effective program before the client proceeds further into recovery. Thus, by the time a client hits Step Three near the end of their first year of entering recovery, they are looking and feeling very different to you in the therapy room. Risks are still present, they always are, but the instability in mood, behavior, and overall health should have greatly receded.

GENERAL THERAPEUTIC CONSIDERATION

Paying Dividends

Not surprisingly, by the ninth or tenth month of sobriety and recovery many of the person's impairments show at least some modest gains. The marked improvement in other deficits is fairly shocking. Here are the areas you can look forward to evidencing consistent and stable improvement:

- Improving health conditions secondary to effects of using (blood pressure, STDs, blood sugar levels, lung or sinus problems, healing track marks or burns, dental problems, etc.). Included in this, clients should be generally feeling better and physically improved.

191

- More regular and routine sleep patterns that have now adjusted to the client's operating world (dependent on work schedule, other obligations like caring for a sick family member, etc.).
- Improved hygiene (overall cleanliness, dental care, grooming, etc.).
- Improved appetite and weight correction from using (regular eating schedule, decrease of binging eating behaviors common in early recovery, weight gain if emaciated after using, etc.).
- Exploration or incorporation of sober fun, hobbies, recreation, even to the point that the client begins to feel some satisfaction with their life.
- Exploration or incorporation of physical self-care through exercise.
- Exploration or incorporation of spiritual self-care through yoga, meditation, mindfulness, church, prayer, and so forth.

THE TIDE OF BATTLE BEGINS TO TURN

Apart from the overall improvement in general functioning, the client's work in therapy also opens up in approach and content. This is made possible through the hard-fought gains of recovery. Improvements are noticeable in sober social skills, memory retention and recall, attention and focus, emotional management and ability to self-soothe, and the diminishing impact of PAWS. The client's relationship with their sponsor is generally well-established along with sober support and fellowship. A client's meeting schedule should be stable and generally fulfilling, and the client begins to find themselves sharing their stories in efforts of helping those newcomers coming into the Program.

Given these improvements, the pressure eases somewhat in the therapy's hyper-vigilant work of relapse prevention, and moves into a more integrated format that allows for incorporation of other treatment modalities and insight-oriented work. Trauma or complex psychological issues may be reintroduced if there are sufficient achievements made in client resourcing (techniques of mindfulness, grounding, self-soothing, etc.) and if the client can tolerate these limited explorations without becoming triggered. Although the tide is turning in psychological functioning, there remains areas where the client is vulnerable.

Remaining Struggles With Egocentricity and Fix, Manage, and Control

With each success, the client continues to gain a great deal of self-confidence in their abilities to remain sober. This is a monumental success for sure! Unfortunately, it is also one of the reasons why egocentricity comes roaring back. The client continues to battle within to let go of the need to be right and being unteachable about recovery. This is best demonstrated in several areas: reemergence of rejecting all forms of suggestions, overconfidence in recovery skills, underestimating the "cunning, baffling, powerful" nature of addiction, and the reemergence of denial in therapy to presented risks. Expect even your best performing clients to struggle in this area. At the very least, the concept of building an ongoing conscious awareness of their egocentricity and/or their need to fix, manage, and control is a struggle for all but a small minority of clients. These patterns are highly ingrained and difficult for clients to observe on their own. Time and time again, clients in this phase are oblivious when a therapist points out this dynamic to them, sometimes even after years of recovery.

Trust

When people, processes, and things demonstrate reliability and consistency, it builds trust. When people, processes, and things demonstrate unreliability and inconsistency, it generates distrust. It is hoped that at this stage in recovery, clients are experiencing enough consistency and reliability in their Program, sponsor, therapist, support system, and ultimately themselves to trust. Each bump that comes along to derail that consistency and reliability causes the ingrained propensity of the client to want to retreat back into a protection-mode, raising their defenses and suspicions. If recovery has any chance to succeed, processing and resolving these bumps in the road are key.

Learned Thinking and Behavior Patterns Linger on in Other Forms

Remember back to our discussion about that very large network of memories of impulsivity, obsession, and compulsion that the client learned through the practice of substance use, abuse, and dependence? Well, even at this stage of the game, that network is still well and active. These thought and behavior patterns begin to be expressed in areas other than the substance use itself. For instance, these obsessive, compulsive, and impulsive patterns often show up in exercising, eating, sex, new hobbies, gambling, and dating.

Need for Review

By the time your client reaches this phase, they have covered a great deal of territory in meetings and in your office. This new learning and perspective is often still fragile and not fully integrated for clients. The aggregate lessons of trigger management, "easy does it," "break it into manageable steps," the four quadrants of using versus staying sober, and the concepts of Step One as well as Step Two are understood, but not yet fully applied. These lessons can be especially difficult to recall during times of stress.

STEP THREE: MADE A DECISION TO TURN OUR WILL AND OUR LIVES OVER TO THE CARE OF GOD AS WE UNDERSTOOD GOD

Key Concepts

Since we are fond of caveats, why not add another? Our first caveat before delving into the concepts of Step Three is that we are not going to stick with the original wording in Step Three. We broaden Step Three to include all forms of Higher Power(s), not just a god. We do this because we have experienced too many clients who initially enter Step Two and Step Three with a broader definition of Higher Power or a dislike of the term "God." For some, the broader definition of Higher Power remains static over their recovery, yet for others they move to a more god-based understanding of Higher Power as their spirituality develops over the long-term. Why do you think this happens? Consider this following account by a client:

> Victoria, a 48-year-old biracial lesbian, came into therapy for cocaine and alcohol dependence. She struggled with 12-Step initially given the sexist and heterosexist language in both the Big Book and the meetings. This shifted when she began to attend women's meetings in AA. Victoria had particular difficulty with Step Two and acceptance of God. All through her childhood and adolescence she heard her clergy condemn homosexuality, and later she rejected religion altogether. Although she rejected religion, she remained very spiritual and described having a "strong connection with God through my prayers."
>
> Once she came out, Victoria was introduced to cocaine on entering the bar scene. She announced her lesbianism in a smaller midsized impoverished city in the south, where drug and alcohol use was widely accepted in the bar scene, regardless of sexual orientation. Her use was managed fairly well for about 20 years, but quickly spiraled out of control after she turned 40. Very rapidly, she lost all that she had worked hard for: her partner of 16 years, her home, her job, and all of her savings and retirement funds.
>
> She pleaded with God incessantly throughout her using, offering grand bargains to be saved. As her repeated pleas to be saved from her addiction went unanswered, the stronger her anger and disaffection became with God. Her bottom came when she was arrested and charged for possession. Due to procedures not being followed correctly by the police, those charges were dropped but the arrest scared her enough that she decided to seek sobriety on her own. She began attending AA meetings and individual counseling.
>
> In early recovery and therapy, Victoria struggled with her anger with God, especially when it came time to move to Steps Two and Three. She and her sponsor were wrestling to help her discover her Higher Power, but they focused on finding it as a concept of a deity. Therapy work helped her instead realize that her faith was strongest in a 12-Step Program itself, and thus the Program became her Higher Power. Over the course of two years, Victoria and her therapist explored her anger and disaffection with God. With building sobriety time, Victoria was able to account for how her drug and alcohol use damaged her relationship to God in a similar manner as in her other relationships. Eventually, Victoria transitioned to God as her Higher Power.

Remember to think conceptually about the Steps in the following fashion. Step One is the recognition that our lives embody insanity, becoming impossible to manage. It is also the decision point to make a determined effort to stop the insanity. Step Two defines the purpose and ultimate goal of the 12-Steps themselves: the restoration of sanity (sobriety). This sanity can only be achieved through learning from sources outside of ourselves since we have proven ineffectual at stopping the insanity. Step Three is the decision point to open ourselves to learn from, and be supported by, these outside sources of sanity. For the more succinct among our readers, Step One is an admission of "I've made myself a mess," Step Two is the acknowledgment that "there's hope for me," and Step Three is "That hope will be brought into my life."

Therefore, Step Three is all about making and executing the decision to turn all aspects that are directly related to the restoration of sanity (sobriety) over to the will of our Higher Power(s). It is the recognition that those who are influenced and changed by and through substance use are unable, and will *continue* to be unable, to save themselves from their addictive thinking and behavior being left to their own devices.

This boils down to what Alcoholics Anonymous (2001) calls "self will run riot" (p. 62). It is that understanding that alcoholics and drug addicts alike—through their manipulation, lying, deceit, fixing, managing, and controlling—attempted to play God and failed miserably because they couldn't see the whole picture. During active addiction, their mentality is that if you can get the deck chairs arranged just right, the *Titanic* won't sink.

While we agree with the concept of "self will run riot" to describe active addition, we find that this phrase is also used inappropriately. Sponsors sometimes interpret any deviation from their suggestions as "self will run riot"; failing to see their own "self will run riot" in their codependent behavior with their sponsee. It is important to take a more exploratory approach when dealing with this conflict between rejections of suggestions versus hard-line thinking.

There is a secondary process involved with this Step, the notion of "turning it over." Remember that requisite in "to fix, manage, and control" is worry. While they were using, your clients attempted to do this with many aspects of their life, typically causing them lots of worry. In Step Two, clients work to identify when they are attempting to fix, manage, and control. The next step, Step Three, asks the client to take this awareness and then decide if they are responsible and if they have power within a situation. If they have power and are responsible, they should act in the situation. If they don't have power or responsibility, then the only action they should take is to wait, not worry, and turn the situation over to their Higher Power. In this way, Step Three becomes a step that revolves around boundaries and a path to reduce worry.

Key "Bumper Sticker" Sayings

The bumper sticker sayings at the Step Three level require little explanation. They are often reminders to turn to your Higher Power for guidance and, most importantly, to listen and trust.

"**Happy, Joyous, Free.**" In tune with the Promises, the more you work your program, the more they come true. Also means that sharing your struggle of sobriety releases you from having to come up with all of the answers.

"**Let Go, Let God**" and "**Turn it Over.**" Both are the simple instructions for working Step Three. This is where you enact your Program by sharing with your Higher Power.

"**Worry Is Negative Meditation.**" All people should try incorporating this reminder into their lives. It will do everyone some good!

F.A.I.T.H. (For An Instant Trust Him—or—Finding Answers In The Heart—or—Finding Answers In The Higher Power).

H.O.P.E. (Hang On, Pray Everyday).

H.O.W. (Honesty, Open-mindedness, Willingness).

K.I.S.S. (Keeping It Simple, Spiritually).

L.E.T. G.O. (Leave Everything to God, Okay?).

P.A.U.S.E. (Patience And Understanding Succeed Everytime). This is a gentle reminder that sometimes you have to wait for your Higher Power to respond.

P.R.O.G.R.A.M. (People Relying on God Relaying A Message).

Therapeutic Issues Within Step Three

Unresolved Issues With Previous Steps

Most people in recovery accept the first part of Step Three with ease: turning over their lives to the care of a Higher Power. This should come as no surprise, as in the case of Victoria, many attempt to do so as they are spiraling toward their bottom. The struggle in both the prerecovery and the third Step is to untangle the concept of turning over to a higher power from that of acknowledging the consequences of the use of intoxicants. This may seem like simple semantics, but it is much larger than that. Recovery efforts will undoubtedly fail if the focus is on minimizing or avoiding consequences versus ending the using itself. If this pattern emerges during the working of Step Three, it really is reflective of some unresolved issues of powerlessness and unmanageability as reviewed in Step One. At this juncture, return to Step One and assess client goals for therapy and recovery. Are they there to avoid consequences, or to give up the using of intoxicants? Until this is fleshed out, recovery will stall as you and the client are most likely on separate pages.

Additionally, therapists are recommended to keep an assessment of whether or not the client's selection of a Higher Power is one that is working for them. Sometimes, clients select Higher Powers that, when evaluated or viewed through the lens of Step Three, do not provide the care or guidance necessary for recovery to occur. When explored in therapy, it usually turns out that their Higher Power was in fact another source. Let's visit the case of Ivana:

Ivana came to therapy complaining about the difficulty she was having in understanding what it meant to turn over her life and will to God. She lamented that her trust in God's willingness to be helpful and caring to her was minimal. She described being grateful for her recovery, but did not attribute that to God.

Ivana: "My sponsor and I keep going back and forth on this. She keeps trying to convince me that I should be grateful to God for my sobriety. I keep telling her that I don't see it that way."

Therapist: "How do you see it then?"

Ivana: "I don't know, that's the thing! I don't know what else there would be."

Therapist: "I'm not sure that's true. What do you do when you have an urge to use?"

Ivana: "I either call my sponsor or someone in the Program. Otherwise I hightail it to a meeting as soon as I can."

Therapist: "What if none of those is available at the moment you need them, then what?"

Ivana:	"I carry my Cocaine Anonymous book with me everywhere I go. I usually pull that out and read it. I don't care where I am or what people think when I do that. I do that a lot at work. I'll go to the bathroom and read it in the stall where I won't be disturbed."
Therapist:	"It sounds like you are consistently turning your life and will over to the Program; your sponsor, other people in the Program, and the text. It sounds as if your Higher Power is the Program, not necessarily God."
Ivana:	"Yeah. That *feels right*. I look for direction from them all. I don't pray when I am in trouble; I reach out to the Program instead. How do I talk to my sponsor about this?"

Going "All-In" With Recovery

Steps One through Three are all geared toward the client making the choice to accept the foundational principles and beliefs of 12-Step. Step Three is the point where doubt about the Program is eliminated or overcome enough to have clients begin investing in the "work Steps" (Steps Four through Twelve). In effect, the sober person realizes that they lack the requisite knowledge for sobriety and are willing to have others with more experience suggest a course of action.

This is not to say that they have to follow every suggestion. However, they do need to acknowledge that the suggestions, even though they personally reject them, still represent a path toward sobriety. Clinicians are recommended to listen when clients quickly reject suggestions without any other reason given except "that won't work for me." To be clear: we are not suggesting that you do this with the intention to change a client's mind. In fact, quite the opposite. We want you to pursue this exercise under the guise of an explorer to discover what is motivating the rejection itself. When a client outright rejects a suggestion, that is where you can have the most impact in a client's recovery. Even though 12-Step is a program of suggestions, sponsors and other recovery support often engage in power struggles when a member rejects a suggestion.

Specifically, suggestions that are rejected outright are often representations of the remnants of active addiction still alive in the recovering person. Often these difficult remnants involve feelings resulting from cutting off access to the intoxicants, practicing vulnerability, letting go of control (or the illusion of control), rejecting fear, and daring to be disappointed. Let's view how this might go in therapy:

Giovanni, a 30-year-old chronic marijuana user, sought treatment for his inability to stop using. At the point where he entered into Marijuana Anonymous (MA), he was smoking 3 to 5 bowls a day. He was unable to function at work and often called in sick. He was placed on administrative leave while being evaluated for termination due to high absenteeism. In that there were only two MA meetings where he lived, he attended a combination of MA and Narcotics Anonymous (NA) meetings. While working on Steps One through Three, Giovanni was given a suggestion by his sponsor to get rid of all of his paraphernalia. Giovanni agreed, but was adamant about not getting rid of a bong that he insisted was "an art piece" that he "paid $300 for." This was a constant source of tension between Giovanni and his sponsor, as his sponsor was worried that it was too tempting to keep around. Giovanni rejected that relapse or his recovery had anything to do with his decision; it was made solely because of its worth as an "art piece I spent a lot of money on."

Giovanni (in sarcastic tones): "I am so sick of my sponsor. 'Giovanni, have you thought some more about my suggestion to get rid of your last bong?' Again and again, all he ever talks about is my bong and that it is around. Shitfire! It's an art piece alright?!? I'm not going to get rid of it. I told him, I don't have any cravings. I only used it twice to get high. Twice!"

Therapist:	"I hear a lot of frustration and anger. I'm not sure I understand though. You were able to shrug off suggestions before that you didn't agree with, like that one about attending a 90 and 90, even when your sponsor suggested it over and over. Why is this one bothering you so much? What's going on?"
Giovanni:	"I don't know. I am bothered by it."
Therapist:	"Okay, stay with this for a moment. Describe how your body feels right now as you think about getting rid of your bong."
Giovanni:	"I feel tense all over, my heart is beating faster, and I feel flushed."
Therapist:	"I see your hands are also clutched tightly together. Now tell me what emotions you are feeling."
Giovanni:	"Anger. Frustration. Anxiety."
Therapist:	"Notice anything about this experience that compares to your past?"
Giovanni:	"Yeah. Two things. One, this is how I feel when my father tells me something to do that I hate, because I know he is right. And the other is how I felt right before I started MA when I thought about giving pot up."
Therapist:	"Interesting don't you think? You said that it reminds you of your father when he is right. That makes me believe that you must feel that your sponsor is right about something here. What do you think he is right about?"
Giovanni:	"That keeping it is a risk. I'm not ready to give it up."
Therapist:	"What is the 'it'; the bong or the pot?"
Giovanni:	"The bong . . . the pot . . . I don't know anymore. I feel like I don't want the pot, but I also know that hanging onto the bong keeps me connected to my pot."
Therapist:	"Okay. You agreed to turn your life and your will over to God, is that right?"
Giovanni:	"Yes."
Therapist:	"Do you still believe that today?"
Giovanni:	"Yes."
Therapist:	"Then knowing all of these things that we discussed, as God certainly does, what do you think is God's plan for restoring you to sanity? I ask this because your reactions to your sponsor's suggestion about the bong feel like insanity to me, especially when we reviewed your thoughts and feelings."

Turning It Over

As shown in Giovanni's case example, the practice of turning it over is simply sharing that you are struggling. By that simple act, you open yourself up for help. As you read in the section on the key bumper sticker sayings of Step Three, they speak to the development of people in recovery to consistently ask for help when they recognize they are confused or do not have the answer to a conundrum. This helps to remind them that, at any point in their sobriety, they have the ability to reach out for help or consultation by "turning it over" to another—whether a person in recovery, an etheric being, a 12-Step meeting, one of the texts of 12-Step, or even something or someone unrelated to the Program. It is little wonder that therapists are involved in this process as clients practice "turning it over" to us all the time.

In addition, turning it over also involves invoking the Serenity Prayer for guidance. When clients utilize the Serenity Prayer, the act of reciting it has the client pause and reflect on a couple of different factors: what is causing the distress, what is out of the person's ability to influence, and what changes can the client make to help bring about relief. It is an exercise in critical thinking. Clients begin to learn that a great deal that is distressing to them is out of their control and, in effect, needs to be "turned over" to their Higher Power to handle. This releases the client to then refocus their efforts on what they can control—themselves, and their boundaries. This process generally results in the client developing awareness that they have the greatest impact on themselves (e.g., to self-soothe, self-advocate, etc.).

Radical Acceptance

Radical acceptance is another skill set applicable to this stage in Step Three work. It represents two notions. One is an unequivocal acceptance of oneself; rejecting all forms of judgment and criticism. It is unabashed acceptance of yourself with all of your qualities and history—good, bad, or neutral. It carries forward the work from Step Two and amplifies it; moving beyond the concept of "faking it until you make it." The client begins to incorporate the belief that they are worthy of sobriety, not because they earned the right to be sober but because they are worthy of being sober. In this act, the client minimizes any judgments about themselves. To be clear, this approach does not grant permission to walk around in a narcissistic bubble. This approach has the client accepting all parts of themselves rather than just the things they like.

The second part of radical acceptance is the slogan "life on life's terms." In active addiction, a person attempts to play God and control everything around them: he or she attempts to not face any uncomfortable aspect of life, choosing instead to use to cope, or both. This is the living embodiment of "fix, manage, and control." Practicing "life on life's terms" means accepting that good and bad things happen in life and you face them to the best of your abilities. Newcomers to recovery often misread this expression as a form of extreme passivity. "Look out! A truck's going to hit you! Get out of the way!" "What? Oh well, life on life's terms." If this was what "life on life's terms" meant human extinction would be fast-tracked.

In applying this slogan, yes, sometimes passivity is called for with life, but that is just one of many reactions possible to life's ups and downs. The key in this slogan is to become aware of your expectations of life, and how you respond when life doesn't meet them. Do you go back out to using? Do you try to control the uncontrollable, or refocus control on how you are going to respond? Do you worry about a joyous event ending instead of enjoying the event itself?

Formation and Maintenance of Faith in the Recovery Process

At this juncture in the recovery process, it is hoped that most clients are having some of their desired results come true. With each success the newly sober person experiences, faith builds that the Program can deliver on its promise for the restoration of sanity and thus sobriety grows stronger. However, just as success can help build that confidence in the Program, each failure or bad experience threatens to derail that construction of faith.

If there is an honest and realistic portrayal of the realities/shortcomings of the processes in the Program and therapy, clients are able to tolerate these failures by the Program, clinicians, or themselves. It helps them not to see the world, or recovery, through rose-colored glasses. The more honest clinicians are about the strengths, challenges, and limits of therapy, 12-Steps, ourselves, and themselves, the more we help to rally faith rather than shake it. It also helps to build the therapeutic alliance when the therapist is honest with the client and shares a balanced perspective.

Relapse and Step Three

Step Three's Role in Relapse Prevention

If all is working within the execution of Step Three, the most protective benefits are realized two-fold. One, the person has reached critical mass in faith in a 12-Step process and is now "all in" with recovery. The second is that this total plunge into the pool results in the person beginning to sufficiently utilize the tool of "turning it over," thereby becoming teachable. This result bears repeating; most people underestimate the power of their triggers and overestimate their recovery skills. This vulnerability is minimized when clients turn to their Higher Power(s) for help and guidance. This includes their personal definition of a Higher Power, a 12-Step program, additional recovery programs, and others who are knowledgeable about recovery who support their efforts. If they are able to remain teachable and open to learning new ways of responding to old ways of thinking and behaving, they are in good shape. It is when they become resistant to suggestions (i.e., choosing to ignore those factors that continue to put them at risk) that risk for relapse is greatest.

Other Relapse Prevention Concerns During the Seventh Through Twelfth Months of Recovery

Return to obsessive patterns. As was discussed earlier in the chapter, it should come as no surprise that on occasion a client reverts to the same obsessional pattern of thinking and behavior that was common in the times of their intoxicant use. Again, assisting the clients to identify their underlying motivations and rewards, and implementing self-soothing techniques that work, are critical if you are to avoid the client fleeing to relapse for relief.

Stress Reactions. As with any emotional disorder, old dysfunctional trends resurface when an individual is stressed. Earlier issues, feelings, and addictive behaviors all tend to resurface during periods of stress. Clients can be shocked to realize that their cravings, which were becoming weak and infrequent, are now strong and almost constant after a bad work review. Or, after being given an eviction notice, they may find themselves walking past their old favorite bar on a street they haven't walked down since they sobered up nine months ago. Again, remember that this pattern of regression is a typical reaction to stress. Simply sharing that with clients can be helpful. Processing the triggers and reviewing the strategies used to cope with the reemerged behaviors are the best responses. It is also helpful for clients to attend meetings more frequently or increase their contacts with sponsors and fellowship.

Overconfidence of recovery. We cannot emphasize the importance of this symptom's reemergence as indicating a huge vulnerability for relapse, and we are not just talking about the client's overconfidence. Clinicians can become complicit in this overconfidence in several ways. First, they can be wrapped up in their own egos about their effectiveness in teaching recovery skills, and assume inaccurate abilities to their clients, or blame clients for all that goes wrong in recovery, therapy, and the therapeutic relationship. Second, they can unwittingly become wrapped up in a remnant of the client's antisocial adaption, pulling them into an enabling fugue (blackout) state about the client's increasing risk taking with triggers. Third, therapists may further fall into the trap of overgeneralization of skill ability. For instance, since a client went to one party and did not relapse but managed quite well, the client is therefore sufficiently prepared to go to *all parties.*

Clients demonstrate these same vulnerabilities in regards to overconfidence of their abilities in recovery. While in the midst of coming to terms with their powerlessness, it is extremely deceiving for a client to believe that one incident proves that they are able to control their using (never mind the other 42 failed attempts in a row), any more than one time successfully managing their triggers demonstrates recovery. There is often talk about the all-or-nothing thinking of substance dependence, and it quite often bleeds over into recovery, specifically in this area. Clients in early recovery love to believe that because they avoiding using with this one person, place, or time, then all persons, places or times are safe. As we instructed in Chapter 7, it is the clinician's job to help the client see the nuances in each triggering situation and prepare appropriately.

Boredom with 12-Steps. Oh, the big "B" comes through on this one loud and clear. In our estimation, boredom with a 12-Step program carries both opportunities and concerns. To name a few, complaints about boredom in 12-Steps can be related to the pace of progression with the Steps, themes in meetings becoming repetitious, contemplation of going back to using, feelings of inferiority or not fitting in with 12-Step group, or the reemergence of egocentricity and becoming unteachable. For some clients, they approach 12-Steps in ways that are similar to their substance use pattern—by binging! This pattern makes up the large share of complaints over boredom: the client obsessively focused on 12-Steps and now the wonder and excitement has worn off.

Clinicians can be caught between a rock and hard place on this one. Given a client's lack of social structure not related to using in early recovery, 12-Step or other recovery programs are the best option you have to immerse the client in recovery and build sober support. However, this immersion can create these feelings of boredom as recovery progresses, and the risk is that the bored client drops out of treatment completely. Conversely, in early recovery if you attempt to caution the client and pace the involvement in 12-Steps too much, you run the risk of the client not becoming sufficiently connected with the program, recovery concepts, and supports. This can have the opposite effect of the client's increasing their reliance and connection with the using world—a world that you are stringently trying to have them distance themselves from.

Instead, opt to have the clients involve themselves heavily in 12-Steps in the beginning stage of recovery to rapidly build that support when they need it most.

Warn them, though, that by doing so they may become bored later on. Most clients, while not exactly scoffing at the idea, generally give us a bemused look not believing that possible. When boredom eventually raises its inevitable head, strategize with the client how to "mix it up." This may mean going to a few new meetings while maintaining contact with the most important old ones, a talk with their sponsor about picking up the pace of Step work, switching sponsors, engaging in other recovery programs, or building other social/recreational activities along with their recovery efforts.

Anniversary dates. Nothing stirs up relapse like a good ol' anniversary date of sobriety. We know it seems counterintuitive, but hear us out. While anniversary dates of sobriety are certainly a cause for celebration, they are also a source of tremendous anxiety. Can you think why? If you guessed that each date represents the reality that they really have quit their intoxicant, and will never experience that again if they remain on their present course—winner, winner, chicken dinner! As celebratory as it is with clean time, this time also highlights the growing absence of their intoxicant and all of the perceived benefits that came with it. Our clients relapse the most within the first 20 days of their last use, although others have relapsed on or right before anniversary markers (30, 60, 90 days sober). Often, we have witnessed clients relapsing just before engaging in Step Four work, which reviews a moral inventory, and also the point where they have decided to go all in with recovery through Step Three.

Continued interpersonal difficulties. In our long-term work (several consecutive years of therapy) with clients in recovery, interpersonal difficulties continue to be a large trigger for relapse. Social skills training should never leave the docket of the therapeutic agenda. During an entire course of treatment, continue to focus on all of the social skill training that we talk about throughout this book.

How Step Three Can Be Utilized to Process Relapse When Relapse Occurs

It is understandable that relapse at this stage in recovery can be incredibly demoralizing, especially the closer they are to the first year anniversary of their sobriety. Specifically in regards to Step Three, relapse can feel like a betrayal by their Higher Power or 12-Steps. Clients can lose enough confidence in these two "safety nets" that reentry into recovery is a longer process. They no longer trust that "turning it over" works. How could it, they relapsed after all?

When clients reenter into recovery and treatment, they are often at the beginning reviewing Step One and evaluating where they were not fully practicing the Program in their recovery efforts. Depending on the severity of PAWS, you generally find that you are able to do some critical thinking work with them. Specifically, in an effort to determine where the system broke down, work with clients in therapy to evaluate their relapse through the lens of the Serenity Prayer. Was it an overestimation of ability or underestimation of trigger? What did they think they could do that was not within their power or control? Did they have the ability and wherewithal to avoid a trigger, but did not? Did they hide their choice to take risk or did they "turn it over" to have the decision vetted?

1. Name four expected improvements in a client's functioning at this stage of the recovery process. What are two ongoing concerns for clinicians to attend to during therapy?
2. Recite Step Three, and list the key concepts in that Step.
3. Name two "bumper sticker" sayings appropriate to Step Three.
4. Name two therapeutic issues in Step Three, and corresponding clinical interventions to address those issues.
5. How is Step Three helpful in preventing relapse? What are some behaviors clients can engage in following adoption of Step Three?
6. How can Step Three be utilized in therapy to process relapse?

12

An Afterword for Experienced Clinicians Beginning Work with Substance Use Clients

We find that psychotherapists, especially insight-oriented ones, struggle with the concepts expressed in this text. We recognize and appreciate this struggle, since as therapists we are trained that everything is grist for the mill. We learn to look at how things are said, how meaning is embedded, how it is expressed, and then ultimately repeated in the therapeutic relationship.

Chemical dependency seems to be the perfect fit for this insight- and relationship-oriented approach. The addiction itself is full of meaning: the client's pattern of sabotaging and shattering their lives via the excessive use of an intoxicant; the pattern of attempting to control others around them while being unable to control themselves; existential crises caused by their own or other people's overdoses or near-death experiences; and then there's that whole self-medicating aspect. For example, when clients use substances to somehow perform a psychological operation by the intoxication effect itself: some drugs numb out feelings, some short-circuit defenses, some promote uberconfidence, and some simply increase sensations.

This field is so incredibly enticing for a clinician. Added to its attraction is the fact that these clients seem in real pain, and thus truly motivated to do the work, sometimes for multiple sessions in a row. They work hard and appear truly motivated to get to the complete picture of *why they use*. Only to have them later say things such as: they understand things better now, but they used again . . . or, they got too upset, so they felt like they had to use . . . or, they'll report improvement, and over the course of time . . . you'll savvy up and realize that they're still using. In all these scenarios, we've been there with clients . . . and at times, we are still there!

This isn't to say that we haven't had any success using an insight-, relationship-, or even a humanistic-oriented approach with clients. We've seen a small number of clients who seemed to respond to these approaches and achieved long-term sobriety. Each met the criteria for abuse. One met the criteria for dependence (just barely), and they did not have physiological dependence. In every other case where we attempted an insight-oriented approach, the clients failed to remain sober. We have also had many clients attempt to find sobriety through insight. Looking back, this approach may fail for a few reasons:

1. Our years of experience leads us to the conclusion that insight and relationship approaches are not the most effective with antisocial adaptations, especially for those clients who are unable to allow the formation of a truly empathic relationship.
   a. This dynamic seems most evident when a client is looking for some gain from being in treatment. Perhaps it's to mollify a partner, or to satisfy an employer's demand, or to qualify for some other gain. These cases often appear that the client was never truly motivated to stop using, despite their statements to the contrary.
   b. Clients who are deeply invested in the urge-compulsion-use loop who then fix/manage/control to enable their continued use find it difficult to engage in the therapeutic process. The therapist becomes pulled into the client's dynamics in a way that's all but inescapable.
   c. The antisocial adaptation rests on a foundation of a lack of motivation to change, preventing a therapeutic contract. Insight approaches are typically ineffective without this form of contract.
2. Insight and relationship approaches do not address the underlying dynamics related to triggers or urges to use.
3. While insight and relationship approaches address the massive uses of denial, rationalization, and minimization, they do not focus on revealing the underlying dynamics that empower using to continue, such as denial, the negative consequences of using, or the impact that using has on others, to name just a few.
4. The goals of insight and relationship approaches often focus on a general sense of wellbeing, improved functioning, relationships, and so forth. These are valuable goals, but they are unreachable for the substance dependent person if they continue using. These goals are unreachable until they attain sobriety.

For these reasons, we generally present sobriety as the treatment of choice for our substance-dependent clients. However, this doesn't mean that we abandon insight approaches. As we work through sobriety with our clients, we stay very aware and take close notes of the meaningful material that the client exposes during the search for sobriety. We store this information for later use. Once a client is in a more firmly established recovery pattern, typically at a minimum of one year's sobriety, we begin to offer and shift to a more traditional psychotherapy. This blended approach continues to offer support for the Steps, but it also increasingly uses a more traditional psychotherapy style to begin exploring and uncovering underlying motivational materials. However, even as we do that, our eye is on the goal of sobriety, and we continue to stay alert for signs of relapse.

Given all these factors, we hope you now feel more prepared to work with your clients to move toward sobriety/recovery as the primary goal. Most therapists and counselors have strong skills to bring to bear to this problem. We hope we've explained the premise behind this book and know that it was written with our desire to make this difficult process a bit easier.

References

Alcoholics Anonymous World Services, Inc. (2001). *Alcoholics Anonymous: The big book* (4th ed.). New York, NY: Author.

American Psychological Association. (2000). *Diagnostic and statistical manual of mental disorders, DSM-IV-TR* (4th ed., revised). Washington, DC: Author.

American Society of Addiction Medicine, Inc. (2001). *ASAM patient placement criteria for the treatment of substance-related disorders* (2nd ed., revised). Chevy Chase, MD: Author.

Curry, S. J., Marlatt, G. A., & Gordon, J. R. (1987). Abstinence violation effect: Validation of an attributional construct with smoking cessation. *Journal of Consulting and Clinical Psychology, 55,* 145–149.

Kupfer, D. J., First, M. B., & Regier, D. A. (2002). *A research agenda for DSM-V.* Washington, DC: American Psychiatric Association.

Laing, R. D. (1971). *Sanity, madness, and the family: Families of schizophrenics.* New York, NY: Basic Books.

Matrix Institute on Additions. (2005). *The Matrix Model: A 16-week individualized program: Therapist's manual.* Center City, MN: Hazelden Publishing.

Miller, W. R., & Rollnick, S. (2013). *Motivational interviewing: Helping people change.* New York, NY: Guilford Press.

Narcotics Anonymous World Services, Inc. (2008). *Narcotics Anonymous* (6th ed.). Chatsworth, CA: Author.

Calley, J. (Producer), Nichols, M. (Producer/Director), & Fisher, C. (Writer). (1990). *Postcards from the edge* [Motion picture]. United States: Columbia Pictures.

Prochaska, J. O., DiClemente, C. C., & Norcross, J. C. (1992). In search of how people change. Applications to addictive behaviors. *American Psychologists, 47*(9), 1102–1114.

Rogers, C. R. (1951). *Client-centered therapy.* London, UK: Constable.

Shapiro, F. (2008). "Who wrote the Serenity Prayer?" *Yale Alumni Magazine, Vol. LXXI/6.* Retrieved from http://www.yalealumnimagazine.com/articles/2143?page=1

Yalom, I. D., & Leszcz, M. (2005). *The theory and practice of group therapy* (5th ed.). New York, NY: Basic Books.

Index

About the Authors

Dr. Kevin A. Osten earned a BA from the University of Wisconsin—Milwaukee, and a Psy.D. in Clinical Psychology from the Illinois School of Professional Psychology. He has worked in psychiatric hospitals for most of the past 20 years, most recently as the Clinical Coordinator of Adult Outpatient Services at Chicago Lakeshore Hospital, where he remains on staff today as an Allied Health Professional. In the past decade, his work has focused on providing clinical care to those in the lesbian, gay, bisexual, transgender, and queer community coping with severe mental illness and/or addictions. He became the Director of the LGBTQ Mental Health and Inclusion Center at the Adler School of Professional Psychology in 2011, where he is also a member of the core faculty in the Doctor of Psychology program. He remains active in his private practice utilizing an integrative approach in psychotherapy.

Dr. Robert Switzer earned a BA from The State University of New York at Buffalo and a Psy.D. in Clinical Psychology from the Illinois School of Professional Psychology. Since 1990, his professional work has concentrated on psychotherapy and diagnostics, with a focus on substance abuse and substance dependence. He works in inpatient and outpatient settings, primarily with adults. He has been an adjunct faculty member at The Chicago School of Professional Psychology since 2000, and a core faculty member since 2008. He continues to be active in his private practice, where he provides individual psychotherapy using an eclectic approach, including aspects of psychodynamic, cognitive-behavioral, Rogerian, and 12-Step techniques. His interests include substance abuse and addictive disorders, 12-Step work, depression, psychodynamic psychotherapy, severe personality disorders, diagnostics, personality assessment, and a recent interest in integrative psychotherapy. Dr. Switzer is also an avid cyclist and can often be found bicycling around the Chicago area, even during weather when he really should be indoors.